About This Book

Why is this topic important?

The wheel of the learning and training revolution turns quickly. We are continually hearing news of the latest technologies and their great potential for change, but we rarely hear the firsthand accounts of those whose everyday lives are affected. One certainty is that people will always be the most important part of the learning experience. Advancements in technology change the face of business and learning so quickly that personal stories are rarely recorded. But there are many stories to be told. If technology is meant to help people, we need to understand how they feel when they use it. How does it change their everyday lives? Via "bursts" of original thoughts from our numerous contributing authors, this diverse collection of passionate, personal, and honest stories recounts how technology is transforming how we learn today and what we can expect in the not-too-distant future.

What can you achieve with this book?

While purposely refraining from focusing on any specific method, product, or technology, this book serves as a common ground for all learners and trainers. It sheds light on factors both beneficial and detrimental to the changing learning experience. Its very readable nature is not meant to advocate a specific tool or technique or serve as a reference, but rather to give you a reading experience to which you can relate. We also invite you to internalize your experience by similarly raving, ranting, and/or reflecting on your own—we are sure that you also have many personal and professional stories to tell!

How is this book organized?

This book is divided into three distinct parts. Part One provides general perspectives about the current world of learning or about experiences as a learner. Part Two contains real-life case studies and in-practice organizational examples and lessons learned. Part Three features the vision for the future and the technologies to be employed. What are they? How can we begin to prepare now? What can we do individually and collectively to ensure success for ourselves, our employees, and our organizations?

About Pfeiffer

Pfeiffer serves the professional development and hands-on resource needs of training and human resource practitioners and gives them products to do their jobs better. We deliver proven ideas and solutions from experts in HR development and HR management, and we offer effective and customizable tools to improve workplace performance. From novice to seasoned professional, Pfeiffer is the source you can trust to make yourself and your organization more successful.

P **Essential Knowledge** Pfeiffer produces insightful, practical, and comprehensive materials on topics that matter the most to training and HR professionals. Our Essential Knowledge resources translate the expertise of seasoned professionals into practical, how-to guidance on critical workplace issues and problems. These resources are supported by case studies, worksheets, and job aids and are frequently supplemented with CD-ROMs, Web sites, and other means of making the content easier to read, understand, and use.

P **Essential Tools** Pfeiffer's Essential Tools resources save time and expense by offering proven, ready-to-use materials—including exercises, activities, games, instruments, and assessments—for use during a training or team-learning event. These resources are frequently offered in looseleaf or CD-ROM format to facilitate copying and customization of the material.

Pfeiffer also recognizes the remarkable power of new technologies in expanding the reach and effectiveness of training. While e-hype has often created whizbang solutions in search of a problem, we are dedicated to bringing convenience and enhancements to proven training solutions. All our e-tools comply with rigorous functionality standards. The most appropriate technology wrapped around essential content yields the perfect solution for today's on-the-go trainers and human resource professionals.

Pfeiffer
www.pfeiffer.com

Essential resources for training and HR professionals

Learning Rants, Raves, and Reflections

Elliott Masie, Editor

Pfeiffer
A Wiley Imprint
www.pfeiffer.com

Published by Pfeiffer
An Imprint of Wiley
989 Market Street, San Francisco, CA 94103-1741
www.pfeiffer.com

For additional copies/bulk purchases of this book in the U.S. please contact 800-274-4434.

Pfeiffer books and products are available through most bookstores. To contact Pfeiffer directly
call our Customer Care Department within the U.S. at 800-274-4434, outside the U.S. at
317-572-3985, fax 317-572-4002, or visit www.pfeiffer.com.

Pfeiffer also publishes its books in a variety of electronic formats. Some content that appears
in print may not be available in electronic books.

Library of Congress Cataloging-in-Publication Data

Learning rants, raves, and reflections/Elliott Masie, editor.
    p. cm.
  Includes bibliographical references and index.
  ISBN-13 978-0-7879-7302-5 (alk. paper)
  ISBN-10 0-7879-7302-5 (alk. paper)
  1. Organizational learning. 2. Learning. 3. Employees—Training of. 4. Educational
technology. I. Masie, Elliott.
  HD58.82.L42 2005
  658.3'124—dc22

                                2005003711

Acquiring Editor: Lisa Shannon

Director of Development: Kathleen Dolan Davies

Developmental Editor: Susan Rachmeler

Production Editor: Dawn Kilgore

Editor: Rebecca Taff

Manufacturing Supervisor: Becky Carreño

Editorial Assistant: Laura Reizman

Printed in the United States of America

Printing   10 9 8 7 6 5 4 3 2

Contents

Introduction

Getting the Most from This Resource

The realms of training and education are continuously metamorphosed by new learning technologies, rendering the constant evolution of the learning and teaching experiences. There are those who see learning technologies as wonderful tools changing the face of education. What are their stories? What obstacles have implementers overcome to see their plans become realities? There are the learners. What have their journeys been like? Have they been rewarding or frustrating? Were their expectations met? There are those who dedicate themselves to studying e-learning. Why did they choose this field? There are those whose mission it is to evangelize learning and advance the profession. How do they see learning and training changing the world? How do they see us participating individually and collectively?

We have faith that the diverse group of contributing authors for this project will motivate you with their passion for learning and technology and with their provocative views on the state of learning and training today and in the future. Each was given a substantial amount of freedom in writing his or her piece, so the contributions are fairly unique. In fact, we feel that lack of restraint and suggestion on our part prompted contributors to write more personal and honest accounts. As a result, they collectively give the sometimes intimidating face of technology-enabled learning a human voice.

The purpose of this book is not to advocate a method or serve as a reference, but rather to give you a reading experience to which you can relate. Where many new distance learning tools are meant to connect people to one another, they often result in frustration and feelings of loneliness as a learner, leaving the learner to wonder, "Am I all alone in this? Are others going through the same thing?" Although these feelings are often recognized as the negative aspects of self-directed learning, nothing can be done to remedy them until we understand from whence they stem.

Since our goal is to present a snapshot of the diverse experiences people have with technology-enabled learning as well as learning and training in general, accounts of negative learning experiences and perspectives as well as positive ones are included. And in order to serve as common ground for all learners, we have purposely refrained from focusing on any specific product or technology.

This book was written primarily because it has not been. There are scores of books on training, implementing technology, organizational learning, and education. This book idea has indeed been birthed from these topics, but it is a much different work. Our hope is that it captures the human side of learning and training (with or without technology) and how people really experience it—one that compels the reader to remember that our goal is to develop and connect people and information, not replace them.

Audience

The primary target audience for this book is comprised of corporate executives, training professionals, and higher education personnel who are charged with designing, developing, implementing, and managing training and learning and the critical role that it plays in the lives of workers, customers, and students and in the business world. A secondary audience are suppliers of learning products and services and professional consultants. Third, this book has an even wider appeal because of how quickly and pervasively the face of technology is transforming the world. In fact, it is relevant to all learners everywhere—a trainee who has taken an e-learning or blended learning course, a college student who has taken a class that has been enhanced by technology, or a doctor who has made a more accurate diagnosis thanks to meeting with expert colleagues through videoconferencing.

How This Book Is Organized

This book is a compiled publication of well-rounded essays and perspectives from our numerous carefully recruited contributing authors. Short biographies of the authors are included at the end of the book.

Part One features general stories about the current or near-future world of training or learning or about individual experiences (both positive and negative) from learners. Included are topics dealing with next generation solutions involving knowledge management, performance support and learning, selling and promoting learning to executives to garner their support for our products and services, driving learning through instructional outcomes and content versus via technology, maximizing business relationships by partnering with vendors and suppliers for mutual benefits, the new professional mind-set and contract required for today's changing workplace, disengaging from the past in order to move learning from efficiency to the transformational stage, the critical importance of copyright laws and why we need to pay attention and get involved, and developing and maintaining our human capital and our business processes via a "people architecture" framework.

Part Two consists of the art of training and learning in practice. Our authors relate their experiences when implementing learning in their enterprises. Real case studies from Saudi Aramco, IBM, Michelin, McDonald's, and the U.S. Secret Service are supplemented with practical tips, techniques, and lessons learned. And in the chapter on mobile learning, numerous working organizational implementations from varying disciplines are showcased.

Part Three encompasses the vision of two of the most recognized visionaries in the learning field, Sam Adkins and Wayne Hodgins. Sam informs us about the emerging technologies we need to keep an eye on, while Wayne calls us to action to make the vision where everyone is learning not a dream, but a reality.

Although the chapters have been grouped into these sections for ease of organization, they are independent pieces and do not need to be read sequentially. We have built in the flexibility so that your preference, time, and needs will drive that decision.

Key Terms

The reader is assumed to have some basic familiarity with training, learning, and technology. For a good way to get up-to-speed or a refresher, you may want to refer to the chapter on operational excellence and next generation blended learning first. Each author has further defined and elaborated any key terms critical to the comprehension of his or her individual piece. This is particularly the case in the more technically oriented chapters.

The other terminology we want to acquaint you with before you begin concerns the three key words in this book's title. What do we mean by rants, raves, and reflections? And what guidelines were given to the various authors to help them brainstorm for their pieces?

Rant (about a particular experience or technology): Think of an experience when training or learning was thwarted, when you were excited to have a learning experience and something got in the way and prevented you and the group from learning. Examples of this might be a new technology that didn't work as planned, the learning experience was too technology-based, the instructor was incompetent, there were technical problems, something else didn't go as planned, people in class didn't get along, or it was poorly designed.

- I hate when I want to learn something and . . .
- I think it is distracting when . . .
- I think the easiest way to ruin a learning experience is . . .
- I think this situation could have been turned into a positive one if . . .
- I will avoid future experience such as this by . . .
- If you encounter an experience like this again, how would you react to or remedy it?

Rave (about a particular experience or technology): Try to recreate an experience while touching on these topics:

- I get energized about learning when I think about . . . (that is, new technologies, experiential learning, simulation, research tools available to me, a great instructor, an online component).
- I get excited about the future of learning when I think about the possibilities of . . .
- What I love most about learning is . . .
- The best learning experience I've ever had took place . . . It was so memorable because. . .
- Parts of this learning experience that should be a part of every learning experience are . . .
- The greatest lesson I learned from this experience is . . .

- *Reflection* (about you as a learner and the world of learning): What comes to mind first when you think about the world of training and learning?
- What comes to mind first when you think about learners, collectively and individually?
- What about the nature of learning connects all learners?
- As a basis for your reflection, imagine you have just won a Lifetime Achievement Award in Learning. How would your acceptance speech read? Possibly include anecdotes of one or more learning experiences.
- What is your vision when you think about the future of learning?

Resources

Several authors include relevant and influential books, articles, websites, and other sources of information within their individual piece. We highly encourage you to follow up with each to gain additional insights and knowledge from these value-added resources and selected publications.

LEARNING RANTS, RAVES, AND REFLECTIONS

A Personal Essay

Elliott Masie

Learning is a topic that yields an incredible volume of rants, raves, and reflections. It is one of the only topics about which almost every person on the earth has a strong set of opinions that he or she can quickly articulate. Over the past three decades, thousands of people sitting next to me on airplanes have been asked a few gentle questions about their feelings and perspectives on learning, and during this time I have listened and learned.

Learning is something that is human and natural. Some of the most complicated tasks that we will ever learn—speaking our first sentences or taking our first steps—are accomplished without the assistance of a certified teacher or graduate of a train-the-trainer program. Instead, we have nature and the human touch of our parents. I often wish that we could recapture the natural aspects of learning in our organizational efforts.

Learning is something that often happens in spite of official efforts. Ask anyone how he or she learned to do a job and 95 percent of the time you will hear about informal processes, including observation of peers, conversations with fellow workers and managers, reading, and even web browsing. In many instances, the learner will tell you outright that the formal course (classroom or online) was of little assistance.

Learning is something that is deeply personal. What works for you may not work for your colleagues. Some people learn in a very logical, end-to-end process. Others, like this author, like to start at the end and make their way backwards in a trial-and-error process. For some people, the PowerPoint® slide is a great structuring tool. For some, we want to pull out a shotgun and blast the screen when the fifteenth slide appears in a training program. Learning also changes for us throughout our lives and throughout the year. When you are starting a new job, full of expectations and excitement, low on relevant experience, a residential orientation program may be a wonderful launching process. Yet six months later, self-paced learning may be the only training model that will help you gain new information or continue to build/refine your competencies.

Learning is often social. There is something so exciting about working with a group of fellow learners on the acquisition of new knowledge. When the team is clicking and the content is relevant, the social nature of story telling, context seeking, peer remediation, and work-based learning is awesome. Then again, there are those who prefer to learn on their own. I can feel schizophrenic about the social nature of learning. Personally, sometimes I need to retreat to the solitude of my office or den at home, sip a cup of tea, and tackle my learning solo and in a quiet setting, while other times, I thirst for the social interaction of a great class.

Learning gets dangerous lip service from leaders. It is so easy to say that "We are a learning organization!" or to tell an employee that "We want you to continually improve your skills and we will support you." Yet when real workers want real time and resources to do real learning activities, the commitment is challenged. Just yesterday, I found myself denying two of my staff's requests to go to a week-long institute on meeting planning. I looked at the cost and the calendar and made a reflexive decision and said, "Let's look for something else." I know that I will try to find an alternative, but even this executive in an organization that is very focused on learning could be accused of giving token support. I worry about whether the widespread interest in e-learning is always a commitment to expanding learning or if it reflects the desire to minimize the impact, visibility, disruption, and cost of learning.

Learning is a longitudinal and long process. As organizational trainers, it is always tempting to confuse the delivery of learning activities with learning. Trainers can always deliver more learning faster than learners can or want to absorb it. Let's go back to the infant taking first steps, learning new words, or even tackling bladder control. We would never think of sending that infant to Potty School. Rather, learning encompasses an integrated intervention, changed environment, evolving culture of support, reward, feedback, and ritual. Learning takes more time and happens more continually than most organizations admit or integrate into their planning.

Learning may not be seen as learning by the learner. Most of the best learning was not done at a moment when the person thought of himself or herself as a learner (or even a student/participant). When I was in college, the best learning that I did took place in the offices of my professors and at the big round table at the back of the snack bar. I discovered that most of my professors actually were in their offices during the hours posted on the door . . . and were impressed that a freshman or sophomore would want to stop by and chat. I made it a habit of visiting and entering into content dialogues with my professors. It wasn't brown-nosing in an attempt to up my grades. But it had more value to me than most of the lectures or seminar discussions. Likewise, the conversations with friends and occasionally with strangers in the Harpur College snack bar were filled with great knowledge acquisition. In both of these instances, I didn't feel like a learner or a student. And I continue to wonder if the best organizational learning happens when the learner isn't aware that he or she is learning.

Learning in the age of Google is different. To continue on this point, look at how people use search engines like Google. Got a question? Type a few words into Google and you get a massive, random, and imperfect list of resources. One of them might contain your answer or launch you on a new discovery pathway. Today's Google is just the beginning. In a few years, we will see much more personalized, social-network-based, Google-like learning tools. The system will know my learning style, my job focus, my past searches, my reference group of peers and mentors that I trust, my language skills, my text versus graphic preferences, and other knowledge acquiring traits.

Learning in the age of technology is totally different. The impact of Google is only a sliver of the broad spectrum changes that the world of learning and training is feeling from the explosion of technology. In many ways, there is a revolution of knowledge afoot that resembles the impact that the Industrial Age had on the nature of making things. Just as we went from craftsmen to factories, there is a parallel shift underway from taking courses to flows of knowledge. This profound change can be seen more clearly from the learner's experience than from the language or actions of training professionals. Learners quickly "get" the big deal that technology adds to the knowledge process. They in fact see e-learning more as a natural extension of the web and the browser. If learners can confirm the status of the checks that they have written or investigate the best and cheapest airfare for an upcoming trip, it is a short leap to see the web as a natural vehicle for gaining the skills, information, or knowledge that they need to do a task or a whole job. In fact, most learners don't see e-learning as learning. They experience it as yet another marvelous way in which the web shrinks the world and explodes their access to "stuff."

So with these observations, let me use my role as editor of this book to share my personal rants, raves, and reflections about the "L" word, learning. I write these with a sense of trepidation, since our field is changing at an incredible rate. To hedge my bets, and to cover the likely reality that much will change between the time that I type these words and when you read them, please go to www.masie.com/rants/ in order to read the latest version of this chapter.

Rants

These passionate "bursts" of thought reflect things that anger or frustrate me:

Learning and Training Are Not the Same Process! I become really incensed when I see organizations confuse their training efforts with employee learning. Training is the set of activities that the organization provides for workers to (hopefully) assist them in gaining key skills, knowledge, competencies, and certifications. Training is an occasional activity that represents only a small percentage (usually less than 1/10 of 1 percent) of an employee's time at work. Learning is the process by which a worker gains some of those skills, knowledge, competencies, and certifications. Many learners succeed *without* participating in training. Many learners succeed *in spite of* the training. And many training activity participants *do not* learn anything. We need to be much clearer about our use of the terms learning and training. For example, I could argue that many learning management systems (LMS) are really more like training management systems.

Invite Thy Learners! Organizations must do a much better job of the invitation process. This is the process by which learners are invited to participate in a training or learning activity. There has been much research over the past four decades about the critical role that *invitation* plays in the success of a training experience. Yet most organizations have actually taken a step back in their investment and support of invitation. For example, if you contracted with me to provide a briefing at your company, there would be a flurry of activity to make sure that the room was filled when I arrived. Yet if you contracted for an online seminar, the invitation process might be reduced to a simple email that was blasted out to hundreds of employees. We know that personal and managerial invitation is very powerful, yet we have fooled ourselves that we can use technology to lower the time spent on the motivational elements of the invitation. Here is a simple step that our field could take to deal with this:

Learning management systems should build in potent invitation systems to identify, invite, and re-invite learners to participate in critical learning activities. Consider this an Invitation Wizard, which would systematically invite workers to participate in learning. It would use style, demographic, and HR data to personalize and target both the content and spirit of the invitation. The Invitation Wizard would do more than just send out emails. It might "ping" a key manager with a message to have him or her call or meet with an employee and invite him or her to a future learning process. Hey, if Amazon can find ways of inviting millions of customers to future purchasing moments, our LMS technology can be used as a high-powered invitation "engine."

Managers Give Mixed Learning Signals. One of the major reasons why there are "no-shows" at classroom-based events is that the manager of a learner changed his or her mind at the last minute. When first approached about a worker attending a three-day class, the reaction was positive and supportive. But once the class appeared on the calendar for the upcoming, very busy, and hectic week, the *value* of attendance was less than the *value* of the worker staying at his or her desk.

Even in the world of e-learning, the message from the manager can be mixed. A manager might be excited about a learner saving travel time and expense by attending a class online. But there might be an unstated assumption that the e-learner should do the learning on his or her own time, or at least find a way of doing all of his or her current work without any "give" to allow the learner to focus on the e-learning assignments.

Give Them a Chance to Apply New Skills. Wow, this is one of my most blood pressure boiling rants! When learners have gone through a class, course, or other knowledge acquisition process, they *must* be given a chance to actually use their newly gained skills. We have to view this as a non-optional step in the road to *transfer*. Without a chance to apply the newly gained skills, they slide into a fuzzy and risky tentative zone.

Sometimes, one must do training a while before the actual application is available. Sometimes, cross-training is provided as a succession or emergency capacity. But even in those situations, the absence of a real-world need to use these skills changes the learning and retention process dramatically. I believe that our LMS systems should actually track and measure the application of newly acquired skills. When a learner is registered for a program, I would have the system ask for the real-world application that he or she will accomplish.

Stop Using Silly Numbers. Measure What Counts! There are so many "silly" numbers in the assessment and measurement of training and learning. My colleague, Naomi Karten, calls these "silly numbers" because they give us very detailed and meaningless data points. Here are just a few silly learning numbers:

- *Total Learners Trained:* Every organization has a graph with the total number of "butts in seats" in class and online. Why is this silly? What does it really tell us? Very little. It does not tell us who the learners were, why they went to training, who was *not* trained, and what the difference in performance was between the trained and non-trained.

- *Learner Evaluations of Classes:* Kirkpatrick won't like me for this one. But the older I get the more "ranty" I become on this topic. Why do we always ask learners if they "liked" the class? Why do we focus on the delivery dimension of customer satisfaction in the training department rather than other departments? We have all filled out really damning evaluation forms for instructors and seminars only to find the same people teaching the same stuff over and over again. I think we should stop asking! Let's really get to Level Four and Five *now*!

- *e-Learning Completion vs. Abandonment Rates:* When was the last time that you "completed" a website? Did you "finish" your visit to a corporate intranet or Google page, or did you "abandon" it? As e-learning proliferates, we have to give up our fixation on completion. By definition, learners will be leaving most online courses before the "end." Unless there is a penalty or reward, learners will take the components they need and then move on to other work tasks. Yet our LMS systems kick out these elaborate indicators of "completion." But it is not the fault of the LMS alone. We have to start at the instructional design and look at competency as the point to target and measure. And many times competency won't happen until the learners finish with the learning phase and do some real practice and application. So let's not do the silly measurement of "completion!"

Universities Are Off Base on Instructional Design Programs. Every week, I receive several emails from undergraduate students asking for advice on where to go for a master's degree in instructional design. I always have to take a deep breath before answering these students. We want them to go into our field. We need lots of motivated and talented people to help design the next generation of learning and knowledge systems. Yet many of the current graduate programs in instructional design are legacy in nature and way out of step with future trends in our field.

Design Does Not Have to Take Long. One of the phrases that rolls off the tongues of line-of-business managers these days is rapid learning development. They have already been sold on the experiment of e-learning. And now they want it to shift from the pilot to the fully enterprise level. This translates into *scalable, massive,* and *affordable content.*

Organizations are starting to ask for really large amounts of content to be developed in a short amount of time, with minimal disruption to subject-matter experts and at a cost level that is significantly less than what we are currently spending on development.

This requires a marked change in the minds of training and learning professionals. We come from a tradition of spending enough time on learning and development to get it "almost perfect." Often, a response to the question of "How long will the design take?" has been: "Eighteen weeks!" This makes sense when you are doing a full-blown training analysis and are doing customized content and introducing a new form factor for the learning delivery. This makes sense when you are developing a highly branched computer-based training type of e-learning, loaded with behavioral oriented design elements. This makes sense when the content is stable and is going to be used by a large number of learners over a long period of time.

But it does *not* make sense in the era of rapid development. Organizations are needing brand new models for learning design. They want content to be developed quickly and used often. They want content to be dropped into templates that can be populated by subject-matter experts. They want the outcome to be less behavioral and to be able to be "digested" in small chunks. They want it to be searchable in Google style, printable in job aid format, and leveraged as a performance support tool. In other words, they want their content to be massive, scalable, and affordable.

The era of rapid development is already upon us. The only enemy of rapid development is our tradition and fear of the new. We must find a way to say "*yes*" to rapid development. We must find a way to embed great instructional wisdom into stable templates and form factors. We must evolve our metaphor for the role of an instructional designer from a person in a monastery with a quill pen who is hand painting each pixel to a learning "assembler" in a CNN newsroom who is doing an edit to transform news feeds into personalized content that yields performance for each worker/learner/viewer/user.

Rapid does not need to be weak, dull, shallow, or boring. Rapid development is moving the learning process to the speed of business. It will be the future. My hope is that the wisdom of instructional design will find its way into this new model. Let's be open to it, so that we can influence and direct its future.

Content Is Lonely Without Context! While I love content, I totally adore context. Content is the authored wisdom of an organization. It is typically well-structured, organized, approved, and often the result of great thinking about how to acquire new knowledge or skills.

Context is the stuff that makes content come alive. Context is the story that the instructor tells about how he or she actually uses the procedures detailed in the content. Context is what other learners say about their reactions to the content. Context is what the learner herself discovers about the usability of the official content. Context is social. Context is current. Context allows the learner to sort, filter, and relate to the content.

Most courseware and learning design focuses on content. Trainers often add the context in their classrooms. Online, context can arrive as part of an electronic discussion board or via interactions with the instructor. Sometimes, context takes place covertly, at the coffee break or in an instant message between two participants in a web conference session. We have to start *designing* for *context* as well as *content*! Instructional design needs to increasingly include the activities, formats, and cultures required to help the learners access and create context.

As the title of this rant suggests, content is lonely without context. And learners are lonelier learners without context.

Sometimes Learning Should Happen Slowly . . . Even "Drip" Style. Advocates for e-learning will often talk about our ability to use this new delivery method to accelerate the learning process. I have given hundreds of talks about the need to operate faster and at the "speed of business." Yet, there is another side of the opportunity that e-learning creates—slower and stretched out learning.

Imagine if you could enroll for an MBA program that took ten years. You would not have to stop anything that you are doing. Perhaps you could take a half course every few months. Ah, the ability to pursue something slowly, rather than at a rush.

I know that I would enroll in several new courses of study today if I could take them slowly. If I could have a low intensity "drip" of learning, it would be a delight. Organizations might see this as a great way to deal with cross-training and skills for succession.

So let's try to avoid the concept that fast is always better. Some learning might take a while, and if I don't need it all today, why not turn that slow drip on?

Raves

My raves are in the form of a personal list that I have been building over the years of things that I really appreciate about learning and training:

Great Teachers.   The joy of being a student with a great teacher is unbelievable. I have always asked participants in my class to write a few words about their favorite teachers, the ones who had the most impact on their lives. Here is what I say:

> Mrs. Ham. She was my second grade teacher at PS 173 in Manhattan. Mrs. Ham had the accelerated class, twenty-five high-energy and smart kids who were put on a track to learn as much as possible. Mrs. Ham used two techniques that I have practiced myself over three decades as a trainer:
>
> • She asked impossible-to-answer questions. She would ask questions that didn't even have a real answer, but that provoked maximum learning opportunities. For example, one day she asked what it would be like to eat peanut butter in a zero gravity environment like the moon. She posed the question at 8:30 a.m. and said we would talk about it at 2:30 p.m. For the next several hours, my mind roamed and rambled around that impossible-to-answer question. She trusted the discovery process.

- Mrs. Ham used peer learning as a key tool. When she gave us a quiz, she would have us grade each other's papers. She would have us provide feedback to each other, and that was in the second grade. When she taught a new set of content, the first thing she would do is have us group in clusters of three or four students and have us re-teach the new concept to each other.

Books as Learning Tools. As a learner, I love to find new books to read. I regret that with the growth of information at our browser's fingertips, the formal use of books in classes is descending. The immersion in a great book is an incredible learning process. Here are some suggestions for keeping books alive as organizational learning tools:

- Create At-Work Reading Clubs: Oprah has done it for her viewers. Why not replicate reading clubs at work? One might focus on leadership or other management issues. Another might be vertically focused on procurement methods. Or they might be a heterogeneous mix of fellow employees who meet to share their learning from a common book recently read. The book club can even meet using a virtual classroom system.

- Peer Group Best Seller List: No insult to the *New York Times*, but I am not very interested in what the top ten books in the country are on a given week. But I am intrigued by what the current best reads are for the executives in my company or for a peer group of colleagues across the country. That is a piece of context that really helps.

- Enter Thy Books into the LMS: Make sure that there is a way for books to be engaged by the LMS process. For example, a course might kick off with the common reading of a book, followed by an online dialogue, followed by corporate procedures taught in an asynchronous fashion.

- Write Your Own Books: Why not ask some of your subject-matter experts to create a multi-author book on a key topic?

Publish it as a PDF. Students in a leadership program would be fascinated to read a book on leadership successes written by twelve executives from around your company.

Learning Objects. Build them small, make them reusable, give the learner more control!

Quick Videos. Set up a small studio in your organization, perhaps using a simple $1,000 camera. Have it ready to roll at a minute's notice. Get into the habit of taping small interviews with key staff members and outside resources. Video does not need to be produced to Hollywood standards. Start experimenting with small, focused, and just-in-time video objects. They work and are deeply appreciated by learners.

Talent Search. Experiment with emerging systems for locating key staff members with relevant talent or expertise. It is funny to find out that someone sitting three cubicles from you has twelve years' experience at a company that you are just starting to work with. We have to find ways of cataloguing and accessing the knowledge and talent resources within our organizations. Every time that I have done this, I have been absolutely impressed with how much talent and how many resources are available throughout the organization.

Local Localization. For years, we have assumed that content needed to be translated and localized at headquarters to maintain consistency. In fact, a number of companies are successfully implementing local localization. The idea is simple. Develop content in a primary language such as English or Mandarin. Then provide the graphics and text to contacts in each region throughout the world. Give them a template where they can "add" additional content in the local language as well as provide local information and perspective. This can be done overnight throughout the globe at a really low cost. By also providing the primary language to everyone, there is a built-in quality control. People will tend to correct inappropriate translations or localization. If we are to operate globally, we have to learn globally as well.

Food as a Part of Learning. I am not joking! Most good learning experiences have involved some form of eating. I discovered early on that my end-of-class assessments rose as I added better food. This is probably a good complaint about the value of end-of-class assessments, but it is also a great comment about the central role that food plays in our learning.

But do use food wisely. One corporate university recently asked leadership class participants to bring a "covered dish" to the first and last sessions of their executive class. It built a level of sharing and communication that was unique. Use food as metaphors, engaging the learners in the themes of eating. Also, remember that every food has a chemical effect on the body. There are topics that should *never* be taught the first hour after lunch. And there are times when I want to have a doughnut dispenser at every table to issue a sugar rush to all of my learners (just kidding!).

Don't Forget the Jackets. Just as food is important, so are symbols. e-Learning participants deserve the trinkets and jackets that attendees at events often receive. These symbols become interesting "totems" in the organization. One company stopped giving a leather jacket to each participant in a blended learning model of a management class. They received strange and negative reactions from the employees, who were looking forward to returning to the factory floor with their jackets. Symbols are important . . . and just sending a graphics file won't cut it.

Usability Testing Rocks! We must find a way to increase the amount of usability testing that is done on e-learning projects. It can be done internally, with a few sample sessions and a trained observer. But we must also find a way to test the usability of our learning efforts. Too often, testing stops at the systems level. It is "done" when it does not crash. But in a usability sense, it is not "done" until learners can easily access the features, functions, and value of the assets. Your learners and your learning investments deserve better. Test for usability!

Reflections

Last, here are some of my reflections to help serve as a common ground for all learners, organizations, and the world of learning:

The Fourth Stage of e-Learning. Our field is entering the fourth stage of e-learning. The first stage was the Pilot. Could we actually design and deliver learning via the Internet? The second stage was the Technology phase. Would our systems handle growing levels of e-learning usage? The third stage was the Management phase. How would we manage and track enterprise use of learning? This stage brought forth learning systems such as LMSs, learning content management systems, and collaborative systems. I call the fourth stage the Scalable and Integrated stage, one in which organizations are striving to:

- Scale Content: This takes us back to the rapid development approaches. Organizations are asking how they can develop large amounts of content and deliver them throughout the enterprise.
- Integrate Systems: e-Learning must integrate with a host of knowledge and HR systems, including learning content management systems, simulation systems, document management systems, enterprise resource planning systems, human capital management systems, calendaring systems, and others.

Yet the Infancy of e-Learning. While we are in this exciting fourth stage of e-learning, on another level we are just in its infancy. Go back and look at how primitive websites from just four years ago appear. That is what our current e-learning will seem like four years from today.

The Deconstruction of the Course. We are rapidly moving toward the deconstruction of the course. The unit of learning will less and less be the class or course (online or in person). Instead, learners will access a series of designer-constructed or self-constructed learning pathways. We will graze content, sample elements, test vigorously, and personalize to the max.

Benchmarking on Steroids. Organizations will seek high-powered benchmarking with other external reference points. In our Learning CONSORTIUM, Fortune 1000 companies benchmark with one another on key factors related to learning development costs, competency models, and design formats. In the near future, we will see the growth of balanced scorecards for learning and training efforts and other increased resources for peer-to-peer as well as industry-wide benchmarking.

Learners Are Evolving. The most exciting aspect of this field is that learners are evolving faster than our methods. The learner, empowered with a mouse, browser, collaboration tools, the Internet, search engines, and global access to peers and resources, is defining her next stage of learning. What we have to do as learning professionals is simple:

- Listen closely to the learners.
- Experiment honorably with new delivery and design models.
- Provide multiple pathways to knowledge, as people are quite different.
- Design collaboratively, using subject-matter experts and learners as key partners in the process.
- Don't worry what we call stuff. In fact, you call it "stuff" if it works. New inventions don't start with a new name; they start with cool thinking that yields real results. Later, you can always name or brand it. This is not a marketing exercise; this is about creating a new science and art for knowledge sharing.
- Be seriously playful about learning.

Part One

Here, Now . . .

or Arriving on the Scene Very Soon

Part One features the following articles about the current or near-future world of training or learning or about individual learner experiences.

Operational Excellence and Next Generation Blended Learning by David Metcalf

Operational excellence is prevalent in the automotive, aerospace, and manufacturing industries (among others) and so it is no surprise that it is now a growing trend in the training and learning industry. How do you create a blended learning process and infrastructure to support OE? Training, learning, performance management, and knowledge management all play a role and need to be linked together in a comprehensive fashion. David's proposed model addresses these three components, and specifically how to align each with a blended learning strategy.

Dining with the Executives: Doing the Right Kind of Training That Will Get You a Seat at the Table by Beth Thomas

Training should be high-value, simpler, and more intuitive. Isn't this the case with how our children learn, how we interface with ATMs and kiosks, and many other examples in our everyday lives? Beth challenges us to redefine how we work, de-complex the situation, and be less structured. How? Include more mentoring, coaching, and stretch assignments. And be sure to sell training and learning to your executives and show them how you can help. And, of course, proudly market your successes.

The New Social Contract by Murry Christensen

In today's business environment, at every level, there is a very different set of driving principles. Long-term employment is no longer guaranteed and, given that, neither is employee loyalty. For better or worse, individuals are more in control of their professional development. Murry advocates that you need to become personally responsible and adopt a new mind-set—one that begins at your job, encompasses your career, and culminates at your profession. There is a new social contract (if I do *this*, then I expect *that* to happen)— and it is in *your* hands.

Are You a Vendor or a Partner? by Scott Sutker

Improving client and partner relationships begins with the terminology. But the expectations around this "marriage of equals" will also allow you to build and manage relationships in a new way. What can partners provide? What should clients expect? Scott, who has been active in both roles, thinks it makes good business sense to work in tandem to support each other and to connect the joint outcomes that are shared.

We Thought We Could, We Think We Can, and Lessons
Along the Way by Larry Israelite

In recounting the history of education, Larry points out how we have always been attracted to "things" (hardware, technology, the latest gizmos, and so forth) and how these same elements interfere with our ability to clearly apply them to build great training and learning programs. Yes, these "things" are necessary, but they are not sufficient—the training and learning experience still has to be well designed. The challenge then becomes how to use technology to support a realistic working model and not become diverted by industry fads and products. The more things change, the more design is still at the heart of it all.

Messing with the Primal Forces of Nature: Transforming
Learning by Lance Dublin

Lance is mad, and can you blame him? We can all relate to our industry's collection of data just for the sake of it, our lack of business knowledge, our seizing of ROI as a way to prove our worth, and other such activities that have not always won us the respect we have so actively pursued. He follows the history of training and learning in connection with civilization. Yes, we're now efficient, and yes, we can be effective, but we need to move on now to the transformational stage and to new mental models if we are to meet today's needs. Let's disengage from the past and look beyond the automation mentality in order to prove our worth in meaningful ways. Lance argues that the answer is not in the definition of "e"— but within each of us and what we can do collectively.

The Blue Pill or the Red Pill? by Mark Oehlert

Mark's rant, a "bombastic declamatory utterance," addresses a subject that has largely been ignored by the training and learning industry—copyright and patent law. What does this mean to you? Why should you even care? Well, just imagine that all our past efforts at training and learning are snatched away and that interoperability and object sharing are not possible—not due to technology, but to laws. Current and emerging developments in copyright and patent law represent a serious threat to the future of learning, and you need to be aware. Mark challenges you as to whether you want to remain in your comfort zone or to understand and begin to discuss the implications of this love/hate topic. It's all about choice—yours.

People Architecture: A Holistic Approach to Building, Maintaining, and Expanding Your Learning Infrastructure by Vicki Cerda

When acting as co-editor and project manager for this book, Vicki noted a gap in relation to business processes and the role of people in providing the internal and external services that support any learning organization. The "people architecture" chapter is the result of her addressing this opportunity and of her desire to unify the different author topics in an optimized vision. Using the analogy of building a house, she engineers a holistic and balanced infrastructure consisting of five "building" components that connect people to other core elements of the blueprint. But as we all know, the blueprint is not enough, so she drills down via detailed questions and strategic objectives to allow for practical and immediate application to your needs—in this case more like consulting an interior designer than an architect. What does your house look like? Is it part of the neighborhood and connected to the community? Is it time to renovate, rebuild, or even tear down?

OPERATIONAL EXCELLENCE AND NEXT GENERATION BLENDED LEARNING

David Metcalf

How do we meet the challenges of providing more with less in our organizations? Constant innovation in the areas of process improvements is necessary to achieve the most efficient organization with excellent operating processes. Learning and knowledge are key components of this trend toward operational excellence. Many companies are putting strategic initiatives in place to provide additional efficiencies and cost savings through the unique combination of several disciplines. These interdisciplinary efforts often carry the moniker of "operational excellence" (OE). Learning and knowledge professionals can play a key role in this area of emerging interest, especially as the rate of knowledge needed to innovate grows exponentially. This is an area of huge excitement for me as I see more organizations embracing this and raising the visibility of learning to meet organizational needs. Operational excellence is a goal everywhere! Leveraging an expanded view of learning to meet the challenges and promote additional efficiencies is a worthy goal for us to aspire to.

In this article, we'll first explore what disciplines are being corralled under the Operational Excellence label before drilling down into the specifics of how learning, knowledge management, and performance support are being leveraged for OE. We'll delve into the specific techniques and a few key examples of how blended learning techniques that incorporate online learning, knowledge management, and performance support come together as key factors for OE.

To conclude, we'll look at the longer-term implications for blended learning in OE and other strategic initiatives and how you can make an impact.

What Is Operational Excellence?

While the term means many different things to different audiences, the essence of OE is the synergy of transformational strategic and tactical areas that leads to high performance in an organization. Sample disciplines include change management; process management, including outsourcing; ERP optimization/leverage; six sigma; balanced scorecard; lean thinking/manufacturing; knowledge management; and education/training/learning (see Figure 1). Key to the success is a holistic view of how these disciplines work together. Some call it organizational efficiency as a discipline, but the intent and potential mix of interventions that improve operating performance are the same.

Figure 1. Overarching Strategy

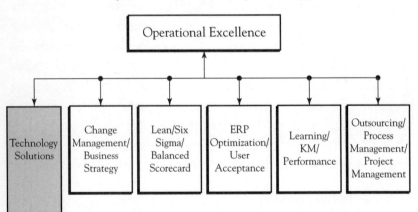

Many organizations have taken a more limited view and would say that this expanded definition is too broad, as much of the initial focus on operational excellence has been in manufacturing quality and measurement initiatives. Some of the most successful examples of OE in action have incorporated at least some of the services beyond the traditional quality improvement interventions, such as lean manufacturing, six sigma, and process measures like gap and root cause analysis.

Operational excellence is a growing trend, with the increased focus on reducing operating overhead and improving overall quality of the focus on process automation. Blended learning, particularly when it involves an extended view that includes knowledge management and performance support, is fundamentally a support mechanism and one strategy for automating the process of learning and performing important tasks with high quality and fidelity. A continuum of people, process, organization, and technology (see Figure 2) typically leads to improved performance and operational excellence. Of these elements, the *people focus* is the key.

Figure 2. Operational Excellence Elements

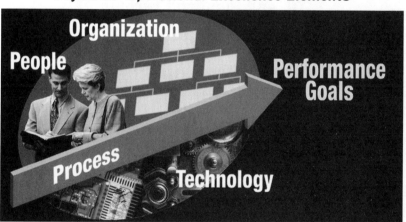

©RWD Technologies®

Operational excellence has substantial traction in the corporate arena. OE seems to be most prevalent in the following industries/segments:

Aerospace

Automotive

Contract manufacturing

IT/infrastructure

Pharmaceutical

Telecommunications

Some examples of companies that use this term include:

DaimlerChrysler

GlaxoSmithKline

Boeing

Nokia

NASA

Verizon Wireless

Rationale for Implementing
OE and Blended Learning

The value proposition of OE for a CEO, CIO, COO, and others involved in high-quality business and personnel performance is that the savvy learning leader can approach the topic of adding blended learning techniques at a strategic level with maximum potential impact on key areas such as IT or manufacturing. Tying to these larger areas of the organization raises the focus of learning in the organization and can also show direct return on investment (ROI) or, more importantly, a return on knowledge (ROK) that shows growth of the business rather than just savings through increased knowledge. The other key benefit to OE is that it ties together existing human performance efforts in a comprehensive, logical fashion.

How Does Blended Learning Factor
into Operational Excellence?[1]

Based on the overarching strategy of combining multiple disciplines to take a holistic look at organizational improvements, how does a blended learning model factor in? The following sections discuss an expanded view of blended learning that connects to various other disciplines that converge in an operational excellence group or initiative.

Most training and development organizations or departments in the world today are talking about the "blended learning model," and yet what's interesting is that they're not necessarily talking about the same thing. This is not surprising, however, since learning—which includes all types of training interventions as well as the various forms of continuous education—is a costly, complex, and time-consuming task for most companies at a time when they can least afford it. So to most people, *blended learning* simply means combining instructor-led training with some form of e-learning in a way that makes sound business sense—that is, an approach that reduces cost or increases performance, preferably both. But in this chapter we'll explore ways that *blended learning* can equally and simultaneously mean a blend of enabling technologies in order to create a hybrid model that merges elements of *online learning, electronic performance support,* and *knowledge management.* The expanded model not only makes immediate business sense (ROI) but also offers a strong return on knowledge (ROK)—or the expansion of intellectual capital for competitive advantage and innovation.

Consequently, a more thoughtful and detailed answer to "What is blended learning?" is that it can mean both *blended delivery methods* and the *blending of technology-based learning solutions* that are aimed at attainable performance goals. This latter type of blended learning solution is sometimes referred to as simply "e-learning," which somewhat masks the larger convergence of technologies and practices that are taking place. And yet e-learning projects have allowed many businesses and organizations today to discover approaches that integrate the best features of e-learning with other means of sharing knowledge in a powerful way, and the Internet and the web have given us many new and exciting options for blending our overall learning, training, and knowledge management strategies. For example, it's now possible to deliver not only self-paced instruction over the web, but also rich media simulations, group collaborations, real-time synchronous learning sessions, on-line assessments, and performance support solutions.

This expanded definition of blended learning that includes elements of knowledge management and performance support is a key component in serving the needs of the people involved in achieving operational excellence and defining measurements for successful learning.

Creating a Blended Learning Process and Infrastructure to Support Operational Excellence

So what might a blended learning process model look like, and how can we best build an infrastructure to support it? When we think about a blended learning infrastructure, we are tempted to visualize a hub-and-spoke model in which the management of learning or learners is at the center of the process. But from a business point of view, a blended learning model that is driven by performance objectives and business metrics would more likely look like the process depicted in Figure 3.

Figure 3. Blended Learning Infrastructure

Reprinted by permission of RWD Technologies® with special recognition of Ken Rebeck and Rick Contel for their contributions to the Model.

Such a model affords a powerful and cost-effective continuous learning solution that combines the following elements:

- *Learning*—Whether it's classroom, workplace, web-based, or intranet/Internet based, and delivered in a "live," just-in-time, or self-paced mode (see Figure 4).

Figure 4. The First Building Block

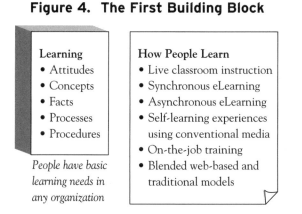

Learning
- Attitudes
- Concepts
- Facts
- Processes
- Procedures

People have basic learning needs in any organization

How People Learn
- Live classroom instruction
- Synchronous eLearning
- Asynchronous eLearning
- Self-learning experiences using conventional media
- On-the-job training
- Blended web-based and traditional models

- *Performance Support*—Job-specific, workplace-resident, paper-based, electronic, context-sensitive, and embedded support mechanisms such as job aids (see Figure 5).

Figure 5. The Second Building Block

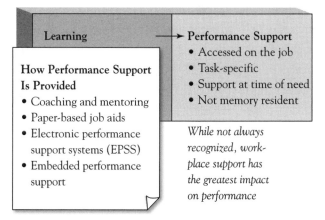

Learning

How Performance Support Is Provided
- Coaching and mentoring
- Paper-based job aids
- Electronic performance support systems (EPSS)
- Embedded performance support

Performance Support
- Accessed on the job
- Task-specific
- Support at time of need
- Not memory resident

While not always recognized, workplace support has the greatest impact on performance

- *Knowledge Management*—Those key documents, expertise directories, lessons-learned databases, best practices, and communities of practice that reflect and deliver knowledge to learners at a particular time of need.

Most importantly, this kind of blended learning model is derived from a clear understanding of the business objectives and how these can be translated into specific targets for human performance, which is often most dependent on two critical components: knowledge and skill. The learning, performance support, and knowledge management model acknowledges the fact that the basic categories of skill and knowledge are imparted differently. As a result, it focuses on optimizing the mix of classroom instruction, web-based online learning, and workplace performance support to maximize the total impact on human performance.

The learning component of the blended learning model relies on blending classroom, asynchronous e-learning, synchronous e-learning, and on-the-job training to support the delivery and retention of the knowledge and skills needed to produce performance improvement. Similarly, the performance support component of the model provides access to the knowledge base in the workplace—both before and during job performance—to help direct and guide task-based activities. Here, performance support activity can draw from elements found in learning or knowledge management, or those specifically designed for performance support. Each of these core components of the blended learning model can stand alone; however, when properly integrated, they form a powerful strategy for achieving performance objectives, creating consistent and predictable performance, and allowing organizations to efficiently and quickly convert new knowledge into practice. (See Figure 6.)

Figure 6. The Full Blended Learning Model

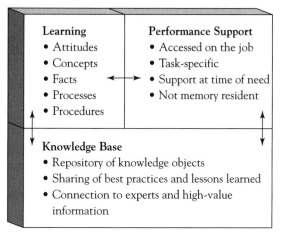

Launching and Tracking Blended Learning Solutions

Many organizational e-learning projects begin with the implementation of a learning management system (LMS), which typically can help with the launch and tracking aspects of training management, performance measurement, and a career plan of a learner's continuous development needs. Thus, a typical LMS-focused system should be able to track training activities, including completion of those activities, track the performance of learner, track their assessment results, establish a learning plan or curriculum for learners, and allow learners to register for upcoming training events or self-service e-learning opportunities, such as a typical web-based training course.

It's also essential that the LMS be able to manage instructor-led classes, self-paced web-based training, real-time (or synchronous) e-learning sessions, access to discussion boards, best practices databases, assessments, communication tools like the now, chat, and instant message applications, curriculum maps, and other learning resources, such as the web, audio and videotapes, books, magazines, journals, and so on. This will allow the learner to self-select the materials that are most useful to him or her and also give the instructor or curriculum developer the most possible options for the delivery of sound instructional content.

Many other critical functions also contribute to a successful blended learning strategy. For example, learners should have access to communities of practice where they can interact with their peers, mentors, and trainees to provide a high level of social learning. The system should also be able to track tacit (experiential, judgmental) learning and individualized learning, as defined by the learner. A knowledge management component to a system will allow this to occur, and the ability to launch a wide variety of e-learning activities will be central to an effective blended e-learning strategy.

Other elements of the infrastructure are very important to the overall process of an effective blended learning system. For example, a synchronous learning tool or several synchronous learning tools will allow real-time classes and training. Some organizations are choosing to host these services internally, while others are choosing to address these needs externally through an ASP (application service provider) model.

Learning Challenges and Applying Knowledge Within the Blended Learning Model

In a more practical sense, all organizations seem to struggle to create blended learning solutions that optimize the mix of classroom instruction, structured on-the-job training (SOJT), and web-based learning. The process requires a thorough approach for conducting the planning, analysis, design, implementation, and evaluation phases relating to training interventions and can be applied to a full range of business situations, from basic course or curriculum conversions to development of a virtual corporate university.

Thus the blended learning development process must also include extensive criteria for making sound decisions on course content conversion, the level of student/participant interactivity, assessment, and testing/certification, as well as the media delivery strategies that will be used. Here, solid planning ensures that a comprehensive solution can be created that satisfies a company's complete needs for rapid and cost-effective learning, performance support, and knowledge/content management.

The *learning* component, in most cases, will support the delivery and retention of the knowledge and skills needed to produce performance improvement, for learning describes "how" information and knowledge are delivered to the learner. It draws its content from the knowledge base, which often includes predefined granules that the learning management system (LMS) needs to organize and present to blend traditional training and e-learning interventions. We will also examine the elements of performance support and knowledge management that are part of our larger blended learning process.

Learning has three phases:

1. Prior to job performance (training). This includes how to do tasks, how to use performance support, and how to participate in knowledge management practices. Its objective is to bring people up to a prescribed level of knowledge and skills.

2. During job performance (when actively doing the job). This includes structured on-the-job training (SOJT) and self-training using performance support. Its objective is to bring people up to a prescribed level of performance.

3. During job performance (when not actively doing the job). This includes participating in knowledge management. Its objective is to allow people to access and share the knowledge needed to exceed previously defined levels of performance.

In *learning*, "what" involves the knowledge being communicated, taught, learned, applied, evaluated, and archived and it has a significant impact on "how" that material is best conveyed for maximum comprehension and retention within the organization. Embedded within the KM component of a blended learning solution are five categories of knowledge that can impact performance: attitudes, concepts, skills, processes, and procedures.

Attitudes are developed to help people make sense of, or interpret, other pieces of knowledge within the context for learning. Attitudes are often culturally based and strongly influenced by peer groups. Attitudes can be acquired and form the early part of organizational learning that is often thought of as change management.

Concepts include generalizations and structures into which more detailed pieces of knowledge can be formed or housed to give them a context within the whole. Mental models, process flows, and knowledge taxonomies are all examples of concepts.

Skills are the explicit capabilities individuals must have to support the execution of complex tasks.

Processes are the interlinkings of tasks that lead to specific accomplishments.

Procedures are the core knowledge elements that lead to performance improvement, the "how to" of job-related tasks. For example, to understand how to apply a procedure, the performer must have a working knowledge of its five essential aspects, including why, who, when, where, and how. These five dimensions are not equally easy to communicate or learn. And becoming proficient in executing procedures requires the acquisition of both explicit (step-by-step) and tacit (experiential/judgmental) knowledge around each of these aspects.

Each of these basic categories of knowledge potentially contains a mixture of tacit and explicit knowledge. *Explicit* knowledge (for example, how to make a photocopying machine produce multiple copies, collate the pages, and staple the results) can easily be put into a static knowledge base and used within a performance support system, whereas *tacit* knowledge (for example, what I've learned to do when the copier jams) can be extracted from subject-matter experts through protocol analysis, what-ifs, and teach-backs before it is recorded into an explicit form. However, *complex explicit knowledge* (for example, how one keeps a nuclear reaction "in balance") poses such demands on most people's information processing capabilities that performance support technologies can be useful to augment people's limited memory capacity and information processing speed. While knowledge management can be hard to get one's arms around, it is a driver in knowledge sharing and building communities that OE teams can thrive in. Operational excellence teams require integrative technologies and processes that help the teams from diverse backgrounds work more closely together and understand others' disciplines.

A sufficiently large knowledge base can also be useful in recording a model of the system plus its dynamics. In contrast, *complex tacit knowledge* (for example, in making this decision, how I ensure that Group A's interests are not perceived as having higher priority than Group B's interests, even though that is the case) is not easily represented within a knowledge base, nor is such knowledge readily teachable, except in circumstances that foster mentoring and apprenticeship experiences. This is where the integrated nature of the blended learning model is most powerful. It can address the needs of different learners and performers at different times in their learning and performance lifecycles.

Successful Blended Learning Solutions

Because of their synergistic and multidisciplinary nature, blended learning solutions often exhibit several key characteristics that allow them to dramatically and positively affect training and development activities. The following list describes several key attributes of an effective blended learning solution:

- *Formalized:* The solution is based on sound research and development in the field of adult learning and also reflects e-learning "best practices" in the industry.
- *Systematic:* The solution relies on a strong methodological and project management approach with measurable outcomes or predictive metrics.
- *Repeatable:* The solution can be widely deployed across disparate parts of the organization by a diverse workforce with similar positive outcomes.
- *Scalable:* The solution is not prototypical, but rather scalable to an enterprise-wide implementation.
- *Manageable:* The solution can be easily managed as an internal or outsourced training solution with strong ROI.

- *Adaptable:* The solution is not brittle and can accommodate a wide array of learning styles and organizational training contexts.
- *Standardized:* The solution uses standard approaches and measures for instructional design, outcomes assessment, and system interoperability, such as AICC (Aviation Industry CBT Committee) and SCORM (Shareable Content Object Reference Model).
- *Integrative:* The solution synthesizes a variety of existing training models, typically involving other systems such as ERP and CRM. This is key to operational excellence integration.
- *Synergistic:* The solution combines the complementary elements of online learning, EPSS, and knowledge management to build a total solution that is greater than any of these technological approaches alone.

Armed with these heuristics for successful blends of knowledge, learning, and performance, it is possible to connect these areas to support the functions of operational excellence. In order to create this synergy, some level of organizational realignment or outsourcing often makes sense in order to augment skills and produce good operational excellence results. Rounding out an internal training team's capability and raising the level of contribution to the overall organizational mission often requires partnerships both inside and outside of the organization. The other key element to achieving the efficiency and effectiveness possible with blended learning is a strong focus on performance metrics that use both business analytics and training analytics. Measuring key performance indicators to define success and operational excellence will take your learning organization to new levels and prove the value of blended learning.

How Do You, as a Learning Leader, Become Involved in Operational Excellence Initiatives?

The overall goal of this rave has been to take a look at how the next generation of blended learning solutions that involve knowledge management, performance support, and learning can be effectively accomplished within key strategic initiatives that improve the overall performance of the organization. Whether you call this operational excellence or use some other term does not matter. Good businesses are looking for anything that can make them more efficient and allow excellent operations. I hope you are catching the vision for ways that blended learning can have a huge impact on your organization's operations.

You as a learning expert, responsible for infusing a learning culture in your organization, can make a difference in these efforts by becoming involved early with these emerging initiatives. Rather than being relegated to a corporate overhead cost, smart learning experts are seeking out opportunities to make significant financial and operational impact on their organizations. This secures their future and the future of the business lines they support by promoting the best practices of blended learning in the trenches of operational business lines, where it counts most. What are you waiting for? Promote operational excellence throughout your organization through next generation blended learning!

The alignment of next generation blended learning with the needs of the organization can position the learning function to help achieve the vision, mission, and goals. Long term, this approach, more than any other technology or individual process, can lead to breakthrough performance for individuals and for the organization. Leaders in this area will be armed with the organizational impact that leads to personal advancement and, perhaps, the fulfillment of the vision for a true learning organization that espouses operational excellence as its mission.

Note

1. Adapted from Bielawski, L., & Metcalf, D.S. (2005). *Blended e-Learning: Integrating Knowledge, Performance Support and Online Learning* (2nd ed.). Amherst, MA: HRD Press.

DINING WITH THE EXECUTIVES

Doing the Right Kind of Training That Will Get You a Seat at the Table

Beth Thomas

I love learning. I love everything about it. I love its successes, its failures, and especially the unknowns. There is so much to reflect on over the last fifteen-plus years I have been in the industry; however, the topics of choice are a rant about the fact that there is too much structured training, that is, the world is on "training overload," and a rave that training finally has a seat at the "table." We've finally been invited to dine with the executives!

Why Do We Have So Much Training?

Processes, systems, and behaviors should be much simpler to learn. For example, why is there no training needed for kids playing the Xbox®, Nintendo® Game Cube, Game Boy® Advance, or PlayStation®? This audience just "gets it" without any training at all. How about an ATM? How many of you went to training on how to use an ATM to receive or deposit money? Does your local bank offer training courses on how to use one? What about online bill paying? Is there training on what to do once we get into a restaurant or store? How about the new movie theater ticket dispensers? You don't see movie theater "trainers" all over the mall, do you? Of course not. So why in the world do we feel the need to train on everything we do? Perhaps it's job security for training professionals. Maybe they think, "The more training I do, the more indispensable I am." We need to figure out how to build systems, processes, and behaviors to be more intuitive, easier, and a natural part of our everyday culture. We need to be involved in the systems design, jump in on the process teams, become visible up-front, and not just at the end, where training typically comes in to save the day (or to get blamed for all the failures)!

Think about it. How can we get this new type of thinking into the corporate world? We are so busy thinking of how to build dynamic content, e-learning, synchronous learning, asynchronous learning, virtual classes, and so forth that we forget the genesis of the problem. Everything is way too difficult. We need to simplify everything. Everything from our language to our systems to our processes. Learn to observe. Watch. Listen. Have you ever been in a business meeting and not understood a word said? I bet you can find e-learning courses on "Business Speak." What about systems? To utilize some of the systems out there, you need a Ph.D.! I have seen systems training programs that go on for weeks and they didn't even go over the process behind it! How many times have you seen, or been a part of, training on broken processes? Why doesn't anyone ask, WHY are we training on this? Can't we make it simpler so we don't have to have any training? Who should be asking that question? I'll tell you who . . . YOU! It doesn't matter whether you are leading a training organization or are part of the training organization, or are a recipient of the services of the training organization— it's up to YOU to ask these questions. To become an active questioner. Improvements in our industry are dependant on professionals like you. By simplifying the systems and the processes we use each day, training becomes more concise and prescriptive for its learners. It's shorter, it's relative, and it's beneficial. This type of training takes more time in planning, more analysis of what is truly needed and by whom, and structure of the training content to ensure that it's applicable to all who take it.

Taking It All a Step Further

Since we are starting at the beginning and redefining how we work, I would challenge you to go a step further. Once you push back to ensure that what you are training about is really needed and that there is no other better alternative, you must make learning a way of life. An everyday occurrence. Part of your organization's culture. It should even feel "unnatural" if we go one day without learning.

Don't get me wrong; training will always play a part in our world. However, there should be less of it and we should be more creative about how we deliver it. In general, we have come very far with training, learning, and change management. The fact that we have the ability to work from anywhere in the world, be connected, and share best practices is something I never thought I would see. We have finally taken training from an event to a process with this type of connectivity and with blended learning solutions. However, many training professionals and leaders still get carried away.

Today's training options are endless. I never thought this would be a problem. However, it has become one. Training has become almost *too* complex. People are so concerned with the technology they are using, or being the "first" to do something, or with being the best at delivery that they don't step back to see whether it's really working or, more importantly, they don't see whether or not it meets the need of the customers. I can't tell you how many people I have talked to who purchased an LMS (learning management system) and have no idea how to make it work for them! How many people do you know who have bought the latest and greatest technology tools, gadgets, and gizmos without having a clue of how they will support their training strategy?

A Revelation? Hardly.

I'm going to let you in on what some may see as a revelation; for others it's no secret at all. I have found a way to train people that has been proven for hundreds of years, costs almost nothing, doesn't utilize an ounce of technology, and most of all guarantees results! There are several different names to this special "secret" business practice. Are you ready? Here we go. Many would call it shadowing or mentoring or coaching. They are three different things, but all very useful in a learning experience. *Shadowing* is observation of someone doing what you would like to know how to do. *Mentoring* is giving advice to a peer, direct report, or colleague on how he or she can improve or move ahead. *Coaching* is what we all do every day. We help our direct reports, our peers, and sometimes our bosses on ways to avoid pitfalls to better themselves every day.

There is so much to be said about shadowing and observing the colleagues we work with every day. Spend a week with people who are superstars within your organization and you will get more from that one-week experience than you would have with three, even four weeks of training. There are multi-million-dollar training budgets out there, but if you would evaluate what is truly needed, you could cut a lot of money from it if you used this simple type of training-and-development strategy. Too many people measure training and learning based on how many hours they put their people through training. There are even state credits on how many hours you have put your employees through. But what we should be measuring every day instead is whether people are learning. Are they able to exceed their key performance indicators? Are people able to exceed the requirements of their job and, if so, why? I work with superstars every day and watch every move they make: in meetings, in the hallway, even their demeanor on the phone or in the lunchroom.

If you ask anyone to think back and tell you about the best learning experience in his or her life, do you think he or she would tell you it was a great training class or e-learning event? I bet not. I bet you would hear that it was from either shadowing a colleague or being coached by a friend or mentor. Most importantly it could be working on a *stretch assignment*. A stretch assignment is when you are given the opportunity to work on something that you may not know how to execute by yourself. It's beyond your current skill set.

It's beyond your reach, but not your ambition—something where you have to research, learn new things, fail forward (failing in a safe environment and learning from your mistakes), and work harder than normal to succeed. Let's next focus on these two key components— being coached and stretch assignments.

Every Business Person Should Have a Mentor or a Coach

How many of you have a mentor? You don't have to be in corporate America, or own your own business, or even necessarily work outside the home to have a mentor. You can even have more than one. Perhaps also a spiritual mentor or an industry known mentor—as many as you want. So how do you get one? Just ask! In the workplace, it needs to be expected and part of the culture of the organization— this is the model we need to use in business. This in itself is a great training program! Someone to show you the ropes, the political landscape of the company, lessons learned, and what success truly looks like. Note that none of this comes in a training class. It's the real world.

In some organizations, it's tough to find a mentor or develop a program. Some business cultures simply don't encourage, expect, or sustain this. But it is my belief that it needs to be the expectation of every leadership team member, the culture around what they teach and demonstrate every day. People need to be held accountable for teaching and learning—all the way up to the chairman of the Board. You will see that successful companies are working toward this philosophy and already "get it." I bet every company would be able to find a "model" employee for every position who could help coach others or, better yet, help training professionals build training on how to become that model employee. If you could capture what has made them successful, bottle it up, and teach it, you would be a very successful person too! Interview the superstar employees and build programs on how to become that person by modeling his or her knowledge, skills, abilities, and behaviors. I believe that most of my strongest attributes came from within and from observing such successful people—observing people I considered to be the best. Why is shadowing better than any formal training program? Because when you are with the superstars, you can ask any question you want, get information and knowledge you need—a personalized program built just for you. Once this coaching, mentoring, and shadowing become an expectation within your company, it becomes a way of life, a teaching culture. This is truly the best culture to be a part of.

A very important thing to remember about coaching, mentoring, and shadowing is that you cannot do without having a good sense of what you are trying to accomplish in the end. Many people fail in corporate America, and sometimes not because they didn't have what it takes, but because they just didn't know what they needed to do to succeed. How many of you would like to know what the perfect person looks like doing your job? If you don't already know, you'd better find out, as it's up to you to find out the expectations of your role. And if you are in a training organization, it's up to you to understand this for all the jobs you support so that you can build training programs to support these jobs.

S-t-r-e-t-c-h Assignments

Now lets talk about "stretch assignments." How many of you ever looked at a project and thought to yourself, "There is no way I will be able to pull this off" or "This is too hard for me to do," but when you finally did pull it off, it was the best work experience you ever had? That is a stretch assignment—something that perhaps you haven't been trained to do or is much more difficult than what you are used to doing. In the end, it's the best type of development and training that you can ever receive. It may feel overwhelming at first, it may feel uncomfortable and it may feel BAD all at the same time, but after it's done, there is a great sense of accomplishment and confidence that enables you to achieve those same results over and over again, getting better each time. There is nothing more gratifying in the world of work today than to take on something that you don't think you can do . . . and to do it. Now THAT is learning! The best learning that I have had in my career is from having an executive coach, from observing superstars, and from succeeding at stretch assignments. If you can create a work environment that expects and holds people accountable to make sure those things are part of the culture, you will be very successful! And so will the organization.

Dining with Executives

Now let's rave for a bit. I am so proud to be a part of the training industry. I have been in the industry when training was the first thing cut from the budget, when it was looked on as a dead-end career, and when it was a place to go right before you were written off to the great corporate pasture of life. However, now it's a great time to be part of the training industry! The training industry is where to be, where the action is, and where successful people migrate. Let's face it, in today's economy, everyone is fighting to be the best. The only way you will be the best is by having the best people work for your company. Building talent is a top strategic component of any business plan and mission. So how do you build talent? Yes, training is a large piece of it, but it must be coupled with shadowing, coaching, and stretch assignments. The top companies in the world recognize this fact, and the leaders within those companies are creating the "teaching cultures" I spoke about previously. How does that happen? How do you get the top executives in a company to adopt and support a teaching culture? How do you, the training professional, get invited to the "table" and help make training a top priority? I'll tell you how. You educate executives on what training can do. You sell it. You don't sell the tools, the technology, or the classes you have to offer. You don't sell the number of people who need to go through training. Stay away from all that training-specific lingo during any conversations with executives! The way you do sell it is by understanding what the top business goals of the company are, what type of people are needed to get the job done, and how this translates to shareholder value. If you talk to the business leaders in their language, language about what it takes to win, to add profit to the bottom line, and to make customers come back for more, they will LISTEN. Yes, you have to do your research before meeting with them. What is the pain of the business? How can you help? Who are you training? What do they need training on? Why? Do you even know your business? What is its value proposition? Have you ever read its annual report? The business plan? Mission? You have to know your audience and the business in order to gain executive support.

One of the best ways to do this is to know your customer wants and needs. When a customer comes into your company for the products and services you offer, what makes him buy? What does she like and not like? This knowledge also should be incorporated into all your programs. Your goal is to know your customer, understand your customer. By doing this, you will be able to build the talent in your organization necessary to create shareholder value.

Once you have figured out how to help the executives solve their business problems with training, present your plan. After you present your plan, make sure you understand their expectations and in the end make sure you give them a return on their expectations! This means not only developing programs and opportunities to help solve business problems, but also making sure that the programs you develop create sustainable performance that will translate into bottom-line results for the company. And when you win, when you can quantify true performance results from your programs, go back and tell them. Communicate and market your successes. This will ensure you are invited back for a permanent seat at the table. The way you get that permanent seat is by becoming a trusted advisor and colleague and by proving that your programs work. We see people winning awards on great training programs, great use of technology, great use of blended learning, and lots more, but how many times do you see what type of performance improvement it led to for the business overall? Everyone may tell you they loved the training, but how many of you ever go back and see whether the training "worked"? Did you really help build talent? Did you help move the business forward? If you don't go and find out, you will lose the trust and respect of your leadership. It is very difficult to get to a Level 4 Kirkpatrick evaluation (that is, validating the training you delivered translated to true business improvement) but it is a MUST when trying to sustain executive leadership and support.

Executive Sponsorship

A very important tip I received a long time ago is to secure a corporate or executive sponsor for any large initiative you are trying to move forward. Use that person as a sounding board to obtain advice on how to sell and market the program or, most importantly, to obtain advice on what is truly important and what performance goals you are trying to achieve.

And you have to ask the right questions. Why do true training professionals start the instructional design process by doing a training needs analysis? Why not a performance needs analysis? Perhaps training is not the answer. We need to ask the right questions about what we are trying to change or improve. This could drastically impact the program you build or *don't* build! If you do a good job upfront, do your homework, talk to your customers, and plan a program that directly aligns with the goals of the company, you will be a success and have that permanent seat at the table with the executives.

I cannot minimize the importance of executive support. The fact is that, in the end, the only way to get results with training is to have executive support and visibility at the top of your company. It is their job to put learning in the forefront of people's minds and make it a priority, part of the everyday culture in order for you to succeed. You have to understand their expectations of training, of the business, of building talent, and of you. And if they do not set the expectation in the company that it is up to each individual to take charge of his or her own career, development, and destiny, then they truly aren't supporting training and learning within the company. Most executives say they support training and learning. Most executives really WANT to support training and learning. But it is up to you to have them prove it. Are you up to the challenge?

THE NEW SOCIAL CONTRACT

Murry Christensen

"Social contracts" underlie our deepest expectations about risk-reward, tradeoffs, and the role of various actors in the large-scale transactions that make up daily life. If I do *this*, I expect that *that* will happen. *I* take care of this part of the daily life and *you* take care of this other part. Learning is a lot like that. More accurately, expectations about who drives the learning process, especially in an adult context—which is what we'll confine ourselves to here—are a LOT like that.

This article is an exploration of the evolution of the social contract. Every act of navigation requires a compass . . . some guiding principle(s) you can refer to in charting your path. Here's the relevant one for this moment: the social contract that underlies American-style capitalism broke in the mid-1970s and a replacement is still being formed. Among a lot of other things, the social contract influences—if not controls—how a society manages its expectations of what constitutes career and how that identity is forged. But first things first. What is a (usually THE) "social contract"?

What Is the Social Contract?

The social contract is usually defined as that shared set of expectations and responsibilities that define the (most important, non-legalistic) rules by which the various parts of society (individuals, associations, corporations, government) gauge and calibrate their interactions—in short, the mutual bargains that underlie the interactions within society. If I act in *this way*, I can usually assume that somebody else will behave in *that way*. For example, if I politely ask a stranger for directions, he or she will be likely to respond by giving me the information I need, not turn his or her back without answering—behavior deemed by observers to be rude. Nor is he or she likely to respond by deliberately giving me false directions— which an informed observer would call malicious—nor by punching me in the mouth—which would potentially result in the legal sanction of an assault charge. The fact that we just assume those various interpretations is an indication that the social contract is at play.

Why Does the "Old" Social Contract No Longer Apply?

In their provocative (and if we're lucky, prescient) book *The Radical Center*, Ted Halstead and Michael Lind argue that the breakdown of the social contract is a result of the social challenges posed by what they call The Third American Revolution. As they note:

> This is not the first time that America has found itself in this predicament. Twice before, technological and economic progress, along with demographic change, has forced American society to struggle to adapt to a transformed environment. (p. 12)

These transformed environments are thought of as resulting from the effects of the first and second Industrial Revolutions on the particular set of relationships between the three spheres of life: market, state, and community:

> The first American republic, formed in the aftermath of the American War of Independence, was in place by the early nineteenth century. It was a decentralized agrarian republic that lasted until the Civil War. The Civil War and Reconstruction produced the second republic, a regime better suited to the conditions of the First Industrial Revolution. The next wave of change, the Second Industrial Revolution of the late nineteenth century, gave birth to a third

American republic, defined by the New Deal consensus that coalesced between the 1930s and the 1960s. (p. 36)

To these historical eras we must now add the transformation we're currently living through, that occasioned by the Information Revolution. The dawning of a fourth American Republic.

Since societies tend to have a fair bit of hysteresis (lag in response to a change of state), social contracts usually persist for some period of time after the conditions they represent have mutated into something else. Such a change occurred in American society during the 1970s and 1980s, when the relationship between employees and employers was radically rewritten during the period of corporate re-engineering and downsizing. The paternalistic system that traded employment and centralized career direction for the security of long-term employment changed to an especially relentless version of "employment at will," which saw people as "human resources," to be acquired and discarded as appropriate to short-term market forces.

When I was growing up in the suburbs of Detroit in the 1960s and 1970s, a lot of the people I was in school with had the expectation that they'd "inherit" their fathers' jobs at Ford. A nice middle-class industrial job, with steady hours and manageable overtime, a long August vacation every few years when model changeover occurred, punctuated by the occasional labor action during contract negotiations. My father worked for the same company (Michigan Bell) his entire professional life . . . and he was representative of his age cohort. Then everything changed.

Do you remember "re-engineering"? During the late 1970s through the 1980s and into the early 1990s, very large changes occurred throughout American business. Under the rubric of "maximizing shareholder value," large swaths of middle management were cashiered and companies were combined, restructured, realigned, and recast in a new, "leaner" mode. These changes occurred for several reasons. The business environment was changing in response to information technology advances and investments, removing the need for an information "gate keeping" class. Foreign competition intensified, much of which had learned how to operate with faster cycle times and improved quality, at lower costs to consumers. The savings and loan scandals burned up large amounts of monetary value that had to be replaced. Organizations, anxious to try anything to retain or gain a competitive edge, were cycling through management models at ever-accelerating rates, upsetting any received wisdom and amplifying the volatility of change. "The Imperial CEO" rose to prominence, on whose back the revivification of companies was seen to lie, providing a need to "do things differently," whether there was really any need for the change or not.

The result—a business environment with radically different driving principles—as is illustrated in Table 1.

Table 1. The Old and New Social Contracts

Expectations	Old Social Contract	New Social Contract
Corporation	Stability in business landscape over long periods of time (ten to twenty years)	Volatility and change over short time periods (.5 to five years)
	Lifetime (or at least very long-term) employment	"Employment at will"
Individual	Loyalty in return for stability	Perpetual uncertainty
	Centrally planned career development	Individual responsibility for career portfolio
Educational Institutions	Training for a stable career	Career self-reliance
	Received wisdom	Autodidactic
Government	Pensions and healthcare tied to an employer relationship	Portable retirement savings and universal healthcare

Note: For completeness, "education" and "government" are included to indicate that, as a response to a broken social contract, all aspects of society are ultimately involved. For brevity, they're subsequently ignored.

Corporate Expectations and the Social Contract

"Employment at will" means that employment is voluntary for both employees and employers. Employers may terminate you whenever and for whatever reason they want, usually without consequence. Conversely, you may quit your job whenever and for whatever reason you want. (Of course, in common law employment in the United States has always been at will. I highlight it here to indicate the changed volatility of the status in current times.) For this discussion, the upshot of this change is that individuals now have to take substantially more responsibility for and control over their own professional development. The organization views its employees as an expendable resource, to be downsized or upsized as conditions demand. Seen in the best light, this isn't (usually) a result of some heartless or malicious intent on the part of employers. In fact, there's often nostalgia for the good old days. But the reality of the landscape is that prudent business practice demands a particular— and different from previous—view of "human capital." The term itself gives it away. Capital is a fluid resource, easy to move around or redirect. That's its virtue.

But people require a substantial investment to grow and nurture. Internally developed talent is sluggish to redirect, requires investment that doesn't always pay off in quarterly timeframes, and disappears when the employee leaves. Again, it's not that employers deliberately created this situation. It happened and they have to react to it . . . or die. The logic that's been forced on the company is to view employees as a market resource, which the organization will dispose of when and if required and then reacquire when changed market conditions make that necessary. Seen more dyspeptically, it's a result of intellectual laziness, faddishness, and/or shortsightedness.

You can think of it as a structural problem if you're so inclined: there's a mismatch between the timeframe in which external conditions change and the timeframe in which talent can be internally grown to respond to those changes. Training organizations have the reputation of being slow to react, bureaucratic, and divorced from the real business needs. Forgetting the sins of the past, in the world just described any organizational part (such as a department) is going to be subject to the same constraints as the whole. Things take time to develop. You have to build them, which takes time. You have to deploy them, which takes more time. Then they have to be maintained every time the initial impetus changes. With these facts staring you in the face, how can you reasonably expect the training department to keep up with current (that is, lagging) needs, forget about getting ahead of the curve?

No wonder people ask whether instructional systems design is broken. It is . . . and it couldn't be any other way, given the historical facts. It was built to respond to a different world . . . a world that ran on a different clock . . . a world that's in the process of dying away.

Individual Expectations and the Social Contract

In *The Radical Center*, Halstead and Lind argue for an enlargement of *choice* as the core of a new social contract and for benefits tied to the individual, not the job, promoting mobility—political reforms that give voice to a broader range of political options, breaking the increasingly nonfunctional gridlock fostered by our current two-party political structure—an educational system that allows parents greater control over their children's education, introducing competition into a mostly monopolistic landscape—at least for working and middle class families.

Focused as they are on the overall arena of public policy, Halstead and Lind restrict their analysis and prescription of learning to formal K-12 education. But as discussed above, learning doesn't—and increasingly can't—stop with formal schooling. Given the realities of the post-industrial world, that world shaped by the Information Revolution and which, to use their terminology, will birth the fourth American Republic, there's only one solution to this quandary that I can come up with: make people realize that they're responsible for their own careers and their development. *Personally* responsible. Erase the expectation that you can opt out of lifelong learning and the assumption that some paternalistic organization is going to handhold you, spoon-feeding your development diet. Why?

- You ought to; you're the one who benefits from the invested time and energy.
- You have to; it's the way things are and there is no going back to the old days.
- You're closest to the issues; therefore you ought to be able to diagnose the need.

Going back to my own experience, yes we can think about structuring the range of worldviews along a spectrum—starting at *job,* moving to *career,* ending at *profession*—and one in which the direction the progression goes (right-left, left-right, up-down, down-up) is entirely dependant on how you organize the hierarchy.

- *Job*—an honest day's work for an honest day's pay; the industrial-era way of thinking about the social contract, characterized by a time-based value structure.
- *Career*—associate, vice president, managing director; the mid-century "Man in the Gray Flannel Suit" version of the contract, characterized by loyalty to hierarchy and often an employer or a small group of employers.
- *Profession*—not as simple as the other two; for example, you can have a career inside a profession. But the characteristics that distinguish this position are identification with content and/or expertise.

With their ultimate loyalty being to a community of practice rather than any particular employer, the professions have developed external standards (professional licensing and certifications), structures for continuing education (CE and CPE credits and requirements), and, most importantly, an expectation among practitioners that the knowledge they base their continued viability on—both economic and status—is dynamic, changing, in need of monitoring, and portable since it is carried within themselves and independent of location or employer.

A Solution

What I'm arguing for here is the triumph of (more precisely, the necessity for) the adoption of the professional mind-set, regardless of what kind of work you actually do. The tragedy of the job landscape in the past couple of decades (well, one of the many tragedies) is that this change has occurred and there's been no organized societal response. For the most part, we've all been left to figure it out for ourselves. To assemble our resources, construct our networks, create and maintain our portfolios. More critically, there's been very little in the way of organized support or structure to help the individual take charge of that realization, if and when it comes.

Fortunately (or inevitably, since the solution is actually embedded in the problem), the collection of capabilities and applications to make this feasible are starting to come about. Google. Open courseware. Learning objects. Digital rights management. Web services. It's getting to be a pretty rich toolbox. What we need now is an awareness of the changed circumstances, the available resources, and the mind-set to use what's available now and explore what's being added every day.

And *you* say, "Easy for you to say, you just happen to have a personal history, socioeconomic position, and hardwired skills to live that way. Not everybody has the same advantages. Pretty arrogant to be prescribing such difficult medicine to other people." True enough. The problem is that no matter what angle I look at the problem, it won't go away . . . and I can't come up with any other workable alternative. I'm no George Gilder or Louis Rossetto, but the need and the solution—difficult though they might be—seem pretty inevitable.

For Further Exploration

An extreme example of the consequences of a broken social contract: www.manbottle.com/video/Why_men_don_t_ask_for_directions.htm

The *Radical Center: The Future of American Politics* by Ted Halstead and Michael Lind. New York, Anchor Books, 2002.

The New America Foundation, among other public-policy initiatives, works to advance the overall program laid out in *The Radical Center*. For more information on their work, see www.newamerica.net.

ARE YOU A VENDOR OR A PARTNER?

Scott Sutker

It sometimes blows my mind how shortsighted a vendor can be. As someone who was in sales for five years before my current role in a large learning organization, I have now seen both sides of the coin. I certainly don't view our vendors as suppliers—I would much prefer them to be partners!

Let's first look at the definitions (from www.dictionary.com):

Vendor. One that sells or vends: *a street vendor; a vendor of software products on the Web.* [syn: seller, vender, trafficker]

Partner. An associate who works with others toward a common goal [syn: collaborator, cooperator, pardner]

Which would you rather work with: a seller/trafficker or a collaborator/cooperator? It makes such perfect sense that you should strive to create a collaborative and cooperative relationship. Here's why: *Any* mutually supportive relationship is better than a seller-purchaser relationship. The very nature of a partnership causes each partner to seek win-win outcomes instead of win-lose. And each partner looks out for the other's best interest. Let's look first at what I expect from my partners; then we'll look at what I can provide in return.

Partnerships—What I Expect

With priorities that can change on a daily basis, I want our partners to understand that I rely on them to help me during peak times. I want them to understand my business and help me reach solutions under tight deadlines. I expect flexibility, and I am willing to give it in return.

Partners look at long-term relationships and do not view each project as a "cash cow." Partners understand that there is give-and-take and that on some projects they may not make a ton of money, but on the average project, they will make a reasonable profit.

Partners look for ways to add value to my organization. This may include introducing us to new technologies or other vendors and informing me on industry trends.

Partnerships—What I Provide in Return

In the past, I have helped our vendors by:

- Becoming a customer reference. I have hosted telephone calls and benchmarking visits.
- Collaborating on joint press releases, industry awards, and newspaper and magazine articles.
- Hosting regional user group meetings for their customers.
- Providing speakers for trade show events.
- Providing leads of companies looking for products or services.
- Providing industry contacts of skilled employees looking for job opportunities.
- Providing suggestions for their product roadmaps.
- Providing significant return business!!!

Am I crazy here? Does this make too much sense? How come many of the companies that call on me do not see that I want to be partners?

What a Partnership Is Not

I have had many "vendor" relationships, and it has been very clear when the vendor's intention was not to be a partner. Some examples include the following:

Holding Me Hostage

One vendor came to me thirty days before a project was due and demanded that I pay them an additional $10,000 or they would pull out of the project and leave me high and dry. When asked why a $10,000 surprise, they said that they did not manage the project budget well and could not pay all of the contractors they were using. Obviously, they thought I would pay the money rather than risk not meeting the schedule. However, I was able to move internal resources around to finish the project and save the unjustified $10,000 bill. Needless to say, I will never use that vendor again!

Ignoring My Needs for Personal Gain

This example has happened many times. I have worked with vendors and have given them our infrastructure requirements (PC configurations, bandwidth, recording keeping, reporting, and so forth). Many times, the vendors would not test for the requirements or they would ignore them. These vendors wanted to develop content to other specifications so that they would have something cool to show our competitors. It did not matter to them that it did not run on my infrastructure.

Leaving Me with a Mess to Clean Up

Another vendor expected me to do their quality control. They would not test to ensure that all of the branching, testing, and reporting would work before they delivered the code. Not only that, but they would not even spell-check their work. Obviously, they had huge quality-control issues and were always rushing to meet deadlines. Simple errors like misspelled words that are not corrected raise "red flags" that make you question: What else is wrong? If the vendor cannot get the simple things correct, then how about the important things like instructional integrity?

Rejecting an Entry Point

I asked a local vendor to work on a short, thirty-minute computer-based training for which I only had a budget of $12,000 to $15,000. I told them that I would look at this as a "foot in the door" project, but the vendor responded and said that they had a project minimum of $25,000 per project and they would not consider working on a project under $25,000. Wow, hard to believe but true!

Keeping Me Guessing

Turnover. It gets very frustrating when a vendor has high turnover. I like to work with partners who learn my business and therefore have very short learning curves. I have worked with companies where every time I needed assistance, there were new project managers or new instructional designers. The people I worked with in the past had already moved on. If a company cannot keep employees, it can really say something negative about the ethics, morale, and their work environment.

One time when I was looking for a learning management system (LMS), I had three different sales representatives from one company work with me during the request for proposal (RFP) process. It was hard for me to even keep up with whom to work at their company during the inquiry stages of the relationship. This certainly did factor into my decision on which vendor was chosen.

What were these vendors thinking? Were they looking for long-term partnerships to initiate a long-term revenue stream? I don't think so. They wanted to look at the short term and figure out a way to help their own companies without thinking of how to help their customers. How do they think they can be in business long without forming partnerships?

Change Is Painful

Another reason for wanting partners is because change is very painful. If you have a give-and-take relationship with a partner instead of an order-taking situation with a vendor, moving from one relationship to another is less frequent. Change can be difficult in many different instances:

Content Library. When you choose a content library from a vendor or partner, your users become very familiar and comfortable with the courseware. They get used to the learning instructions, the navigation, and the testing mechanisms. In addition, your IT partners also become comfortable with the maintenance of the library. If you decide to change libraries, you must think of the following: bandwidth studies, linking the new courses to competencies, notifying customers that they must finish training because new courses are coming, taking all of the old courses out of the LMS, and uploading the new courses into the LMS. There are probably one hundred other items that you must consider, and it is a long, expensive, and somewhat painful experience to change content libraries.

LMS. If you choose to switch to another LMS, you must think of all of the aforementioned items, as well as the culture change of your organization. When my company implemented a new LMS in 2003, we had 22,000,000 hours of legacy training that had to be loaded into the new LMS. The entire LMS transition process took over twelve months, thousands of labor hours, and many customizations. It was a painful experience.

Content Developer. If you choose to change to a new e-learning content developer, you must think about the learning curve you have already built. This includes:

- Knowledge about your business, products, and services.
- Understanding of the technical requirements and standards.
- Usage of templates and other streamlining tools.

Request for Proposal (RFP). To do a good job of scanning the marketplace for content libraries or learning systems, a formal RFP process is also very painful. I have been involved in finding new training partners, and it usually takes a considerable amount of time. To gather support, resources, and budgets just to go through the process can involve many different stakeholders, including information technology, purchasing, business units, management, legal, and usability testers. I have never been on a team that could get this process done more quickly than ninety days, and the average time to secure a new partner, and do it right, is approximately 180 days. If you add up all the time spent by internal resources during the selection process, it is quite expensive and painful!

What a Vendor Can Do

Before joining my current company, I sold documentation and training solutions. I learned how hard it was to generate business with new companies and how easy it was to generate business within existing accounts. Approximately 90 percent of my sales were generated from three accounts. I was the leader in sales for the company four out of five years, and this was accomplished mostly by partnering with my clients. Some things I did to create a partnership atmosphere included the following:

- Cut prices! Yes, I know it sounds strange, but we had a contract grow from two to three people providing services to eighty. I didn't need to make a ton of money on each person because I could make it up in volume. My customer was shocked and actually presented my company a customer appreciation award at the end of that year.
- Provided speakers for their meetings and events.
- Kept them up-to-date with industry trends.
- Allowed them to hire our employees, which we had placed at the client's site, after ninety days from their start date at no cost (no finder's fee).

- Said "No!" If my customers asked me to do things and I could not meet or exceed their expectations, I would tell them no. I would usually try to help them find another company that could provide them the services they desired.

- Took shared risks. We would do joint projects and share in the rewards or learn together from the failures.

- Provided mentoring and consulting advice to them. I knew what was going on in the industry and I could help them figure out solutions to the problems they were having. I would also arrange for benchmarking visits with companies facing the same problems.

So if you are a vendor, I hope you will consider looking for partnerships instead of sales opportunities. If we wanted to purchase based on pricing only and did not care about forming relationships, we would just look to the cheapest source, including offshore opportunities. If you are worried about your products and services being bought from overseas sources, then do something about it by forming strong partnerships that your customers cannot live without.

If you are a purchaser, I hope you can relate. You really want to find partners who look at entering into long-term relationships. It is easier to deal with partners on a long-term basis and know that they are looking out for your best interests and are not trying to "stick it to you" when they can. Our jobs are too hard for the time and effort vendors require. We want partners!

Take the Partnership Pledge

If you decide it is in your best interest to create partnerships in your business relationships, take the pledge that follows. This pledge is geared toward training/provider relationships; however, the general principals should transfer to any client/partnership relationship.

Vending Partner

I hereby pledge the following to my clients:

- I will look for ways to improve my client's business and impact his or her bottom line. This may include consulting, services, or products. It may or may not involve any "billable" services or product sales.

- I will look for ways to cut my client's costs. This may include reducing my costs or providing new technology that will result in lower costs for my client.

- I will look at each project with a win/win attitude. I will try to make a reasonable profit and not gouge my clients. I will never view them as cash cows.

- I will never hold my clients hostage during the business relationship. This may include using proprietary software/hardware, withholding source code, or threatening to pull out of a project.

- I will never "over design" a project with elements that are not needed or that do not enhance the instructional integrity of the project. This may include adding extra audio, video, simulations, or animations that are not required.

- I will always design to the hardware/software specifications of my client. I will ensure that the products that I deliver will launch and track in the company's infrastructure. All media elements will run within the specifications of that environment (for example, bandwidth constraints and minimum PC configurations).

Sourcing Partner

I hereby pledge the following to my sourcing provider:

- I will always treat my sourcing partner with the utmost respect. I realize that I must work in my employer's best interest, but I pledge to be fair, honest, and respectful to my sourcing partner.

- I will always look for ways to leverage our agreements and help the sourcing partner maximize the contract in our company.

- I will always practice a "no surprises" philosophy and keep the sourcing partner informed on his or her standings in the company and communicate any issues as soon as possible and work with him or her to solve any issues.

- I will always pay invoices on time and per the contractual agreement.

- Upon request and on a limited basis, I will provide customer references to help my sourcing partners create new business relationships.

Signatures:
Vending Partner   Sourcing Partner

_____ _____   _____ _____
        Name   Date   Name   Date

WE THOUGHT WE COULD, WE THINK WE CAN, AND LESSONS ALONG THE WAY

Larry Israelite

My first job after graduate school was designing computer-based training (CBT) programs for one of the first commercially available CBT systems. This was in June of 1981, a scant two months before the release of the first IBM PC. The tools with which I worked comprised a minicomputer supporting up to 128 simultaneous users, a keyboard with an embedded instructional design strategy based on concept learning, a color display (a fifteen-inch Sony Trinitron) that provided twenty-four lines of text with forty-three characters each, and pixel-based graphics. Authoring tools included a highly structured system for teaching concepts, a simulation language, and one of the earliest full-featured graphics editors. This wasn't a bad place to start for a newly minted Ph.D. instructional designer with little practical knowledge and even less useful experience.

Over the next few years we added increasingly sophisticated authoring capabilities, integrated a videodisc player into the system, and, finally, moved to a platform based on the PC (some viewed this as a step backwards). My colleagues and I had the privilege of designing all sorts of interesting training programs, ranging from basic math skills to flight crew simulations to a "driver's education" program for tank commanders that was built around voice recognition technology (this was in 1986!). Our goal was to use technology to enhance the effectiveness and efficiency of the learning process, and technology was the means by which we would achieve that end. In other words, we endeavored to design highly effective and engaging instructional products that took advantage of the technologies available to us. There was no doubt that we were on a mission, and we truly believed all of the hype about computer-based training, much of which we created ourselves. (This was before the phrase "drinking our own Kool Aid®" had entered the vocabulary, but rest assured, had Kool Aid been available, we would have happily and energetically drunk it. We were, after all, about nothing less than revolutionizing the way people learned, or so we told ourselves.)

Were we successful? It's hard to say. For the most part, our products worked. We delivered sophisticated training programs that would, arguably, compare very favorably with many of the e-learning products that are available today. Users learned from them, time-to-mastery was reduced, updates were far easier, and the life-cycle costs were dramatically lower than with more traditional training methods. But commercial ventures are in business to make money, and, like most of the other systems with which we competed, profits proved elusive. So while we might have been an artistic success, we failed as a business.

Our products and services were simply too expensive for all but the most well-heeled customers. The company was sold once or twice to large defense contractors, both of which served a well-funded market. But the company and its products eventually disappeared, as did almost all of the other large CBT vendors of the early 1980s. And so ended what might be viewed as the first generation of what we now call e-learning. Or, more cynically, one might say that this was the first of a continuing series of failures in our ongoing search for a business model that simultaneously creates enriched learners and satisfied investors, something that has remained, for the most part, elusive for more than twenty years.

I offer this small bit of somewhat self-serving history to illustrate a simple point that is at the root of what I believe is our industry's single largest challenge—we simply don't, can't, or won't learn from the past. The essential elements of the story I told about the start of my career could apply to several other generations of learning professionals. Many great learning products have been created; many people have learned from them; many employers have benefited from the outcomes of that learning. But we haven't achieved the penetration or percentage of learning delivered through technology that we all believe is possible, and, of course, very few businesses have figured out how to generate the kinds of sustained profits that current-day investors require. So no matter how we look at it, we would be hard-pressed to declare victory.

So what haven't we learned? What is it that keeps preventing us from experiencing the success we keep searching for? Why is it that we have been unable to find the formula to achieve the impact that we all believe is possible? I believe there are three specific mistakes we continue to make, and that these, in tandem, make our success more elusive than it ought to be. They are

- We are attracted to things instead of thoughts;
- We keep looking for ways to exclude learning professionals from the creation of learning products; and
- We put too much stock in the words of pundits who tend to divert us from our search for solutions to everyday problems.

Toys Are Us

We like things—stuff, toys, trinkets, junk. We are the nation of pet rocks and then electronic pets (the Tamaguchi). We have an economy built on home shopping channels and infomercials. We buy $250 remote controls that can change our channels, dim our lights, open our garage doors, and even start our cars. We have cell phones with features we don't need and computers with features we don't understand (what is an 800mhz front-side bus anyway?). We even buy SUVs, although we live in locations that haven't seen snow since the ice age. We simply love to have the latest gizmos, whether we need them or not.

This attraction to things extends beyond consumer purchases. We behave the same way in our professional lives. We listen to, believe, and respond to the claims of the creators of new technologies.

We invest heavily in them, fully expecting to achieve the incredible results promised by those who sold them to us. Moreover, inevitably, the results are not achieved, and then we again begin the search for the next product that will solve all of our problems.

This phenomenon didn't begin with computer technology. I remember, for example, showing up at school one year to find TV monitors suspended from the walls of my classrooms. Educational television was going to revolutionize public education. The teaching profession was to be changed forever. And learning, of course, would never be the same.

Unfortunately, no one had really taken the time to figure out how the new technology would be used in the classroom. And there was a pile of questions no one was ready to answer. Was there programming? If programming was available, was it consistent with the curriculum? Was it any good? And after all that, could the district even afford it? Apparently, the answer to the last question was no, because I don't recall seeing anything that was professionally produced.

So some enterprising educational bureaucrat figured out that one solution might be to produce programming locally. We had good teachers, good content, and, after all, a pile of expensive technology. So this idea seemed to make sense.

That's where Mr. Strackbein comes in. He was my science teacher, and he was very knowledgeable, extremely well-organized, and deeply interested in his students. But he would never have been mistaken for someone with a dynamic personality. We managed to get through his class because every now and then we got to see him do something really interesting. He mixed chemicals that smoked, hissed, flashed, changed colors, and smelled. He talked about what he was doing and we got to ask him questions, which he answered in a language only a few of us actually understood. But his answers sounded impressive. And perhaps best of all, he was live and lifesize; he was present. At the very least, the classroom stimulated all of our senses and made what was a challenging learning experience slightly less so. I think we may have even learned a few things along the way.

I think they tried to tape Mr. Strackbein just once. That was all it took. What was arguably tolerable in the classroom was simply lethal on TV. The sensory experience was gone, no one could ask questions, and anyone more than a few feet away from the screen couldn't see anything anyway. I don't know how much my school district spent on all of that equipment, but bulletin boards would have been a much better investment, as that is the purpose many of those TVs served. School districts all over the country spent millions and millions of taxpayer dollars on technology and had little to show for it. They had bet on the possibility that the characteristics of television would be a suitable replacement for those of a good teacher. It was a bet that most of them lost.

Good leaders argue that making mistakes isn't a crime. Not learning from them is. What we should have learned from this experience is that what works in a classroom won't always work on TV. Some of us didn't. Fast forward to the mid-1990s. Technology that allowed for "interactive broadcasting" had been invented. In simple terms, this meant that people at remote locations could watch a television broadcast and be linked to the studio through the use of a small keypad. Viewers could ask questions, respond to instant polls, and interact with the instructor in a way that approached the interactions found in a traditional classroom.

A successful training company contracted with leading universities and business schools to offer their executive education programs remotely. The instructors were well-known faculty with a great deal of experience at working with corporate clients. Clients were being offered interesting technology, good, relevant content, and excellent faculty, all at a reasonable price. What could go wrong? The answer is plenty.

Clients had to install special satellite dishes and then outfit each classroom with keypads and a special receiver. Classrooms had to be set up and tested prior to each session, and a technician had to be present to deal with any problems that occurred during the broadcast. Then, of course, the equipment had to be broken down and stored between sessions. This was a lot of work, but it seemed like a worthwhile investment in return for access to such high-powered content and faculty, delivered using technology that would provide remotely the level of interactivity typically found in a classroom.

Unfortunately, things didn't work out quite as everyone had planned, but about on par with what we should have expected. There were technology problems, and the programming wasn't all that good. It seems that the business model didn't include a sufficient design budget. And many of the faculty wouldn't have cared anyway. Rather than create new designs that took advantage of the technology, they simply wanted to do what they had typically done—stand in front of the classroom and talk, just like Mr. Strackbein. When everyone is in the same room with a very compelling presenter (or when there are chemicals involved), this model can work. But when the room is virtual, comprising dozens of classrooms scattered around the country, and the presenter is inside of a twenty-five-inch box, personal charisma and interesting content are no longer sufficient. And simply adding the ability to ask and respond to questions using the keypads doesn't make all that much difference. So course evaluations were low, people stopped attending, and the business quickly disappeared.

In some ways, none of this makes sense. If you have a great or, at least, a good teacher combined with a delivery medium with which everyone is comfortable, effective learning should be possible. That isn't to say there haven't been many situations in which video has been an incredibly effective learning tool. But in those cases, the television was a delivery system for an instructional event that was designed to take advantage of its characteristics. It wasn't used to display something originally designed for a different delivery method.

We have made several mistakes like this over the past twenty years in both our schools and our businesses. In the early 1980s, we invested in personal computers to deliver CBT (or computer-aided instruction [CAI], as it was sometimes called). Interactive videodiscs were next, both independently and in conjunction with a personal computer. In the 1990s, we switched to multimedia, and then the web brought us what we now refer to as web-based learning or e-learning. In all cases, we were convinced that a better, newer technology would lead to better, more effective learning that could be delivered less expensively and more flexibly than the more traditional delivery methodologies. And in each case, there were examples of programs and companies that were successful at using learning technology to achieve measurable results. But there is little evidence to suggest that the total investment in each of these technologies achieved the results we expected. Now there are plenty of e-learning libraries installed on corporate learning management systems that are gathering the digital equivalent of dust, just like those TV monitors I found in Mr. Strackbein's classroom. Great ideas, big investments, incredibly high hopes, and, more often than not, minimal results.

Why? The answer lies, I believe, in our attraction to things (new learning technology, in this case) and the way in which this interferes with our ability to think clearly about how technology can be used as a facilitator of learning. Hardware, no matter how we look at it, is nothing more than a content delivery device. It provides features: color, motion, sound, storage, and distribution. But none of these features, individually or together, achieves anything. They are just part of the set of tools the designer uses to construct an effective learning experience. In the examples above, the tools became the ends instead of the means. And the tools (the things), by themselves, simply couldn't achieve the goals we created for them.

It might be reasonable to ask whether or not this was a generational problem that resulted from our collective technological naiveté. Maybe it was just that we were taken with the newness of it all. Is it reasonable to assume, for example, that a generation that grew up with GameBoys® and computers and cell phones and iPods will be more intelligent about how they apply technology when trying to solve learning problems? I can't say for sure, but I don't think so. It seems to me that it's still all about the cool quotient. What's changed is the sophistication of the features and functions. But, I fear, the psychology remains the same.

Things—computers, networks, storage devices of all shapes and sizes—are necessary, but not nearly sufficient, for building learning programs that work. And our affinity for things makes it difficult for us to remember this when we are listening to the compelling promises made by those who sell them. Creating instructional designs that take advantage of the capabilities of the tools is necessary, which leads to the second item in my list of mistakes we keep making—we don't understand learning and don't value those who do.

The Nine Lives of Instructional Design

It's a little odd to hear your own obituary. But I am getting good at it. There isn't a conference on almost any subject related to learning or technology at which the death of instructional design, and by association, the instructional designer, is announced. People speak kindly about us, saying that there once was a purpose for our work and that we were nice people on whom others should look fondly. But then they shake their heads and proclaim that our skills are no longer needed and that someone or something else has replaced us, invariably involving video, graphics, or software development of some sort.

At first, I was alarmed. Had I made the wrong career choice? Did I somehow miss my own obsolescence? Should I be worried about an unanticipated early retirement? These and many other questions flashed through my mind. I began to take stock of the work that designers do in an attempt to figure out what had gone wrong, what had led to our apparently imminent demise. Here is what I came up with.

Designers help identify learning needs or skill gaps. We try to describe what people should learn as a result of the programs we design. We architect the learning experiences themselves in ways that result in the achievement of the learning objectives. We're not perfect, but we usually do a good job at this. Media selection is another activity we focus on in order to make sure that the ways in which a program is delivered make sense, given the needs, the objectives, the content, the audience, and the environment in which the learning will take place. Most of us know how to measure results in ways that provide meaningful indicators of success. And, finally, we understand a thing or two about the psychology of learning, which is the foundation on which all the other activities are based.

Based on this simplified list of the designer's work, I tried to figure out which ones don't matter any more, and I couldn't find any. I don't think anyone would argue that learning experiences have to be designed. But it appears that some may disagree about the underpinnings of the design process itself. It may be that each time someone announces that instructional design is dead, what they are really saying is that learning psychology has been replaced by something else as the foundation. And because of that, instructional designers are no longer necessary. Here are three examples to illustrate this point.

In the mid 1990s, CD-ROM-based multimedia instructional programs were the learning technology of choice (see the prior discussion of our attraction to things!). Since the technology allowed for the use of video in a way that had been difficult to achieve previously, a competence in video production became the foundation on which many CD-ROM programs were built. There were, of course, graphic artists and programmers involved, and many of the production teams included someone with the title of instructional designer. But a producer played the leading role, intended, I am sure, to provide clients with comfort that the project (or product) was in the hands of a competent professional who understood the technologies being used. This is what you would expect from companies whose primary expertise was the production of video.

Unfortunately, I was never comforted. Why? Because it was always so hard to engage in conversations about learning. Instructional designers were rarely included in meetings; it got to the point that they trotted one out whenever I showed up. Discussions about alternative learning strategies and evaluation techniques always took a back seat to effusive praise for the richness of the images and the ways in which special effects would be used to enhance the overall visual image. In a two-day span in 1997, three different vendors went out of their way to show a colleague and me how they used animated lips to make cartoon characters look more realistic. By the time we saw the third demo, all we could do is laugh. The vendor thought we were crazy; we were just depressed.

In fairness to video producers, they weren't the only ones who tried to jump on the multimedia bandwagon without recognizing the value of instructional design. A prestigious New England university published a set of leadership titles based on the work of very well-known faculty members. They had great content and terrific production values, but they weren't particularly effective instructional products. I suspect very few copies were ever sold and those that were sold were rarely used. I could venture a guess that the product line was a failure. I could also guess that instructional designers didn't consume a significant portion of the budget.

The second example involves the World Wide Web, or the Internet. As this technology emerged, its natural home was IT departments and university computer science programs. Tools and languages were developed to make web product development fast and efficient. People began to add the work "web" to their titles—web master, web architect, web designer. And suddenly, we had web-based learning, and companies purporting to do that work popped up like weeds. I used to say, somewhat tongue-in-cheek, that they all were started by twenty-two-year-old computer science majors and their significant others, some of whom happened to be graphic designers. In retrospect, I may have been right more than wrong with my somewhat flippant comment.

Web competence became the foundation of the learning products for this generation. It wasn't clear that this group had ever even heard the words "instructional" and "design" used in the same sentence. So having an instructional designer on the production team would have been unlikely. And I, having learned my lesson a few years earlier, didn't have the energy to even bring it up. So I waited, and slowly but surely, as consumers found out that poorly designed web-based learning programs weren't worth the network bandwidth they consumed, these companies disappeared at an alarming rate. And so went another artifact of the "dot-com" boom and bust.

To be clear, there were many examples of very effective, meaningful instructional products produced during the time span covered by each of the learning technologies addressed in the examples described above. There were many instances of collaboration among a variety of professions, including video production, web developers, graphic artists, subject-matter experts, and instructional designers. But as a rule, I believe that expertise in learning and in how effective learning experiences are created was not viewed as a necessary part of the process. And as a result, product quality suffered.

The third example is very new and it is too soon to tell how it will turn out. At a professional conference in late 2003, a speaker said with surprising certainty that instructional design was dead. Game design, he said, would become the foundation on which learning products would be built. The rhetoric sounds familiar—a seemingly new technology and the profession that uses it taking the industry by storm, profoundly changing the face of learning.

I can't say with absolute certainty that he was wrong. But on the other hand, instructional designers have been creating games for years. Games can be very effective tools for achieving a wide range of instructional goals, when used in the right situation and with the right audience. But they are instructional games. They are created using well-documented and highly reliable design processes and tools in order to achieve specific learning outcomes. And they can be delivered using a variety of media including, but not limited to, a computer or the Internet. Without question, the emerging competence in game design represents an exciting opportunity for collaboration. But if history is any indicator, eliminating learning expertise from the equation will significantly reduce the likelihood of success for an industry based on games intended to achieve learning outcomes. I suppose only time will tell what happens.

The World According to . . .

Later in this same 2003 conference presentation, a suggestion was made that games (designed, of course, without instructional designers) would become the predominant training delivery method in the not-too-distant future. It was another pronouncement much like those of the industry pundits who so willingly forecast our future and attempt to influence our decision making. The problem is that I am not sure pundits actually know what they are talking about, and I am less sure that we are served well by listening to them. I believe their primary mistake is that they draw conclusions based on a sample that is not representative of the population whose behavior they are predicting. Here is an example.

I have three sons. Two I acquired the old-fashioned way. The third became a family member through a weird quirk in Massachusetts squatter legislation: he spent so much time at our house that he acquired family member status. All of them are in college; one at a large state university, one at an elite liberal arts college, and another at a moderately sized private university. They all grew up with computers and are avid (compulsive?) users of instant messaging, which has become our primary form of communication throughout the school year. They are part of the generation that pundits would have us believe prefer computers to classrooms.

So I asked them each, individually, a simple question: "If you had the choice of taking a course in a traditional classroom or taking the same course on a computer, which would you choose?" All three of them picked the classroom. They offered a few caveats. One said, "If the class was in a huge lecture hall and all the professor did was lecture, I would rather just read the notes online." Another said, "If it were a math course and all we did was review problems, I might pick the computer." One of them asked a friend who was in the room at the time how he felt. After a short pause, he gave the same answer. But there was little enthusiasm for removing the direct face-to-face contact that a classroom provides. I was surprised, so I kept probing.

Then I asked about instant messaging. That didn't appeal to them because they thought it would be hard to have spontaneous group discussions. (I might mention here that we once tried a family instant messaging session. We all found it a little cumbersome.) We talked some more and what emerged was one of the principles that guides the work of those not-long-for-this-world instructional designers. All media are appropriate under certain conditions. And for my three sons, these conditions led to a preference for sitting with other people and engaging in meaningful conversation.

It is important to remember that the members of my minuscule sample have been in classrooms since they were two years, nine months old, the age at which children in Massachusetts are allowed to attend preschool. They, as has almost everyone else, have been brainwashed to believe that formal learning happens in classrooms. So adopting any other method of learning will require a significant change in very ingrained behavior. It also will require many thoughtfully designed learning experiences that take specific advantage of the technologies on which they are based (there is that design issue again) and that result in learning they believe is valuable.

I am aware that colleges and universities continue to experiment with different modes of teaching. A very good friend of mine teaches several of her courses using the Internet, and her students rate them equal to, or higher than, her more traditional programs. However, this particular institution is largely a commuter school, and getting to campus can be a hardship. Thus, given the characteristics of her audience and the conditions under which they desire to learn, the delivery media and methods she has chosen are appropriate. But one simply can't conclude that this particular approach is always appropriate or that everyone always prefers it. And this is exactly what the pundits would have us believe.

Now to go back to my gaming friend who suggested that gaming would become the dominant method of delivering corporate training. The reasons, as near as I could tell, were because of the popularity of commercial computer games (he had lots of data on this) and the technology and tools that were available for the design and development of games. I just smiled.

A Mile in My Shoes

By way of background, I am responsible, among other things, for leadership development in a reasonably large company. I have to provide a variety of learning experiences to approximately three thousand leaders at all levels. They come from more than a half-dozen different businesses and range in age from their early twenties to something just this side of retirement age. Some have high school educations and others hold Ph.D.s. They manage blue-collar workers, customer services agents, corporate staff (that is, finance, HR, IT), and highly technical engineers. They lead individual contributors, other leaders, and business functions. Some are just highly paid and very well-respected individual contributors. I almost forgot to mention that they speak English, Spanish, French, and German, and a few other languages that I won't even mention. I have to offer a curriculum that addresses both the company's needs and my customers' individual needs, all on a reasonable, but still modest, budget. I don't think my situation is particularly unusual. Most people who do the kind of work I do face exactly the same challenges, some much more difficult than mine.

In a needs assessment we just completed, the first thing everyone said about prior leadership development efforts was that the most valuable parts of the programs they attended were lunch and dinner. It isn't that they thought the food was all that good. It was the opportunity that meals provided for them to sit and talk to each other; to learn about the business, the personal challenges they all face, and how they deal with them. They talked about customers, and sales opportunities, and job opportunities. They formed communities of practice about being a leader who values leadership. Sometimes they even formed friendships.

My challenge is to figure out how to use technology to support a delivery model in which direct human contact is the most highly valued attribute of the offering. Will I embed some forms of e-learning in the curriculum? Without a doubt! Am I likely to include some form of business simulation in the classroom programs? Absolutely! Would I like to find a way to include a game or two (computer or otherwise) as part of the media mix? I wouldn't have it any other way! But will gaming be the primary form of delivery? Not a chance. Even if I could afford it, which I can't, the designer in me constantly reminds me that the audience, learning environment, instructional outcomes, and the content itself drive media choices, not the availability of new technologies, pundits notwithstanding. So games, interesting though they may be, become just another option in an ever-increasing array of interesting media choices.

What I would really like is for pundits and prognosticators to walk in the shoes of the people who are responsible for improving business performance through learning. Attend the meetings *they* attend, talk to their customers and see the things *they* see, and try to solve the difficult, frustrating, persistent problems they have to solve. Study the constraints under which they have to work as they try to design solutions to address the needs of the businesses they support.

Then, perhaps, pundits might change their approach. Perhaps they would go to conferences and offer suggestions about the kinds of problems new technologies might be able to help solve. Perhaps they would focus more on the outcomes that learning professionals might be able to achieve. Perhaps they would just start being more helpful than they are right now.

One could argue that the role I am describing isn't one that pundits should play. But they have visibility and credibility. They speak with authority. And they have the ability to influence what learning professionals do. Given the enormity of the challenges we all face, a little extra help would be greatly appreciated.

And in the End

Earlier I said that our inability to achieve the success we all desire has, in part, been because we don't learn from our mistakes. I attempted to describe them and then provide examples of how this has played out over the past twenty years. I painted an overly grim portrait of the state of our art. In all honesty, I don't really think everything is as bad as I made it out to be. In fact, I am more optimistic now than I have been for quite a while. Simply, we are becoming more and more creative about the way we go about solving problems, and I think our diligence is beginning to pay off.

But still, we have many more miles to travel. So if I found Aladdin's magic learning lamp, this is what I would wish for:

- That we learn to resist the lure of sexy pretty things (technologically speaking, of course). We should, instead, strive to be practical, always searching for the features and functions that will help us achieve our learning goals.
- That we take on faith that learning is a science and develop a healthy respect for those who understand it and who know to apply that understanding to the creation of meaningful learning products and processes.
- That we not forget that learning professionals spend much more of their time dealing with the mundane than the exotic. It's great to fantasize about the two or three weeks each year that I spend on vacation. But it would probably be much better for me to concentrate on the forty-nine weeks I have to work so I can go on my vacation with a clear conscience.

Cheryl Wheeler, a wonderful folk musician, wrote a song in honor of her father's seventy-fifth birthday in which she describes the changes he witnessed during his life. In the chorus, she asks: "Are you more amazed at how things change or how they stay the same?" I think this is an especially appropriate question for those of us who have been doing this for a while. Which would you pick? Have things really changed? Or are we just walking on a treadmill? I don't have an answer. I am somewhat cynical because it is in my nature to be so. At the same time, I continue to see many new and exciting ways to improve the quality, flexibility, and impact of the learning opportunities we help to create. I guess I am just amazed. All in all, that's not such a bad place to be.

MESSING WITH THE PRIMAL FORCES OF NATURE

Transforming Learning

Lance Dublin

You may know the scene. If not, rent the movie. The movie is *Network*. It was released in 1976. In the scene, the lead character, Howard Beale (played by Peter Finch, who won best actor for this role), completely fed up with the hypocrisy he sees all around him, implores his audience on live network TV, "Get up right now. I want all of you to get up out of your chairs. I want you to get up right now and go to the window, open it and stick your head out and yell, 'I'm mad as hell and I'm not going to take this anymore!'"

First one person opens a window and shouts at the top of his lungs, "I'm mad as hell and I'm not going to take this anymore!" And then another. And then ten others. And then hundreds. Until the whole city seems to be reverberating with the words, "I'm mad as hell and I'm not going to take this anymore!"

I can relate. That's exactly how I feel when I reflect on the state of our industry. "I'm mad as hell and I'm not going to take this anymore!"

I'm mad as hell that for the past twenty-five years—and if I read the literature correctly, for many more years before I came along—learning professionals have been whining about the fact that senior management doesn't understand the value they bring. That we aren't invited to participate in key business decisions. That we get no respect.

In fact, because of this, I've come to term our profession the Rodney Dangerfield profession. For those of you who don't know Rodney Dangerfield, he made a career out of his failure to get respect, capped off by his 1981 Grammy Award for his comedy album, "No Respect."

Sure sounds familiar to me.

I'm mad as hell that we do so little to get respect. We continue to talk in a language that business leaders don't understand. Ask the average senior business manager if he or she knows about Don Kirkpatrick's four levels of evaluation. Or course objectives? Or if he or she even cares? The answer is a resounding, "No!" What managers care about are measurable business results in a language they can understand: profits, cost of sales, time to proficiency, and increases and decreases in key business indicators.

It reminds me of the stereotype of the American tourist on holiday in a foreign country. He's trying to make himself understood. But instead of learning the local language he just starts speaking louder and louder—in English. To corporate leaders, we are that tourist!

I'm mad as hell that we continue to collect and report data that business leaders don't care about. And, of course, technology only makes the situation worse because it allows us to more quickly collect and report data that doesn't matter! If you're a CEO, do you really care about the number of courses your employees take? Wouldn't you rather know how that time spent directly impacts the business?

I'm mad as hell that we continue to search for the "silver bullet" that will catapult us into the ranks of the respected and valued. We don't do the hard work of understanding how organizations operate and how we can contribute to their success. We don't learn to talk in the language of the organization. It amazes me, for instance, that so few learning professionals have MBAs or come from a business background.

I'm mad as hell that, in order to gain respect, we have seized on return on investment (ROI) to justify our existence. All ROI calculations seem to prove is that we can do activities of little perceived value cheaper and faster. But if it's of little value, wouldn't you want to get it as cheaply as possible? Of course! And we wonder why senior management pushes us to do it even more cheaply. You can't save yourself into competitive advantage. To be competitive you must surely be efficient in all aspects of your operation. And effective in the execution of your strategies. But true competitive advantage comes from finding ways to create business value, not necessarily saving money.

I'm mad as hell that we've promoted e-learning as a term for a revolutionary new way for people to learn. Human beings have been learning for millions of years. Learning hasn't changed. What has changed—and will continue to change—is the context in which we live and, therefore, learn.

We Know a Lot About Learning

We start learning with the first breath we take as babies and we only stop learning when either we choose to or we die. We know a lot about learning. And we've learned over these ages what works and what doesn't work.

The earliest humans learned how to survive by trial and error. Those who learned better and faster survived. Children learned from children and adults. Adults learned from adults and children. The learning was all hands-on, hands and tools being the only technology available at the time. Those humans didn't have the "benefit" of Kirkpatrick's four levels of evaluation. It came down to "learn or die." Quite a harsh final exam. And truly pass-fail.

But civilization grew and life became more organized. Villages formed. Work became more specialized in order for everyone to survive and prosper. And it turned out that not everyone was really good at hunting or farming. That among us were singers and dancers, cooks and tailors, metal workers and carpenters. Survival was now a larger group effort, and the larger group needed more to survive.

The ancient Chinese philosopher Confucius (551–479 BC) wrote about learning so very long ago:

I listen and I forget
I see and I believe
I do and I understand

But learning by trial and error alone was too slow. So the skilled began to formalize the transfer of knowledge to the unskilled. Masters took apprentices. Guilds were formed. Priests and politicians lectured to the masses. Using the best learning technology of the day, writing, documents were created to capture information and facilitate the transfer of knowledge.

And then there was a revolution. Not just the social and political kind (there were many of those all the time), but a technological revolution. A means was invented to enable the sharing of information better, faster, and cheaper than ever before. It was called the printing press. The printing press shook up the educational establishment of the time and a new phrase was coined, "book learning." Now we could capture and share the knowledge of the wise with the many. And as civilization developed so did the model of formal education in the form of school and courses.

Civilization continued to grow and develop. Villages became cities. States and nations formed. Inventions catalyzed the development of an industrial economy. We fought two world wars. And now, in addition to "book learning," we could share information and transfer knowledge by radio and then TV. We could take the very best of our teachers and expose thousands of students to them at relatively low cost.

Fast-forward to the 1950s and the famous American educator Thomas Dewey, who said, "All experience is learning." But the predominant learning paradigm continued to be via "telling and showing" rather than "doing and experiencing."

Then the computer was invented and our world changed forever again. Some say as dramatically as with the printing press. Or more so. Computers enabled us to distribute not just "talking heads," but fully developed multiple-media courses and even simulated experiences faster and cheaper.

Next, one stand-alone computer was soon connected to all the computers through intranets and the Internet. Distribution channels extended far beyond one company. And today they have extended to the whole world, in real time. Our challenge therefore isn't understanding learning. Our challenge is to understand how to make learning more effective in today's world.

What's in a Definition?

I'm mad as hell that we have seized on e-learning as a silver bullet. When the term e-learning was popularized around 1999, the world was in the midst of its love affair with anything and everything "e": e-Business, e-Commerce, e-Tailing, e-Toys, e-Cards, e-Dating. Put an "e" in front of it and even the greenest MBA could raise a couple of million dollars.

Those in the training industry surely didn't want to be left behind. Companies that had never before seen an "e" in their business plan raced to jump on the "e" band wagon. Established companies changed their tag-lines, their marketing materials, and even their names to get some of that magic "dot-com" dust. New companies were formed with the millions of dot-com dollars available. And in this race to riches, even individuals became "dot-commed."

Talk of stock options and IPOs was heard at training conferences. Training companies went public and were tracked by industry analysts for the first time. It seemed like a new, more highly valued industry was born. An industry that was current and of-the-times.

But what really is e-learning?

In the "early days" before the Internet was such a dominant force, e-learning in fact wasn't called e-learning at all. It was called web-based training or online learning. Most people thought of it as the logical next step in the evolution of computer-based training (self-paced courses delivered on a PC), which, in turn, had evolved from computer-assisted instruction (self-paced learning courses delivered on a mainframe or mini computer), I should point out.

Since computer-based training was commonly defined as the delivery of courses using a computer, web-based training was defined as the delivery of courses using intranets or the Internet. But as time went by and we began to understand the impact and possibilities offered by this new "e" world, more comprehensive definitions evolved.

From Efficiency to Transformation

We are in fact repeating a three-phase process of technology adoption that has been around for quite a while. New technologies are typically introduced into our culture in these three phases:

1. *Efficiency*—do what we know how to do cheaper and faster.
2. *Effectiveness*—do what we already know how to do better.
3. *Transformation*—do things we have never done before.

Think about it.

As a worker you want to get paid. In the 1980s as companies automated their systems, you most likely were paid by a computer-generated check. And these checks were certainly a more efficient way to get paid than hand-written checks or cash for any number of reasons. But at the same time, you still had to take the check and deposit it in your bank account. At times, banks would put a hold on your check until it "cleared," meaning they had confirmed that there was, in fact, enough money in your employer's accounts to pay you. This could take days.

Then in the 1990s, companies upgraded their computer systems again. And electronic links were developed between institutions. Direct deposit was invented. It is certainly not only a more efficient way to get paid, but it is also more effective. It eliminates the need to go to the bank to make a deposit, it provides access to your pay immediately, and it makes it easier and less expensive for your employer to manage the entire payroll process.

But most of us still are paid bi-weekly or even monthly. Our employer holds on to our salary until payday. But what's so sacrosanct about payday? In fact, the state laws typically are that your employer must pay you on your last day of employment if you leave or they terminate you. Not on your last payday. So why can't we be paid weekly or daily or even hourly? And why can't you have your employer pay your bills directly in the same way they pay into your 401K or retirement accounts? Why can't we re-think the relationship we have with our employers so that the definition of employee changes?

Today, the initial hurdle to accomplish this is the technology. There just isn't enough computing power or bandwidth. But that won't necessarily be true in the future. I, therefore, predict that when the youngest of our children join the workforce, direct deposit will seem as quaint to them as hand-written checks or cash do to us today.

So it is with e-learning. We know how to create courses. Courses have been around since we formalized the learning process to make it more efficient. So it's natural that our first inclination is to figure out how to take any new technology—radio, TV, film strips, video, computers, LANs, WANs, intranets, the Internet— and use it to make the delivery of courses more efficient.

But as we become more comfortable with the new technology and explore its potential, we are able to see ways to make the learning process more effective. We are beginning to realize there is more to learning than just courses. So while we're well on our way to making formal learning more effective, we are beginning to recognize the validity of informal learning as well.

I'm mad as hell that we keep putting the "e" in front of the word "learning." By doing so, we have focused our energies and efforts on applying the "e" to learning as we now most often deliver it today— in courses. Simply put, e-learning = e-courses. Most people in organizations think of learning as courses, even though research proves that most of what people need to know to do their jobs, they learn through informal means rather than formal ways. And that for every hour of formal learning they complete, they spend twenty-five times that in informal learning! But regardless, it seems that courses still rule.

Continually putting the "e" in front of the word learning leads to what I call an "automation mentality" of learning. Take what you are currently doing—'cause after all, you know how to do that—and apply technology to make that process more efficient, to do it faster and at less cost. So often e-learning has been promoted in this way: better-faster-cheaper courses.

But what if you move the "e" to be a superscript to the word learning. Learning^e. Then the focus changes to be on learning and the "e" represents everything possible to impact learning in an exponential manner. That is transformational.

Toward Transformation

I'm mad as hell that the world around us is way ahead of us and we don't seem to be paying attention. In fact, it appears we are looking backward. While we focus on how to apply the "e" to courses, the rest of the world is learning how to apply the "e" to transform itself. Without any formal design or acknowledgement, Google® has, in fact, become the world's most widely used e-learning application for the simple reason that it is designed for today's world.

To Google has become a verb. And "googling" is huge. In fact, Google's 200 million searches *every day* represent only 31.5 percent of all online searches just in the United States. However, if you ask those searchers if they are doing e-learning, they'll look at you blankly. Searching the Internet to find the information you need in order to answer a question or solve a problem very, very quickly is just the way we work—and live—today.

In *Network*, Peter Finch is warned by the powers-that-be, "You're messing with the primal forces of nature, Mr. Beale!"

And again I stand with Mr. Beale. I intend to mess with the primal forces of the learning industry that keep us anchored to old, outdated mental models. I believe people should be angry that the learning industry and learning professionals are not meeting their needs in today's world. I believe people should be mad when the learning industry and learning professionals focus on lame issues and meaningless data that do not address the world we live in and the way we live, work, and learn in it.

It's time to become engaged with the future rather than rooted to the past. The new technologies are changing not what life is, but how we live it. We need to therefore accept that new technologies are also changing not what learning is, but how we enable, extend, and enhance it.

THE BLUE PILL OR THE RED PILL?

Mark Oehlert

So what does every hack writer do when he can't figure out how to start a piece? Go to the dictionary, pick a key word, and use that definition as his starting point. I suppose it's intended to add some sort of authority to the pronouncements that follow. Whatever the case, it just happened to really help me focus in this case. I mean, look at this definition!

> Main Entry: 1. rant
> Pronunciation: 'rant
> Function: verb
> Etymology: obsolete Dutch ranten, randen
> Date: 1602
> intransitive senses: 1: to talk in a noisy, excited, or declamatory manner; 2: to scold vehemently; transitive senses: to utter in a bombastic declamatory fashion
> (*Merriam-Webster Online Dictionary*: www.m-w.com)

What do you notice? The first thing I noticed was that it is a Dutch word. Who knew the Dutch were so pent up and angry? Good for them. Then I noticed that it dates from 1602, which means either we as a species have been ranting for four hundred years or (as I really suspect) we have been ranting as a *defined* activity for four hundred years but doing it informally for much longer. I mean one of the most famous rants of all time has to be Martin Luther's 95 *Theses*; he nailed them to the church door all the way back in 1517! Seems kind of rant-like to me. Anyway, the point is that ranting as a human activity has been defined for four hundred years, enough time for us to really work on it. Then I finally read the definition and was set free! I had been trying to be fairly scholarly about this process and as a consequence stayed fairly unemotional; turns out that's all wrong. By definition of the transitive sense (my favorite), I must proceed to *"utter in a bombastic declamatory fashion."*

I should also mention that these days, anyone writing a "rant" is under an enormous pressure. Dennis Miller[1] has set the bar at such an Everest-like altitude that any soul foolish enough to approach that kind of aerie must be filled with a Sir Richard Branson-esque love of heights. Let me pause here to reaffirm what is a rant. By definition, it is not a "fair and balanced" coverage of a topic. So when I quote from sources or take stances that are obviously biased against the people who are wrong (who also happen to be the people who disagree with me), don't come at me with "Well, you didn't tell the bad people's side of the story." If you want balanced coverage, read a newspaper.

Now what is the second favorite trick of hack writers when they have already cited a definition? That's right—insert a quote. More *supposed* authority. My quote was to be direct from that highly esteemed piece of philosophical celluloid, *The Matrix*. There is a scene toward the start of the movie when Neo (Keanu Reeves) is presented with a choice by Morpheus (www/imdb.com/name/nm0000401/). Neo must choose whether to stay in his dream world or awaken to a harsh reality. The choice that Morpheus frames for Neo is between the blue pill—symbolizing the rejection by Neo of reality—and the red pill—symbolizing the option to accept that the world in which we live is not reality and instead to engage with a truer but uglier reality.

Now I hear what you're saying, "Mark, that's no quote; why that's more of a paraphrase." Well dear reader, you are correct and I'll tell you why it's not a quote: ridiculous ideas about copyright. Yes, I would have had to pursue permission to use that quote in this essay. Somebody tell me when you are convinced that something here is broken. Oh, by the way, I can tell you that the quote in its entirety is posted online at http://imdb.com/title/tt0133093/quotes. Enjoy.

I do love the choice though. As introduced in this pharmaceutical fashion, this rant will be about a variety of things, but in general will concern "our" general willingness to happily gulp down the blue pill and remain blissfully unaware of that which is coming or possible.

Blue Pill or Red Pill; Why Should You Care?

Remember that old saying about "You can't take it with you"? Remember how that phrase gained new meaning with proprietary e-learning systems? Remember how groups like The MASIE Center and Wayne Hodgins and AICC and IMS and ADL/SCORM spent so much time and effort carefully crafting the technological underpinnings of a world in which e-learning systems (and their cousins in training and performance support) could interoperate and in which you could create and share thousands of objects?

Imagine all that work gets snatched away. Imagine we get stuck somewhere worse than before—somewhere that all objects cost money to even share—where interoperability is killed not by technical hurdles, but by the law. That world is coming, in fact is closer than you think. The only thing that will stop the advance of that world is awareness and action; this article represents that first step. Let me be clear: current and emerging developments in copyright and patent law represent the most serious threat to the future of e-learning ever.

Since this is a rant, however, I did want to slam into something else that I feel is a very real threat to the success of not just e-instruction but of instruction in general—a decided lack of play. That's right, I said play. Not play like hopscotch, although that's fine too, but think play as in "room to move." There are serious design implications here in not understanding this concept, and I really want to at least bring it up so that we don't ride out and slay the copyright dragon and just guarantee the ability to produce bad content. Continued ignorance of the power of *play,* in all its many forms, to impact and motivate learners will keep e-learning cut off from a most powerful force for good and will keep e-learning relegated to something that people *must* do instead of *want* to do. So stay tuned for that rant after I get done with copyright.

Blue Pill/Red Pill #1: Copyright and Patent Law

I recently spent some time looking at way too many of the proceedings from the latest round of e-learning conferences. No, I'm not a masochist; I was actually looking for something in particular, something I couldn't find. Let me start, however, by telling you what I did find. I found lots of stuff about content: how to create it, how to author it, how to publish it, share it, reuse it, and blend it. I saw entries on how to work with Higher Ed., what people need to know about employment law, and so on. I found presentations on how to get started and how to present with IMPACT! (which evidently is better than with just impact).

What I didn't find, however, was much, if anything, about copyright and/or patent law. I can hear you out there right now saying, "Why should you expect to find anything about those icky, boring subjects in those conference schedules, Mark?" Well, aside from being almost sure that there were already some icky and boring presentations in there anyway, simply put, I think that these two subjects are the Scylla and Charybdis,[2] the jagged rocks, the hidden reefs upon which the e-learning ship could ground and sink.

Thomas Jefferson once said, "Though [the people] may acquiesce, they cannot approve what they do not understand."[3]

Jefferson was right. Nowhere else in our little electronic world is that acquiescence screaming louder than in our dealings with copyright and patent law. To satisfy the requirements of full disclosure, I must admit that this is not my first rant on this topic. Way back in the spring of 2002, I published a screed on this same topic.[4]

The prep for this essay led me to re-read that "older" piece; geez what a hothead I was! I think I am calmer now, but no less scared. I am still frightened that one day we'll wake up at the very bottom of a slippery slope. I want to rant about this because I think someone should. Now, I'm not a lawyer, I don't even dress up like one in Internet chat rooms. But I do read, and that's about all it takes to start working up a big case of concern.

"Buying" Music

This is an insidious area in which to tread (probably why so few are walking around out here). An example, just to kick things off, would be the innocuous-seeming iTunes[5] music service from Apple. I still love this service but am starting to have some odd feelings about it as well. No less a personage than Elliott Masie, at the 2003 TechLearn,[6] described the content on iTunes as "nano content" (I'd actually argue that the songs are "micro" content and things like ring tones are really nano) and he happily downloaded songs from the stage. Apple really seems to have cracked the code here; they offer popular songs at a reasonable price ($0.99), and you can burn them to CDs or your iPod. But let's look closer.

When you buy a CD, DVD, book, or any copyrighted work in the physical world, you can avail yourself of *the right of first sale.*[7] The net impact of that right is that you can walk into any store or flea market or garage sale or eBay and sell your legally purchased copy of a copyrighted work with NO permission from the copyright owner. The law does prevent you from making copies of that work and selling them. However, this right does not seem to be holding up in the digital world.

Buried within the terms of sale (TOS) of all the music download services (iTunes, Musicmatch, Wal-Mart) is language that restricts the uses to which you can put your newly purchased piece of digital content. The absolute winner for the most Draconian legal language is clearly Wal-Mart. Wal-Mart is now the largest retailer of music in the United States, so it only makes sense that they would jump into the online music world. They have even taken their discount philosophy online and offer their songs for $0.88 to everyone else's $0.99—but man, that is an expensive eleven cents. Here is the language:

> "You may not reproduce (except as noted above), publish, transmit, distribute, display, broadcast, re-broadcast, modify, create derivative works from, sell, or participate in any sale of or exploit in any way, in whole or in part, directly or indirectly, any of the Products, the Service, or any related software. You may not reverse engineer, de-compile, disassemble, modify, or disable any copy protection or use limitation systems associated with the Products. You may not play and then re-digitize any Products, or upload those Products to the Internet. You may not use the Products in conjunction with any other third-party content (e.g., to provide sound for a film). You may not sell or offer to sell the Products, including but not limited to, posting any Product for auction, on any Internet auction site. *All Products are sublicensed to you and not sold,* notwithstanding the use of the terms 'sell,' 'purchase,' 'order,' or 'buy' on the Service or in this Agreement."[8]

Is that clear? You just paid your money and YOU DIDN'T BUY ANYTHING!! You got a "sublicense" to the song and that's it. That should be stunning. That should be infuriating. You paid for something that you don't own. Wal-Mart, for only $0.88, has managed to destroy the constitutionally guaranteed right of first sale. Actually, its worse—they got you to destroy your own rights. I mean you obviously have no right to sell something if you didn't actually buy anything but merely gained access to a sublicense. It is amazing and disheartening that rights that cost so dearly to acquire are so cheaply given away.

There has already been one attempt to sell an iTunes song on eBay[9] and it was eventually pulled by eBay. This kind of erosion of an existing right simply because the content is now digital is all the more troubling since the restriction comes about through our own acquiescence rather than careful legislation. Mark Federman aptly sums up the problem this poses in this blog comment:

> "The danger goes beyond merely not being able to sell music. *The danger is that we are becoming conditioned to accept via contract, that which cannot be enacted in law because of its unconstitutionality.* In other words, Congress gives a nod and a wink and enabling legislation so that companies can regulate through the back door that which cannot be regulated through the front door."[10]

Copyright and the Constitution

As content consumers, this should worry us. It worried Thomas Jefferson so much that he had to be talked into including provisions for copyright and patent monopolies in the U.S. Constitution. The language that went into that document states in Article 1, Section 8 that:

> "The Congress shall have power to lay and collect taxes, duties, imposts, and excises, to pay the debts, and provide for the common defense and general welfare of the United States; but all duties, imposts, and excises shall be uniform throughout the United States; *To promote the progress of science and useful arts, by securing for limited times to authors and inventors the exclusive right to their respective writings and discoveries.*"[11]

Grudgingly though, good old TJ did become convinced of the need for a limited term of copyright. Compared to the current crop of pro-copyright extension freaks, the *small mind* of Thomas Jefferson, however, was so lacking in vision and foresight that he thought a government-granted and enforced monopoly of something like nineteen years should be long enough for artists and inventors to have incentive enough to continue to create. Let's be clear, when I say grudgingly I mean it. Thomas Jefferson originally stated in a letter to James Madison in 1788 that "the benefit even of limited monopolies is too doubtful to be opposed to that of their general suppression."[12] Silly Thomas Jefferson.

Copyright Extension

Now copyright is potentially infinite, and don't let anyone tell you otherwise. By law, copyright can now stretch up 120 years,[13] and even that ludicrous length is not fixed in stone. Far be it for me to quote Phyllis Schlafly,[14] but allow me to quote Phyllis Schlafly. Below, she describes the Sonny Bono Copyright Term Extension Act of October 7, 1998,[15] that was passed in an odd hurry by both houses of Congress in a single day:

> ". . .informally known as the Disney Copyright Law because some consider it a billion-dollar federal handout to the Disney Company. It extended the copyrights on Mickey Mouse, Donald Duck, Pluto, Goofy, Winnie the Pooh, and other cartoons and works scheduled to expire over the next several years. . . . The Disney Law mocks the constitutional requirement of 'limited times' by extending copyright protection to 95 years."[16]

So let's recap for a moment:

- Copyright by law can already be extended 120 years or to infinity, whichever comes last.
- We are "contracting" away parts of the copyright clause that have not been crippled by legislation.
- The primary author of the Constitution and Bill of Rights was opposed to lengthy monopolies.

Yet here we are, meeting at industry conferences and talking about stuff like content creation and learning objects and presenting with IMPACT and NOT talking about how we are going to deal with this wonderful world of content in an increasingly Draconian and locked-up copyright world.

The DMCA

I can hear you out there right now. You're saying, "Yeah, but how does that impact me? I just make widgets." Well Mr. Widget-maker, allow me to introduce you to the Digital Millennium Copyright Act[17] (DMCA), also passed in 1998 (a real banner year for copyright).

Back in 1998, a crack appeared in the surface of the earth and out crawled the DMCA (the DMCA also likes to kick puppies and splash people with mud). Since 1998, the DMCA has become the favorite chilling weapon of content controllers everywhere. It has been used to stop everything from cryptographic research to people who make copy toner cartridge replacements (no kidding).[18] It has even been used by one of our e-learning own—welcome to the stage, Blackboard! A cease and desist letter sent from Blackboard to two student researchers included veiled references to DMCA action. (Blackboard eventually used much nicer federal and state hacking and trade secret laws to go after the dastardly duo.)[19]

The first of the two main sections of the DMCA focuses on making it illegal to deal in or with "circumvention" devices—that is, devices (hardware or software) that could allow a user to get around copyright restrictions (for example, breaking the encryption code on a DVD). The second section deals with the liability that an Internet service provider (ISP) is exposed to via one of its subscribers posting copyrighted work to a website.[20] Keep in mind that neither of these two provisions really deals with crime after it has been committed but instead outlaws actions that have the *potential* for criminal liability. I can still hear you: "I don't circumvent protections and I am not an ISP, so why worry?" You're right, don't worry—don't worry when music is locked up, don't worry when films are locked up, don't worry when educational content is locked up, and by all means don't listen to the legislative counsel of that knee-jerk reactionary group, the American Library Association, when she argues that "sooner or later. . . you'll get to the point where you say, 'Well, I guess that 25 cents isn't too much to pay for this sentence,' and then there's no hope and no going back."[21]

Now I could do a whole rant totally on the DMCA, but I wanted to cover a couple of other topics as well. Keep in mind the focus of this essay is to convince you to take the red pill, that is, to convince you to wake up and smell the coffee. I do need to cover one other DMCA topic though, e-learning.

That's right—there was a provision in the DMCA that expressly directed that a study be conducted to assess the impact of copyright issues on distance education. Expressly the language named the Copyright Office of the Library of Congress to consult with "representatives of copyright owners, nonprofit educational institutions, and nonprofit libraries and archives" to craft recommendations on how "to promote distance education through digital technologies, including interactive digital networks, while maintaining an appropriate balance between the rights of copyright owners and the interests of users."[22]

Well, there was a great deal on consulting and the Library of Congress's esteemed Register of Copyrights issued a rather disappointing set of recommendations. The gist of the ruling was that educators could sidestep the DMCA's rules against circumvention of technology designed to restrict the use of copyrighted materials in only two instances: lists of websites blocked by software filters and instances in which the blocking mechanism is malfunctioning.[23] I know that if you're like me, you were just stunned by the sweeping nature of such imaginative ideas! So now there is this huge report (353 pages), and you can get it online[24] if you're into that sort of thing, and we are really left where we were before the report.

You can't circumvent protection protocols (no matter how ridiculous), you can't design software that may allow someone else to circumvent protection protocols (good thing gun makers don't fall under DMCA), and, as it turns out, you better not even legally research the security of copyright protection protocols.[25] So, toolmakers, I hope your tool doesn't unintentionally circumvent known or unknown security measures in someone else's content or allow someone totally unknown to you to do that. LMS vendors, I also hope you enjoy an environment with weaker security protocols because legitimate research in the field is being stifled by DMCA threats. Everyone else, I hope you enjoy watching the death of the dream of interoperable content and vast repositories of reusable knowledge when the majority of content is locked down by proprietary security systems.

Instead please enjoy the *Minority Report*-like world brought to you by the Sonny Bono Copyright Extension Act and by the DMCA and by the Recording Industry Association of America (RIAA) and the Motion Picture Association of America (MPAA) and all those others who would stand there and convict the rest of us for crimes that we may yet commit. I need a Tums. Oh wait! I forgot to mention patent law.

Patent Law

Here's one for you—ever hear of Raindance Communications? Well, they were just granted a patent covering the "the capability to record all media content shared in an audio or Web conference and play it back at a later date."[26] Sound like it might have an impact on your desktop videoconferencing capabilities? Hmmm, maybe. Not convinced? How about the patent claims asserted by Acacia Media Technologies in 2003 that said it "owned patents on the process of transmitting compressed audio or video online," one of the most basic multimedia technologies on the Net?[27] Wait, I have another one. SBC Communications is sending out letters asserting that it controls patents on—get this—the use of frames in web pages.[28] Don't use streaming media or frames? (Welcome to 1993.) Let me throw one more story in the mix. Test.com is kind of shopping around a patent granted in February of this year that covers "making and posting tests online."[29]

To Find Out More. . .

We are about to move on, but I didn't want to do so until I gave you at least a couple of pointers concerning things you can read or do about the items mentioned above. Probably the smartest place to start following these developments is at the blog of Lawrence Lessig.[30] Lessig is a professor of law at the Stanford Law School, founder of the Stanford Center for Internet and Society,[31] has written

The Future of Ideas and Code and Other Laws of Cyberspace,[32] and is the chair of the Creative Commons project.[33] Lessig also argued (and lost, unfortunately) the Eldred v. Ashcroft case[34] before the Supreme Court (this case was a challenge to the Sonny Bono/ Mickey Mouse Copyright Extension Act). I hope by now you can guess what side of this Lessig is going to come down on. At a 2002 conference, Lessig delivered a keynote address[35] in which he focused on four main points:

1. Creativity and innovation always build on the past.
2. The past always tries to control the creativity that builds on it.
3. Free societies enable the future by limiting this power of the past.
4. Ours is less and less a free society.

This speech is probably the single best source of arguments against the trend in both copyright and patent law. Go read it. It's three pages, or you can listen to the MP3. You need to know this stuff. Lessig ends his section on patent with this challenge that I'll use to segue to the next topic:

> "It's not physics that makes them powerful, it's lawyers and lawmakers and Congress. And the thing is, you can fight all you want against the physics that make a nuclear weapon destroy all of mankind, but you cannot succeed at all. Yet you could do something about this. You could fuel a revolution that fights these legal threats to you. But what have you done about it? What have you done about it?"[36]

The last topic I want to mention here deals with organizations that are fighting the good fight against some of this copyright/patent madness. Understand this: I am staying very much at the top of the food chain on these groups. There are many smaller groups also fighting the fight (Downhill Battle, DigitalConsumer.org, iPAC, and others). Lessig is the single brightest point in this firmament, but he is by no means alone; the same goes for these groups. The following are two of the most important and well-known groups in this fight, and they are not alone either. The first group is the Creative Commons (CC)[37] project headed by none other than Larry Lessig. I am going to include an image here for two reasons: (1) I love visuals and (2) the very sane and readable Creative Commons copyright license[38] that governs use of this work tells me that I am free to:

- Copy, distribute, display, and perform the work
- Make derivative works
- Make commercial use of the work

Under the following conditions:

- Attribution. You must give the original author credit.
- For any reuse or distribution, you must make clear to others the license terms of this work.
- Any of these conditions can be waived if you get permission from the author.

Therefore I offer the following visual explanation[39]:

Creative Commons wants to help define the spectrum of possibilities between full copyright—all rights reserved—and the public domain—no rights reserved. Our licenses help you retain your copyright while allowing certain uses of your work. They help you offer your creative work with some rights reserved.

Simple, right? Just think of CC as bringing sanity to copyright. Do you really need to have all rights reserved to the entries on your blog? Have you thought about what kind of impact concepts like "all rights reserved" have on creative communities?

The last group I want to bring up is the Electronic Frontier Foundation.[40] Its site states that:

> "The Electronic Frontier Foundation (EFF) was created to defend our rights to think, speak, and share our ideas, thoughts, and needs using new technologies, such as the Internet and the World Wide Web. EFF is the first to identify threats to our basic rights online and to advocate on behalf of free expression in the digital age."[41]

Think of them as your watchdog in cyberspace. They are guarding encroachment on your civil liberties in ways that groups like the ACLU are just beginning to understand. They are the guardians of the slippery slope.

Why am I bringing all this up? For the same reason Morpheus offered two pills to Neo. *It's all about choice*. You can continue acting like these things don't affect you and aren't part of your world, or you can take the red pill and start looking around for ways to combat or at least minimize your exposure to or damage from these various ill winds. I promised a wide-ranging *bombastic declamatory utterance*, however. Thus, I feel I must move on.

Blue Pill/Red Pill #2: *Spielraum*

Now I want to rant for a moment about play. I am a huge proponent of the use of games and simulations to teach, but this idea of play is something larger. One of the smartest bloggers I know of is named Anne Galloway.[42] Anne manages to find stuff on the web that is rich and meaningful and wonderful—and by the way, why can't instructional content be more like that? One story she found recounts a meeting at which the philosopher Hans-Georg Gadamer described the difference between game and play (Stop it! I can actually hear your eyes glazing over out there).[43] Gadamer describes how

Americans have created a problem by having two different words, one for play and one for game. The French and Germans, he contends, have only one. The *play* he describes is analogous to the wiggle room (scientific term) that you must leave when tightening the nuts on a bicycle wheel. You can't make them too tight or too loose, he argued:

> "It has to have some play!" he announced pedagogically and a little exultantly, I thought. And then he added, "and not too much play, or the wheel with fall off. You know," he said, 'Spielraum.'"[44]

Ready for a little *Spielraum*? Wow, does e-learning need some of that! At a recent industry conference, people asked me what I considered to be gaming. I was a bit stuck. But I ended up saying something like, "To me, gaming portends not a set of actions or a medium but a different way of looking at approaching content." (I probably didn't say portends.) I wish I had been able to whip off Spielraum as an example! This is what I mean, people—there has to be greater play in e-learning, more wiggle room. Current customers are asking, if not demanding, it and future customers will expect it as the status quo. Want to know why Elliott Masie gave (less than half-jokingly) Google the number one e-learning product of the year award? It's got play in it. It's not customizable or personalizable, but I can bend it to my will as opposed to the other way around. This is why gaming is so powerful. It is permission to play, to fly around a bit and see what happens.

James Paul Gee of the University of Wisconsin wrote an interesting book entitled *What Video Games Have to Teach Us About Learning and Literacy*[45] (read a great review of this book by Marc Prensky[46]). Gee talks about many things, but one point he made in the book that now resonates with greater context for me is the statement that:

> "The learner also needs to learn how to innovate in the domain—how to produce meanings that, while recognizable, are seen as somehow novel or unpredictable."[47]

This ability to innovate of which Gee speaks is play. That's why gaming can be such a powerful teacher. Not only does it allow people to find different paths to learning but it asks them to take that knowledge and do something with it. An example of this from the gaming world (as we most popularly know it) is online right now in the form of a contest. There is a first-person shooter game out right now called *Unreal Tournament*.[48] This game (as with almost all current games) includes an editor, that is, a program or an ability to create new objects, missions, maps, and so forth to be used in the game. That's right, users creating content (known as mods) for free. So the companies that produced this game and a couple of other sponsors got together and decided to hold a contest[49]—to create the best mod and win. Sounds simple right? Well, they also did something very interesting. They got another group called 3D Buzz[50] to stand up an entire website[51] with over 120 hours of world-class game design instruction and made it available to anyone who wanted to learn—FOR FREE!

When is the last time you gave away 120 hours of instruction to anyone who wanted for free?

Think about it. They have now created a vast user community with the tools, knowledge, and capability to create content for their platform (the game), and the users will generate all that content for free. Wait! There's more! The act of training all of these folks as game designers has also addressed a labor shortage that this or any gaming company that uses the Unreal technology could experience. Think about it. What do you think all the fourteen-year-olds who are online right now learning how to design game levels are going to want to be when they grow up? Astronauts? Firemen? I have a hunch that more than a few will want to be game designers. They have already held the first two-day Unreal University[52] at North Carolina State University in Raleigh, North Carolina, USA. Where are the conference sessions that address how to translate that kind of model into corporate e-learning? Trained users are right now creating valuable content for free and are training themselves on their own time, quite happily I might add.

I am going to quote somebody quoting somebody else now. John Seely Brown[53] and Paul Duguid[54] wrote a wonderful paper called *Stolen Knowledge* (more in a moment). They open the paper with the following quote:

> "A very great musician came and stayed in [our] house. He made one big mistake . . . [he] determined to teach me music, and consequently no learning took place. Nevertheless, I did casually pick up from him a certain amount of stolen knowledge." (Rabindrath Tagore quoted in *Bandyopadhyay*, 1989, p. 45)[55]

Again, seems to be dead on to me. You want my rant? Make e-learning follow these models. Give it some play! You say that's hard to do? Maybe it is because we're using the wrong tools. It's hard to turn a screw with a hammer; maybe we need to put down the hammer. Maybe we don't even need tools (Heresy! Heretic!). Maybe what we need to do is change our corporate cultures to recognize and support what is already going on and then work to teach our employees the critical evaluative skills needed to investigate, identify, capture, and innovate with the knowledge they need.

You want innovation? Try the iPod. I gauge the importance of something new by the seismic waves emanating from its development community. There are some great waves coming out of the *Hack the iPod* community right now.[56] This device was meant to be a great digital music player, and it is. I have also seen it used to dual-boot two laptops—one running Windows XP and the other running a flavor of Linux. Talk about the law of unintended consequences. Here is an iPod innovation that has specific learning/training potential: *Read It To Me*[57] is a conversion program that can turn RSS[58] feeds into MP3 files and store in playlist form on your iPod. Get it? You can *listen* to XML! Where are the companies creating content for their employees' iPods? Give them some play!

I mentioned having some more to say about the *Stolen Knowledge* paper, and so here is a great quote:

"Where 'situated learning' talks of learning, questions about educational technology tend to be framed around teaching and instruction. A situated approach contests the assumption that learning is a response to teaching."[59]

That's the "Google Theory of Learning." We talk about e-learning, but what we are selling is e-teaching. Producers don't make e-learning. Producers make product. One hopes consumers of that product use it to create learning, but we must rise above this arrogant belief that anything that we do will produce learning. We might produce a stimulus/response chain, but that's conditioning and not learning. At best we produce opportunities for learning to take place. Am I being unclear? Do you think that learning is taking place right now inside of companies that have no learning management system, no content authoring tools, no instructional design staff? If the answer is yes (and you know it is), then why aren't we studying how to support and focus and enrich this learning that is already taking place?

Back to the Conference Proceedings . . .

You know I said at the start of this piece that I had spent some time searching through the latest e-learning conference proceedings, looking for some things that I didn't find. Well, I also actually spent some time at the conferences and two other things leapt to mind that I hadn't seen: (1) hardware and (2) learners. I was part of a group that did a series of mobile learning (m-learning) sessions and hosted a booth at a recent conference.[60] We weren't selling anything at the booth. We just set up all of the mobile devices we had brought (tablets, Palms, Pocket PCs, and so forth) and a free Wi-Fi bubble. We let people walk up and PLAY with them, and we just talked to them about m-learning. We probably had the most traffic of any booth at the show. That tells me that people are hungry to see the end point at which e-teaching is being delivered. How can you design for end points and not talk about them or show them or have the vendors around who make them? Where are the technology petting zoos at e-teaching conferences? How do you know what will work on a handheld if you aren't working with one?

Finally (phew), the last thing I didn't find at these conferences was learners. Specifically I mean those people who are not instructional designers, who are not corporate trainers, who do not work in HR. This is the huge population that has nothing to do with the creation of content and wouldn't know an LMS if it fell out of the sky and landed on them. They are simply just the majority of the people who are signing up and taking all this training. I have this real problem in continuing to discuss this population with so few representatives from its ranks present at the table. What if we held an *e-learner's panel* at the next conference and let the users themselves tell us the ground truth of their experiences? Scared of what we might hear?

Conclusion

I've been ranting for a while now and I'm getting tired. So what's it going to be? The red pill or blue pill? Are we going to wake up and look at the world, warts and all, or do we stay in our comfort zone until someone comes to take it away? Since I've done it so much already, I figured I'd be consistent and end with a quote as well, actually a paraphrase. At the end of the first *Matrix* movie, Neo is talking to the dictatorial computer overlords. Over a system failure notice, he tells these overlords that his intent—without knowing the final outcome—is to at least wake people up. Neo then becomes the one offering a choice, the same one I offer to you now:

Please check one:

☐ Blue Pill
☐ Red Pill

If you do choose to wake up, then feel free to visit me at http://blogoehlert.typepad.com/eclippings/ and we can continue down this rabbit hole.

Notes

1. www.hbo.com/dml/
2. Aside from being characters in a tragic Greek love story, Scylla was a dangerous sea monster that sat opposite the lethal whirlpool of Charybdis.
3. Thomas Jefferson: Opinion on Apportionment Bill, 1792. ME 3:211
4. http://blogoehlert.typepad.com/eclippings/2003/11/intellectual_pr.html
5. www.apple.com/itunes/
6. http://show.techlearn.com/techlearn/V40/index.cvn
7. www.nps.gov/helpdesk/copyrght.htm#copyrght.2 www4.law.cornell.edu/uscode/17/109.html
8. www.lessig.org/blog/archives/001647.shtml
9. http://george.hotelling.net/itunes_auction.htm
10. www.construct-d.org/mt/mt-comments.cgi?entry_id=477
11. www.house.gov/Constitution/Constitution.html
12. Thomas Jefferson to James Madison, 1788. ME 7:98
13. www.nps.gov/helpdesk/cpychart.htm
14. www.eagleforum.org/misc/bio.html
15. www.loc.gov/copyright/legislation/s505.pdf
16. www.eagleforum.org/column/2002/july02/02–07–03.shtml
17. www.copyright.gov/legislation/hr2281.pdf
18. www.eff.org/IP/DMCA/unintended_consequences.php
19. http://news.com.com/2100–1028–996836.html
20. http://en.wikipedia.org/wiki/DMCA
21. www.nytimes.com/2004/01/25/magazine/25COPYRIGHT.html?pagewanted=2
22. www.copyright.gov/disted/
23. http://chronicle.com/free/2000/10/2000103101t.htm
24. www.copyright.gov/reports/de_rprt.pdf
25. See Professor Ross Anderson, Cambridge University, Declaration in Felten v. RIAA (Oct. 22, 2001), describing ways in which the DCMA is suppressing research into security weak-

nesses in SDMI watermarking technology: (www.eff.org/IP/
DMCA/Felten_v_RIAA/20011022_anderson_decl.pdf).

26. www.learningcircuits.org/2003/mar2003/newsbytes.html#new4
27. http://news.com.com/2100–1023–983552.html?tag=nl
28. http://news.com.com/2100–1023–981446.html?tag=nl
29. http://news.com.com/2100–1023–983709.html?tag=fd_top
30. www.lessig.org/blog/
31. http://cyberlaw.stanford.edu/
32. www.amazon.com/exec/obidos/ASIN/0375726446/eclippadiviso-20?
dev-t=D68HUNXKLHS4J%26camp=2025%26link_code=xm2
33. http://creativecommons.org/
34. http://eldred.cc/
35. www.oreillynet.com/pub/a/policy/2002/08/15/lessig.html
36. www.oreillynet.com/pub/a/policy/2002/08/15/lessig.html?page=3
37. http://creativecommons.org/
38. http://creativecommons.org/licenses/by/1.0/
39. http://creativecommons.org/learn/licenses/comics1
40. http://eff.org/
41. http://eff.org/about/
42. www.purselipsquarejaw.org/about.html
43. www.purselipsquarejaw.org/2003_11_01_blogger_archives.php
#107021573791282629
44. www.purselipsquarejaw.org/2003_11_01_blogger_archives.php
#107021573791282629
45. www.amazon.com/exec/obidos/ASIN/1403961697/eclippadiviso-20?
dev-t=D68HUNXKLHS4J%26camp=2025%26link_code=xm2
46. www.marcprensky.com/writing/Prensky%20-%20Review%20
of%20James%20Paul%20Gee%20Book.pdf
47. www.amazon.com/gp/reader/1403961697/ref=sib_rdr_srch/
103–4439138–3787024?v=search-inside&keywords=innovate
&x=0&y=0
48. www.unrealtournament2003.com/news.php
49. www.unrealtournament2003.com/contest.php
50. http://sv3.3dbuzz.com/vbforum/uunr_about.php
51. http://sv3.3dbuzz.com/vbforum/unr_main.php

52. http://cde.ncsu.edu/uu/

53. http://www2.parc.com/ops/members/brown/jsb.html

54. http://www2.parc.com/ops/members/brown/pduguid.html

55. http://www2.parc.com/ops/members/brown/papers/stolenknow
    .html

56. www.time.com/time/archive/preview/from_redirect/0,10987,
    1101020422–230383,00.html; http://www.ipodhacks.com/
    modules.php?op=modload&name=News&file=index

57. www.tow.com/software/read_it_to_me/

58. www.webreference.com/authoring/languages/xml/rss/intro/

59. http://www2.parc.com/ops/members/brown/papers/stolenknow
    .html

60. http://colab.typepad.com/mlearning/

PEOPLE ARCHITECTURE

A Holistic Approach to Building, Maintaining, and Expanding Your Learning Infrastructure

Vicki Cerda

With human capital as one of the most important assets, learning professionals, just like architects, must make choices about what to build, where to build, how to build, with what to build, and with whom. It is the people who provide the services that support the business, technology, and processes of an enterprise. In order to ensure success, "architecting" your people and the related infrastructure needs to follow the big-picture vision—the blueprint. The five core building components in my vision of the blueprint—Culture and Climate; Job Roles, Career Tracks and Competencies; Workforce Development; Compensation, Benefits, and Rewards; and all related Supporting Processes—are key when building or sustaining your strategies, developing metrics to track and improve operations, and planning for the future. Although applicable to any project or endeavor, I find them particularly well suited to the training and learning field, since this is one discipline in which business, technology, process, and people come together—and sometimes *very* quickly.

Training and learning should not exist in a vacuum—stand-alone, isolated, and disengaged from the rest of the organization. But unfortunately, this is often the case. Our goal as learning professionals is to provide our workforce with an integrated environment and the know-how that will lead to better decision making, ongoing competitiveness in the marketplace, and satisfied customers, partners, and stakeholders. This cannot happen if we are not well rooted in, and supported by, what I propose to you as the five core organizational constructs that serve as common ground within your enterprise. Using the analogy of building a house, I reflect on the overall "People Architecture" framework and present a series of detailed blueprints consisting of potential issues to consider and corresponding business strategies for you to customize and apply to your particular organization and situation. Ready?

The Overview: Building from the Foundation Up

The *culture and climate of an organization* are critical to all other processes. A house too sits on its foundation and footing and needs to be properly constructed to be able to support the structure. Any effort to save on the basics will cost you almost immediately, and certainly in the long term. And surely your maintenance costs will be unafford-able if the foundation is weak. Never, never skimp when it comes to structural soundness; rather, invest as much as you can afford.

How? Define and share your corporate values and the expected business etiquette that define your work environment. (New hire orientation is the perfect place to start, but don't stop there.) Provide the tools, hardware, and software needed so that employees have access when/where needed and can be productive and hassle-free. Leverage corporate programs to the fullest extent. Implement quality as a way of life by integrating continuous improvement in all processes. Manage overtime to prevent burnout. Facilitate the use of technology and collaboration for meetings and training to reduce travel. Recognize and promote the power of workforce diversity and the resulting benefits derived from incorporating new and different ideas and approaches. Invest in the physical and virtual space and the work environment of your people as part of your strategic planning.

Job roles, career tracks, and competencies are your floor plans and elevations. They provide different views of what the finished product will look like. Include enough detail so employees can easily focus in on their current area of interest (learning or training need), but also have the ability to visualize future "additions" (desired development). Grouping roles ("what you do") by specialization, such as business, technical, or management, by competencies ("how you do it"), and by categories such as "core" or "leadership" is helpful for further visualizing how everything fits together. Such groupings can also demonstrate how to move horizontally as well as vertically within the organization.

Your employees and their skills are the "pipes" for the flow of knowledge—much like the electric wiring and plumbing in a home. If there is a break somewhere in the circuit or pipe, productivity will stop. Aside from the obvious and visible area of learning and all its variations and delivery options, other key elements also must be considered as part of *workforce development*. Do you:

- Plan goals with employees and timeframes for achieving them?
- Consistently conduct biannual performance evaluations with all staff and other key personnel?
- Employ a variety of mentoring programs?

"Stacking" elements in this manner can reduce both the costs and future efforts required to build and maintain balanced, well-rounded employees, similar to the savings realized when adding a second floor to a well-planned existing structure.

The bottom line for *compensation, benefits, and rewards* (in any field) is that you need to be competitive, whether you hire an outside contractor or do the work yourself. You also need a wide variety of alternative and recognition programs. Partner with your human resources department to conduct comparative market reviews and other benchmarking efforts.

If the foundation holds up the house, various other supporting members hold up the roof and ceiling. As with a home's foundation, get the best materials you can afford! Sourcing, recruiting, interviewing, managing contractor and vendor services, and other overall value-producing business activities are essential *supporting processes*. It is crucial that these are solid to minimize the small problems and avoid the bigger ones. Take the time to do them correctly or they will have to be repaired again and again, and you will need to live with the consequences. Also critical is the need to communicate,

communicate, and communicate on an ongoing basis, in various ways and via all available mechanisms at your disposal.

Engineering and Managing the Materials and Measures

Assuming you now better understand the five core People Architecture building components, what is next? Each organization has different needs and will want to build a different type of house. For a deeper and more focused reflection, as well as to bridge theory with practicality, I next outline numerous thought-provoking questions and sample strategies to help guide you when customizing your particular design and housing "model." Note that this is the nitty-gritty—more like consulting an interior designer than an architect. The architect plans for a kitchen's space and the wiring, plumbing, and lighting, but the designer helps decide which appliances to buy, how to group the lights, where to put the dining table and chairs, and how many cabinets are needed. Together, the blueprints generated from the five core components ensure alignment of your people with your learning infrastructure by integrating the myriad interrelated strategies and processes that must occur in parallel in order for you to successfully engineer and manage your organization's performance and your workforce's productivity.

Culture and Climate

Is your organization a great place to work? Work and workforce expectations are changing and the lines between employees, contractors, customers, and partners are blurring. Today's workforce is transient and there is an increasing acceptance and reliance on mobility and working at home. In order to drive business value, you have to architect your people, processes, and technology accordingly. Through your culture and climate, you can eliminate time and distance as a barrier to productivity.

Table 1 lists a series of issues, and the related business strategies, to consider when thinking about your organization's culture and climate.

Table 1. Blueprint Elements: Culture and Climate

Investigate, Identify, Assess	Associated Business Objective/Strategy
How many people (or what percentage of the people) are taking advantage of existing corporate programs?	Leverage your organization's programs to the fullest.
Can employees work at home? What tools/software do they need? Do they have the latest version of applications? High-speed connection? Do you have a process/procedure for reporting/resolving problems with software/hardware? What is your turnaround time?	Employees need to have the right tools at the right time and at the right place to be as productive as possible.
Do you have a lot of rework? How about complaints/issues traced back to your department? What are the three largest problems reported? When was the last time you surveyed your customers?	Implement quality as a way of life and as a key element in improving the delivery of your products and services.
How much money is being spent on travel (including training and meetings)? Can similar goals be accomplished via alternative methods such as e-learning, videoconferencing, virtual collaboration tools, and so on?	Facilitate the use of technology to reduce travel costs and increase the use of flexible schedules.
Is your workforce diverse? Does it represent different backgrounds, ages, experiences, and cultures?	Promote the power of workforce diversity. Allow employees to learn from one another, and grow the business by incorporating new and different approaches.
Take a tour of your facilities. Are there improvements needed to the physical space? Do you need to add or eliminate conference rooms? Upgrade or redefine floor space? Are there too many people sharing one printer? Is it too far away? Is more administrative support needed? Is the fax too slow?	Invest in the physical work environment of your employees. And don't forget their virtual space too!
Are life/work balance opportunities encouraged and demonstrated?	Allow staff the opportunity to de-stress and re-energize.

Job Roles, Career Tracks, and Competencies

Your environment is now in place, but are your people assigned correctly? Are they placed in the right jobs? Do they know what they are responsible for and by when? Do they need additional training, development, or mentoring to go to the next level? Personnel need a clear vision of job responsibilities and their opportunities for growth.

As a learning organization, you need to identify "hot" and emerging industry roles and their corresponding accountabilities. As a learning manager, you are responsible for increasing employee productivity and performance by communicating the expected knowledge, behavior, and skills for each key responsibility area within your organization and assisting your employees to prepare for progressions within the same role, promotions, or new/different roles. As a learning professional, you need a clear understanding of your job responsibilities and must proactively develop specific action plans to address any skill gaps so that you can improve your career opportunities.

Table 2 provides a list of questions and related business strategies to consider when optimizing your job roles, career tracks, and competencies.

Workforce Development

This is the area most of us know the best—training, learning, and workforce development in all its formats and glory. But let us not be like the story of the cobbler whose children had no shoes! We need to practice what we preach in our own organizations and with our own people. And yes, the same applies to you. As a manager, you may not need to be an expert yourself, but you will need to be credible and knowledgeable in more disciplines than ever before to be able to direct operations, communicate with technical and nontechnical personnel, and implement business processes and learning innovations to bring competitive advantage to your organization.

Table 2. Blueprint Elements: Job Roles, Career Tracks, and Competencies

Investigate, Identify, Assess	*Associated Business Objective/Strategy*
Are your job descriptions up-to-date and in sync with the market?	Continually evaluate roles, responsibilities, and skill sets to determine whether they need to be updated, combined, or even eliminated.
Are personnel mapped to the correct roles? Do they clearly understand their responsibilities?	Employees have to be correctly mapped to their functional roles and have a clear understanding of their responsibilities and expected responsibilities so that they can be productive and fairly evaluated for their performance.
Are the expected competencies identified by role? Are competencies grouped by categories for ease of understanding? Have the required performance levels of achievement (and how they will be measured) been defined and communicated? Have employees chosen two or three specific ones to develop in the current year?	Define the required competencies, what level of performance is expected, and how these will be measured; have employees develop action plans to address gaps as part of your performance management program.
Does each of your employees know what the next job in his or her career path is and how to get there? How about other options available to them (for example, technical versus management)?	Provide a road map so employees can not only focus on their current area, but can also plan for future growth. And be sure to allow for both vertical and horizontal growth opportunities within the organization.
Do you offer job rotations? How about flexible assignments?	Assist employees to broaden their skills and company perspective by working in different areas and on varying assignments.

Today's learning professionals require a wide range of skills, including business, information technology, leadership, and technical e-learning (authoring tools, collaborative platforms, mobile technologies, and so forth) in addition to specialized industry training skills and know-how. And we need to continually enhance these skills to keep up-to-date. Have you?

The wiring of our house, or the flow of knowledge through our people, is in many ways the most complicated and dangerous part of building our house, or our workforce. For these reasons, this should only be attempted by a qualified professional—electricians or learning professionals, respectively. The payoff for the learning organization is that the knowledge of its workforce directly impacts its competitiveness.

The blueprint provided by Table 3 will assist you when considering ways to enhance your various workforce development programs.

Compensation, Benefits, and Rewards

To initially attract and continuously retain the best and the brightest, compensation is just a fact of life when doing business. Job roles and skills in the learning industry are rapidly evolving and demanding different levels of pay. Do you expect to build a quality house with cheap materials and labor? Do you want your general contractor or a key worker leaving in the middle of a project because his or her skills are undervalued or underpaid? I think not. Additionally, today's workforce is more global and diverse than ever. Do your learning and training programs reflect this?

Table 4 lists a variety of issues and corresponding strategic business objectives to consider for your compensation, benefits, and rewards programs.

Supporting Processes

Due to the many factors and situations that are unique to every enterprise, the process area is easily another chapter. Although each organization differs in its specific needs and implementations, below

Table 3. Blueprint Element: Workforce Development

Investigate, Identify, Assess	Associated Business Objective/Strategy
Do you have a formal training program for new hires? Seasoned personnel?	Minimize confusion for new hires and build loyalty from the start; build in ongoing education and development for your existing staff.
Do you have in place a blended curriculum of classroom and e-learning solutions?	Mix different delivery formats to address different needs, costs, learning styles, reach, cultures, and/or timeframe requirements.
Do your programs include a variety of technical, professional, personal, and business disciplines?	Offer a balanced and diverse range of business, IT, technical, and leadership training in addition to other specialized training-specific skills your employees may need; update content continually to keep users coming back for more.
Do you conduct biannual evaluations with all staff? Plan short-term and long-term goals with employees and the timeframe for achieving them?	Continually grow your workforce and employ a consistent method for measuring and improving performance.
Do you employ a variety of mentoring programs? Encourage your employees to share their knowledge?	Manage and grow your company's knowledge; expect and encourage key people to employ their leadership skills as part of their role; link your work and learning programs.

are numerous areas and metrics to consider as "triggers" for internal and external process improvement opportunities (see Table 5). Much will depend on your size, location, market, resources, and other such critical variables. Supporting processes are a major, and unfortunately often overlooked, component of our People Architecture infrastructure. The term may be "supporting," but without these back-end processes the house's roof would fall down and/or the protective walls would never go up, thus making all else negligible. Remember that although the specific configuration and characteristics of your situation will vary and depend on your business operations and needs, the identified process areas will most likely need to be considered as part of the mix.

Table 4. Blueprint Elements: Compensation, Benefits, and Rewards

Investigate, Identify, Assess	*Associated Business Objective/Strategy*
Are your salaries competitive? Do you consistently conduct market reviews and benchmarking studies? Do you pay extra for "hot skills" and in-depth program experience, industry contacts, and knowledge?	Pay competitively to attract new employees and be able to retain and motivate existing staff.
Do you employ a wide variety of alternative reward and recognition programs?	Recognize that money is not the only motivating factor; be sure to reward achievements—big and small—in different ways and to balance between fixed and variable reward options.
Do you reward for the results you want? Do your rewards target your business drivers?	Measure and reward on the basis of the contributions to corporate profit and/or sharing in the contribution to the knowledge bases of your organization and ensure you strike a balance between absolute contributions and relative performance.
Are your incentive programs realistic? Do they reflect the reality of the marketplace? Do they encourage teamwork?	An ill-thought-out program (for example, unachievable sales quotas) will only result in demoralizing employees and lead to a loss in productivity or sales. Be sure to also foster and promote teamwork, as it is never just about what you do on your own.
Do your programs account for today's more global and diverse workforce?	Continually reassess your programs to determine whether they need to be revamped to include different cultures, ethnicities, and religions.
Do your employees understand the reward system? Do your managers know how to properly manage it?	Communicate your programs across the enterprise and ensure they are implemented fairly and consistently.

Table 5. Blueprint Element: Supporting Processes

Investigate, Identify, Assess	Associated Business Objective/Strategy
Outsourcing/Insourcing: Is it more cost-effective and productive to outsource certain operations or keep them in house?	Business processes are key value-adding activities and are essential for operating smoothly behind the scenes and for providing support and a repeatable structure to all the other processes and goals of the organization; employ a Quality Framework strategy and philosophy throughout; continually explore and balance quality, cost, and service options.
Use of Technology: Are you using technology wisely to streamline and support operations?	
Purchase Orders: Are your purchase orders up-to-date? Do they need to be renegotiated based on volume and changing business conditions? What costs can be avoided? What services can be added "for free"?	
Vendor and Partner Management: Do you need to reevaluate existing vendors? What redundant services or processes can be cut or consolidated with others? Based on changing business models, do you need to forge new strategic alliances?	
Operational: What steps can be automated? Are your processes standardized and well documented? Readily available to all? Up-to-date? Can you minimize any number of steps and dependencies?	
Marketing: How well and consistently do you communicate and market your services across the enterprise?	
License Agreements: When was the last time you inventoried your training license or infrastructure software agreements? Looked for hidden costs and potential savings? Are you paying for more licenses than you are using? Should maintenance fees be renegotiated?	

Table 5. Blueprint Element: Supporting Processes, Cont'd.

Investigate, Identify, Assess	Associated Business Objective/Strategy
Shared Services: Have you explored end-to-end services for breaking down the silo walls between functional groups? Allowed for growth demands through scalable and bundled organizational processes?	
Project Management: For any sizable process, have the scope and requirements been defined? Tasks identified and effort estimated? Appropriate resources assigned?	

How best to architect your supporting processes, whether for learning and training or in a broader sense? Focus on business success versus technology. Manage not only your workforce, but also your external relationships with customers and partners. Integrate and improve your business processes for internal efficiencies. Plan for and manage change. Communicate, communicate, communicate. And fully realize that all of this can only be achieved by another one of your supporting structures—your people.

Providing Balance Through the Final Architectural Dimensions

Buildings serve many purposes and come in many sizes. They consist of materials meant to resist different loads and forces. Building dimensions, while basically a function of building codes and materials employed, can be changed to meet your own needs and tastes. While the method employed may be similar and use the same principles, no two houses will look the same. This is also the case with learning organizations and our set of "structures" (learning objects, learning management systems, learning content management systems, curricula, and so on).

Another point of commonality between the building industry and the learning industry concerns innovation and technology. As new materials are invented and technology continues to advance, our corresponding building elements and practices need to dynamically do the same. But tying innovation exclusively to new technology is expensive and many times unnecessary. Many opportunities for innovation also exist within traditional and "latent" materials. Apply your imagination and ask yourself how best to extend your materials beyond the uses for which they were originally created. Innovation comes from what we have not yet perceived in the commonplace materials—both in architecture and in learning.

Just as engineers consider standing buildings the norm and structural failures the exception, there are many lessons to be learned from failure. Examine, learn, and repair as necessary. Know when it is best to patch or renovate, rebuild, or even tear down.

With the outside complete, the wiring, plumbing, heating, and insulation installed, the floors laid, the walls and ceiling up, a house is virtually finished. While theoretically possible, it is rare that we can say we are "finished" because improvements and additions are constant. An entire book can be written about the hundreds of final decisions concerning your house. Do you want two or three coats of paint? Wood floor or tile? Which light fixtures? What about the landscaping? And that is just the beginning. It's the same with learning.

But in the end, it is not about one house or two or three. The building of cities is one of man's greatest achievements and an indicator of the state of civilization. The test of our achievement is whether we can break away from a fragmented approach and begin to see cities as a whole, as neighborhoods and communities. So it is the case with our people, our processes, our business, our technology . . . and the infrastructure that connects us all. It's the same with learning.

Architecting your people and the key elements of your learning infrastructure are no different than building a house or anything else—they need careful management and vision. How you plan to use the house can affect where you locate it and how you design it. Build that house in a tiered or layered manner to build in flexibility. Use standard components to maximize reusability and minimize costs and integration requirements. Customize the elements of your building plan to your needs and to the specific metrics that make the most sense to your organization, but always leave room for future renovations and additions. Remember that no matter how well the location of the house fulfills all the other requirements, you must be able to access it. Combine elements to maximize total effects. Target your results. Measure consistently. Continue to repair, improve, and re-target/re-measure. Same with learning.

No matter what stage in the various blueprints you are at today, use this framework as a reference point to ensure that your People Architecture infrastructure pieces fit together and support and complement each other. Only then can the big picture be communicated, built, maintained, and continually improved. So go ahead and break (or re-break) ground today. Hammer in that nail—whether it is the first one or the next important one in your individual, your workforce's, or your organization's ongoing building and learning architectural process.

Part Two

In Practice Perspectives . . .

The Art of Organizational Implementations

Part Two consists of the following articles about the art of learning and training in practice.

Grassroots Corporate e-Learning Collaboration Works! by Carol J. Friday

Carol has authored a detailed case study focusing on the growth of e-learning within her organization—a grassroots tale that serves as a model for others and somewhat mirrors the evolution of training and learning in general. Follow her story, told in four phases, which begins with informal knowledge sharing and collaboration to its now formal, strategic, and vital role within the culture of the workplace.

Learning in an On-Demand World by Nancy DeViney

Nancy, a corporate veteran at IBM for almost thirty years, sees a future in which learners are empowered to shape how, when, and where they learn, where learning is continuous and embedded in our processes and roles, and where collaboration transcends the physical boundaries of time, space, and geography. The enterprise itself, the enabler for all this, is the "glue" for linking these pieces together. Is your enterprise ready to differentiate itself in a new "on-demand" world and to think about learning in this way?

A Journey of e-Learning Efforts by David Barton

David reflects on his up-and-down experiences when introducing technology-based learning at Michelin—not unlike the experiences of many others. His ongoing determination for growing learning efforts within his enterprise, as well as the lessons learned along the bumpy road, have now paid off and he is optimistic about the future.

Going Global at McDonald's with e-Learning by Mike Hendon

As businesses become more global, so does our approach to business learning technology. Can you think of a more global company than McDonald's? How did it meet this ongoing, multi-faceted opportunity with its infrastructure needs and globalization and localization challenges? The organization's philosophy sums it up very nicely: "Think global, plan international, act local." After reading this, it may be hard to order a hamburger at your local franchise or when on a business trip to the Far East without thinking about the "behind-the-counter" efforts it took to bring you that consistent experience and quality "deliverable" (the burger).

Simulation at the Secret Service: As Real as It Gets by Paul L. Nenninger

Paul, a retired Secret Service employee, reflects on his experiences in this article. Simulations are a way of life at the Secret Service—and for excellent and not so "secret" reasons. Can you even begin to imagine trying to set up and coordinate large-scale exercises involving numerous departments and agencies within government spaces today? For this very reason, simulations are employed in federal agencies to create critical thinking, plan logistic operations, and increase communications—all indispensable when responding to any catastrophic situation. Specifically, simulations allow for setting up multiple versions of the same scenario, practicing safely, experimenting with changed variables, trying again . . . and all in a realistic but controlled learning environment.

It's in the Air: The Move to m-Learning by Judy Brown

If I can identify one person instrumental in the mobile learning arena, it would be Judy. As work, life, and educational boundaries continue to blur, extending this technology model to the training and learning world is natural. All industry predictions point to more options and devices, with "m" rapidly intersecting with "e" (me!). Where are we going and what are some recent learning examples across different industries? There is more already available than you think, so let Judy be your guide.

GRASSROOTS CORPORATE e-LEARNING COLLABORATION WORKS!

Carol J. Friday

Leaning against the door of the auditorium, I watch over two hundred people who have arrived for Saudi Aramco's Ninth Corporate e-Learning Forum. I think, "This would not be happening today if it weren't for a few individuals from different business lines who got together six years ago to share their knowledge about e-learning."

I work for Saudi Aramco, a large oil company based in Dhahran, Saudi Arabia. One of the most important lessons we have learned—something we clearly want to "rave" about—is that grassroots initiatives often yield excellent results. Especially in new non-traditional areas such as e-learning, a company can benefit from small successes lower in the organization and then leverage these successes into fuller corporate participation.

In 2004, Saudi Aramco has broad-based, cohesive corporate coordination on e-learning across business areas, but e-learning would not easily have achieved a "corporate face" if it had not been for an earlier passionate grassroots initiative.

How did we make this journey? What steps did we take along the way to achieve corporate-wide coordination of e-learning? We went through four phases to get from a situation where separate organizations inside Saudi Aramco pursued their own e-learning agendas, without coordination, to a place where organizations throughout the company work closely together.

These phases were important to our e-learning evolution. In fact, these phases mirrored, to some extent, the evolution of e-learning in general throughout the world during the same time period. I will discuss these phases and the steps we went through over a six-year period during which we moved from informal collaboration and knowledge sharing to where e-learning is a vital part of Saudi Aramco's corporate strategy to prepare our workforce for the future.

Phase 1: Started Informal e-Learning Collaboration, Problem Solving, and Knowledge-Sharing Sessions

Our journey began with a casual conversation back in 1997. A few of us from the training organization met informally with a few colleagues from the area of the company involved with oil exploration and producing. They had some floppy disk CBT (computer-based training) to teach computer skills and so did we. In fact, we discovered that we had purchased similar courses from the same vendor! About the same time, we had another informal meeting with employees working in the area of engineering. They were using a specific professional authoring tool to develop online courses and so were we. Because this tool was complex, course developers from both areas were eager to meet and share lessons learned.

In mid-1998, all three groups decided to meet together. Our first gathering was for seven e-learning practitioners and lasted half a day. Following are some of the major steps/issues we addressed in our first meeting.

Combined Knowledge Sharing with Discussion of Issues of Interest to Members. Our first program agenda was titled "Computer-Based Training (CBT) Technical Exchange Meeting." The purpose was simply for different areas of the company to share what they were doing with e-learning and to air concerns.

Created an Agenda, Asking for Input Ahead of Time from Members. Our first agenda included the following:

- Discussion of what computer-based training is and is not.
- What are the purposes of using CBT?
- What level of interactivity is important?
- How does multimedia fit in?
- Discussion of specific CBT being used.
- Technologies used and problems/challenges.
- User needs regarding content and ease-of-use of CBT. (The training organization had done a needs survey of the entire company, and the survey results were shared with the meeting members.)
- Vendors supplying CBT.
- Demonstrations of e-learning from attendees.

Gave Technology a Major Place on the Agenda.   Because computer-based training used technology for learning, we focused on technology during this first phase. Many member problems were technology related, so it made sense to focus on the technology underpinning e-learning. Some key issues were

- Which technologies were being used?
- What were members' experiences? Of particular interest were successes and problems.
- What about the network and hardware?
- What about CBT course development?
  - What course development tools were available?
  - How should we train course developers?
  - What about multimedia concerns like audio and video?
  - What about a Help Desk facility for end-users?
  - What about outsourcing our CBT development? (Of particular interest were issues relating to contracts, estimating costs, controlling the work, and necessary standardization/standards.)

- Learning management systems (LMS). At that point, learning management systems were proprietary to each set of courseware that we had and therefore were not standardized.

As I think back, we started out with a broad range of topics—all of which were new to everyone who attended. Many of these same topics are still on our agendas today.

As we progressed through Phase 1, additional steps were taken.

Expanded Session Length and Topics as Needed. Later that year, we expanded to a full-day sharing session to give e-learning course developers time to discuss their nuts-and-bolts issues concerning authoring tools.

Meeting agenda items included demonstrations of two courses developed by the training organization's curriculum development and by engineering curriculum development, respectively. Also included were demonstrations of off-the-shelf courses for technical and IT skills. A presentation was given on how to evaluate third-party courseware—with both good-quality and bad-quality examples. Learning centers were on the agenda also, as they offered an important service for employees without direct access to a computer at their work location. Items on web design and the need for search tools to find e-learning were added, as members had expressed keen interest in these topics.

Opened Participation to All Who Were Interested. During the next few years, we held meetings about twice a year, adding practitioners from more areas of the company. These areas included refining and distribution, medical, and community services. (It may seem strange that Saudi Aramco provides e-learning for medical and community services, but we are a fully integrated company that provides many of its own support functions.) These meetings and between-time collaboration were still very much a grassroots initiative driven by e-learning practitioners.

One of our fundamental premises was inclusion. As word spread, we received more requests to attend the next session. We had decided early that anyone who was interested in the field of computer-based training should be included. This was a grassroots initiative, and we gave no formal invitations. It was an informal way to "spread the net" and also to ensure that there was a sense of equality—that we were all part of the same team with the same overall objectives for e-learning at Saudi Aramco.

Included Information Technology Staff. In 1999, the training organization met separately with the IT organization for a "Training/IT Initiative-Sharing Session." That same year, IT invited a group of about fifteen people from several different areas in the company to form a "Media Streaming Group" to share what we were doing with videoconferencing and streaming over the network. Saudi Aramco's IT organization was becoming more and more involved with e-learning, and representatives started attending the e-learning sharing sessions.

Changed Name to Keep Up with a Broadening Scope. We changed the name of our session to "Distance Learning/CBT Sharing Session." We added "distance learning" in order to accommodate the activities of the refining and distribution area of the company. They were piloting distance learning as a way to offer professional employees university courses in economics and finance for nonfinancial management. Some courses were taught via videoconferencing and some via the Internet.

Kept Agenda Items Fresh and Pertinent to Members. As computer-based training grew, more employees attended relevant worldwide conferences. New agenda items included:

- Conference summaries from members who had attended conferences about authoring tools, online learning, and distance learning.

- Installation issues related to putting vendor courseware on the intranet. (This was the first time we discussed putting course-ware on the company network, as vendor CBT had become network-enabled.)
- Philosophy of computer-based training and distance learning. How would CBT and distance learning change the way employees accessed learning and utilized learning on the job?
- Learning culture changes that would be required of our employees and the change management challenges we would face.

We also continued our tradition of including at least one practical "how-to" segment with an authoring tool tutorial.

Adjusted the Venue as Numbers Grew.   For our next Distance Learning/CBT Users' Sharing Session in 2000, we had to move to a bigger venue. We moved to our Leadership Center, which had a room for forty people. As it turned out, we had standing room only, when about fifty people showed up! We also added the word "user" to our title, because we wanted to maintain the emphasis on practitioners and not formal presentations to management.

Invited Management as Guests at Sharing Sessions.   We invited a few unit heads and division heads as guests at our 2000 session. Until then, no management personnel per se had come to any meetings. We had on occasion invited supervisors who were interested in e-learning to attend. However, they had not come wearing a "management" hat.

Phase 2: Established a More Formal Knowledge-Sharing Forum: The Corporate e-Learning Forum

We decided to establish a twice-yearly formal showcase to highlight members' e-learning accomplishments. Our name changed to the "Corporate e-Learning Forum." We had grown in size to about fifty practitioners. During this phase, the following key changes were enacted.

Requested Management Support and Participation. We asked one of the vice presidents to open the fall 2000 Corporate e-Learning Forum. His address was inspiring. He congratulated all practitioners on their productive e-learning work. He mentioned the value added to the company through the use of e-learning. In addition, we invited other key management from around the company to attend.

Sent Invitations to a Broad Spectrum of Company Employees. We made a strategic decision to open the Forum to people who may not be e-learning practitioners. e-Learning had grown enough at this point that the Forum was a good way to market the concept. We also hoped that many attendees would become e-learning advocates in their respective areas.

In order to be fair, we sent invitations to all administrative areas in the company, allocating a certain number of places, based roughly on the size of the administrative area. We then reserved seats at the Forum, based on feedback.

Moved to More Formal Venue. We moved into a large auditorium in case we needed the extra space—but frankly we did not expect many people to come. As it turned out, reservations streamed in and we almost filled the auditorium. A strong interest in e-learning was growing throughout the company as the real value of e-learning as a corporate strategy became more evident.

Increased Support Staff. We needed a larger staff to plan and implement this more formal Forum, so we enlisted the help of the core e-learning community. Throughout Saudi Aramco, there were e-learning practitioners who had been attending our informal e-learning sharing sessions for years. Now we called on them to help organize the new, more formal event.

Created a More Formal Look for the Forum. We designed and printed posters and formal agendas. Because e-learning was becoming more visible in the company, it was important to provide a more formal appearance to the Forum.

Phase 3: Reinstated Separate Problem-Solving/Knowledge-Sharing Meetings: The Corporate e-Learning Working Group

The period 2001–2002 was very important in the evolution of e-learning at Saudi Aramco. During this time, the training organization worked with IT on a project to acquire both a corporate learning management system (LMS) and a virtual classroom collaboration tool. In addition, the training organization established the Corporate Integrated Learning Services, which supported the LMS and virtual classroom tool and also offered corporate-wide learning consulting services and e-learning technical and customer support.

Much of the input to develop the learning management system requirements came from core e-learning practitioners from around the company. e-Learning had truly become a corporate initiative. In Phase 3, we took some steps to re-focus our work.

Realized We Needed to Go Back to Grassroots in Order to Discuss Nuts-and-Bolts Issues Again. In the beginning, we had combined our sharing sessions with problem-solving meetings. With the advent of the learning management system and virtual classroom tool, however, there were many more installation and implementation issues to discuss among practitioners. How could we address these urgent issues in the Forum?

The Corporate e-Learning Forum's formal presentations were effective as a way to share major initiatives, but they did not lend themselves to addressing nuts-and-bolts issues. Members certainly did not want to discuss in a formal setting problems with a vendor's products, for example. Several key members said that they missed the close collaboration when they had originally met with other practitioners in an open dialog about e-learning problems and challenges.

Established a Separate Working Group of e-Learning Practitioners to Address e-Learning Concerns.   In 2002, we returned to our roots and brought back the idea of problem-solving sessions where e-learning practitioners could focus on e-learning concerns and ways to address these concerns together. The Corporate e-Learning Working Group was born. Approximately thirty-five members from across the company participated in the first meeting. Each meeting usually showcased one member's presentation about his or her latest e-learning initiative, followed by a round robin where members presented e-learning news or issues.

Extended the Membership of the Corporate e-Learning Working Group to Ensure Its Success.   All areas of the company were invited to participate if they were involved with e-learning. We reached out to include areas beginning to be involved with e-learning for the first time. We still had our core e-learning practitioners who had started with us several years before. However, because of the advent of the learning management system, the Corporate e-Learning Forum, and e-learning marketing initiatives (including mass e-mail announcements, presentations, and articles in the company newspaper), more areas of the company were utilizing e-learning and were interested in locating specific courses for their employees. Chairmanship for this group rested within the training organization, with the head of Program Development and Technical Support. In addition, key support people from the training organization attended all meetings in order to support member e-learning needs.

Phase 4: Established a Small Group with Higher-Level Representation to Determine and Address Strategic Corporate e-Learning Concerns: The Corporate e-Learning Advisory Council

By 2003, we had both the Corporate e-Learning Forum (where all areas of the company could formally present their e-learning initiatives) and the Corporate e-Learning Working Group (where practitioners could address their e-learning concerns).

But something was missing. We still needed a way to address key e-learning issues from a higher, more strategic corporate viewpoint. By the end of 2003, there were over eight hundred e-learning courses in the learning management system. Management was increasingly aware that e-learning could add considerable value to Saudi Aramco. It was imperative to strategically align e-learning with major corporate goals, initiatives, and strategic imperatives.

To achieve this alignment, we took the following steps in Phase 4.

Created a Small, High-Level Strategic Advisory Group.   Bigger issues were arising regarding e-learning. We needed a more structured way to obtain business area input, direction, support, and help promoting e-learning. We needed high-level representation from the business areas in order to shape a strategy that would support corporate strategic directions and strategic objectives. So we started a new advisory group called the Corporate e-Learning Advisory Council.

Used a Group Structure to Maximize Effectiveness.   Each major business area had one representative on the Council. In addition, there were representatives from several other key administrative areas, for a total of ten members. Several members were heads of their areas' continuing excellence initiatives. Others were members of senior management staff. Members were chosen for their keen interest in e-learning and their willingness to attend meetings and to interface with their management as necessary. Also, members understood that they would work together with their Corporate e-Learning Working Group counterparts from their business areas. This new council was chaired by the general manager of the training organization.

Developed a List of Strategic e-Learning Concerns Focusing on Aligning e-Learning with Corporate Objectives, Initiatives, and Imperatives. The Corporate e-Learning Advisory Council spent its first two meetings working on a charter and developing an initial list of strategic e-learning concerns. Some key concerns were

- Providing access to e-learning to all employees, including those without an assigned computer in the workplace (such as in the plants) and those in remote areas.
- Ensuring that e-learning was aligned with and supported key corporate initiatives, such as self-development.
- Ensuring that e-learning was aligned with key corporate strategic imperatives, such as to prepare the workforce for the future.
- Promoting e-learning to employees so that they could learn both at work and from home.
- Sharing knowledge across the company by linking with other corporate knowledge-sharing and knowledge-management initiatives.

Created Strong Communication and Support Links Between the Advisory Council and the Working Group. The Corporate e-Learning Advisory Council linked with the Corporate e-Learning Working Group to create a system where each group helped and supported the other. The council provided advice and information to management on strategic direction and strategies for e-learning across the company. The working group was responsible for identifying e-learning challenges, concerns, and success stories from their business areas and for sharing that knowledge. They also performed research, conducted surveys, and helped market and promote e-learning. If the council needed e-learning information to give to management, they asked the working group to do the research. Likewise, the working group elevated any concerns that should be addressed at the corporate level up to the Corporate e-Learning Advisory Council, and the council addressed the concern to management.

Shared e-Learning Successes and Concerns with Management.   Also in 2003 we presented our e-learning services and vision to executive management. e-Learning was accepted as a key strategy to prepare our workforce for the future, one of our corporate strategic imperatives, and was recognized as one way to add real value to the company. Over eight hundred e-learning courses were available online to employees' desktops and in approximately thirty-five learning centers. There was one specific website for e-learning—one access point for any employee to take e-learning courses from several different vendors. Course completions were tracked to employees' permanent training records through our enterprise resource planning system.

Collaborated Closely Across All Areas of the Company.   Saudi Aramco now had strong ongoing e-learning collaboration across the entire company. At our 2003 Corporate e-Learning Forum, over two hundred people gathered to hear fifteen different e-learning presentations and demonstrations from various areas of the company. Several areas had made great progress with e-learning—to the point where real cost savings and added value were evident and quantifiable. For example, several employees from a gas plant gave a presentation about taking e-learning courses available on the company intranet and then applying what they had learned directly to their jobs. One employee was able to inspect boilers more effectively. An engineering specialist talked about transforming his classroom course into a blended course using e-learning. He was able to offer his expertise to many more employees in a shorter timeframe and was able to quickly reduce a years-long backlog of engineers awaiting classroom training.

Summary

At Saudi Aramco, e-learning is now a key corporate strategy. We have developed structures and mechanisms for sharing e-learning knowledge and for determining an overall strategy for e-learning. We journeyed through four phases to develop e-learning coordination, collaboration, knowledge sharing, and steering/advisory functions.

- Phase 1: Started informal e-learning collaboration, problem solving, and knowledge sharing.
- Phase 2: Established a more formal knowledge-sharing forum: The Corporate e-Learning Forum.
- Phase 3: Reinstated separate problem-solving/knowledge-sharing meetings: The Corporate e-Learning Working Group.
- Phase 4: Established a new higher-level group to determine and address strategic corporate e-learning concerns: the Corporate e-Learning Advisory Council.

Yes, e-learning at Saudi Aramco—which started as a grassroots initiative—has grown into a key corporate strategy to prepare our workforce for the future.

LEARNING IN AN ON-DEMAND WORLD

Nancy DeViney

I am clearly a product of a learning organization, having worked for IBM for my entire professional career of twenty-nine years. During that time I have grown from an entry-level administrative position into various technical support, sales, services, marketing, management, and executive positions before assuming the role of general manager, running one of the largest corporate training organizations in the world. The changes I experienced in my professional career required a constant need for re-skilling, professional development, and risk taking. So I certainly qualify as a lifelong learner. And watching how my children learn and prepare for a rapidly changing world has been an eye-opener. I suspect that many of you reading this chapter can relate to this set of real-world experiences that qualify so many of us to engage in a dialog about where we believe learning can and must go in the future.

I spend much of my time thinking about the future of learning and collaborating on this topic with learning, HR, and business executives around the world. I have concluded from these discussions that organizations are changing and transforming in some rather significant ways. There is a need for learning to play a more strategic role in enabling and accelerating change to contribute to top-line results. Aligning learning investments with an enterprise's priorities and transformational initiatives is now imperative. This trend places more emphasis on innovative learning approaches to enable higher levels of individual, group, and organizational performance.

This view is supported by CEOs who recognize the importance of a skilled workforce and leadership team to drive growth and innovation. A recent survey of over 450 CEOs worldwide, conducted by IBM (*Your Turn: The Global CEO Study 2004*, May 2004), tells us that chief executives know that organizational responsiveness in meeting customer needs is critical in driving growth. They also acknowledge the need to build new internal capabilities and skills while enabling their leaders to be change agents. Aligning learning initiatives to address these challenges is of paramount importance as companies move toward an "on-demand" environment.

The "On-Demand" Enterprise

IBM defines an on-demand business as one that can respond with speed to any customer demand, market opportunity, or external threat. To accomplish this, organizations must become more responsive to shifting market needs; more flexible in how they operate; more focused on their core competencies; more nimble at partnering; and more resilient to external market forces. On-demand organizations require on-demand thinking and behavior at every level of the organization. Learning can play a key role in engendering the change in people to adapt to this new way of thinking and operating.

So how is learning evolving to support "on-demand" environments? Although tremendous progress has been made, e-learning is still far from ubiquitous. In many organizations, training budgets have been flat or down, and a high percentage of learning is still taking place in the classroom. Many executives, managers, and teachers still have a very narrow view of what is possible with e-learning. Initially, there was a lot of hype around e-learning, not so dissimilar to some of the dot-com hype. This led many to think of e-learning primarily as a way to shift classroom courses onto the web, which would reduce travel-related expenses associated with formal, face-to-face training. Avoided costs are real, but are only part of the story. This view does not consider the business value delivered by technology enabled learning in supporting organizational transformations and performance.

The Next Generation Workforce

To understand how to think about e-learning differently and more broadly, let's begin by looking at our school age children, as they are the next generation workforce. For example, my two children have desktop computers in their bedrooms. They are growing up with computers and access to the web as the major source of entertainment, information, connection to friends, and support for their school work. Their computers are much more vital to their daily lives than TV or radio, as opposed to our generation. They are the interactive generation.

My nine-year-old son's primary use of his computer is to play games and write an occasional school paper. He learned how to develop PowerPoint presentations in the third grade! Games like Reader Rabbit and Math Blaster quickly gave way to more sophisticated games like Roller Coaster Tycoon and exploring various Internet connections for online games. One night while playing Roller Coaster Tycoon, my son shouted out from his room, "Hey Mom, what's a marketing program?" At this point I sat down to better understand this new game, and, much to my surprise, he was actually learning how to run a P&L for an amusement park, including making decisions on marketing programs to increase park attendance! The concepts he was learning were concepts that I hadn't heard of until college. What wasn't so obvious to my son is that he was actually learning while he was playing. For him, the lines between playing computer games and learning are blurred into a fun, interactive, and engaging experience. He will be in college in eight years and the workplace in twelve years. Are we thinking about e-learning or the learning process this way? Will we be ready?

My seventeen-year-old daughter uses her computer for instant messaging and exchanging emails with friends and teachers, doing research on the web, completing school reports and projects, shopping, listening to music, submitting college applications, getting SAT coaching, and communicating with her college mentor. She navigates complex search engines and performs cut-and-paste functions on the web far more skillfully than her parents. She has her own instant messaging language (r u there, c ya, gtg = got to go, ttyl = talk to you later) for social chit chat and can easily handle upwards of ten simultaneous online conversations. Some of these actually involve real work such as collaborating on group projects for school or asking a question of a classmate or a teacher to clarify a homework assignment. In fact, it is often while collaborating with other classmates that she will finally grasp a concept that she didn't quite get in class. She will be in college in a few months and will enter the workplace in just four years. Are we thinking about e-learning this way? Will we be ready?

I share my personal experience with my children to illustrate what is staring us right in the face. The next generation workforce is already using a broad set of technologies to enhance their learning process: games and simulations, search engines, instant messaging, file swapping, expert locators, cell phones, PDAs, laptops, broadband, and wireless. Organizations will not achieve dramatic improvements in learning until these capabilities are leveraged to make learning more interactive, collaborative, engaging, and, ultimately, more effective. The next generation of learners will expect these tools to support their roles, making them more productive and enabling them to make the best use of the greatest commodity of all . . . their time.

Blended Learning for Impact

For purposes of this chapter, e-learning is defined as the use of innovative technologies and learning models to transform the way individuals and organizations acquire new skills and access knowledge. This is a very broad definition of e-learning that recognizes the intersection of learning, knowledge management, collaboration, and performance support tools and technologies. It also recognizes that new learning methods and models are emerging as we seek to embed learning into our real-time work flows, making work, life, and learning more seamless.

To enable a more robust learning environment, we see organizations applying blended learning in a number of initiatives, including management development, sales force transformation, compliance training, and on-boarding and assimilation of new employees. This blended learning framework, outlined below, has been implemented for several priority initiatives at IBM to help us deliver the right blend of learning content and experiences to the right people so they can develop the right skills and apply them in the right timeframe. The ultimate goal of the blended learning framework is to achieve the desired learning and business outcomes.

The key methods that the 4-Tier Blended Learning Framework™ leverages include:

1. *Learning from Information* encourages self-directed access to performance support information, including static information (for example, web books, reference materials, web pages, videos, and so forth).

2. *Learning from Interaction* implies that the learner is engaged in techniques to "try out" or practice scenarios through tools such as simulations and gaming.

3. *Face-to-Face Learning* is the traditional classroom model, where the students are physically in the same place at the same time with other students and instructors/mentors.

4. *Learning from Collaboration* enables learners, instructors, mentors, and subject-matter experts to come together online using collaborative tools and technologies (such as instant messaging, team rooms, and live virtual classrooms), enabling learning in groups, and leveraging joint experiences. Learners do not necessarily need to be online at the same time, since asynchronous methods also allow collaboration.

This framework is illustrated in Figure 1.

Figure 1. The 4-Tier Blended Learning Framework™

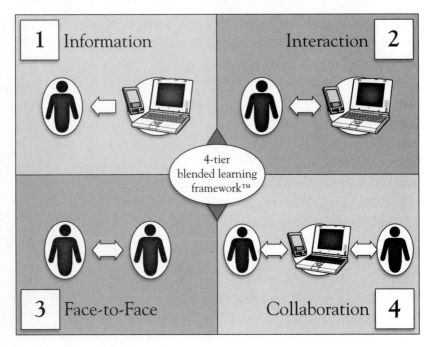

What are the implications of this type of blended approach to learning?

- Learning will be integrated with performance support, collaboration, and knowledge management to enhance productivity and performance.
- More content can be deployed to a dispersed network of learners.
- Learning environments will support a continuum of formal and "ad hoc" opportunities. This is critical since most adult learning occurs outside the classroom . . . on the job and through interactions with others.

- Courses and curriculums can be established that take advantage of multiple delivery approaches to create much more impactful learning experiences.

It is now clear that this broader set of tools, technologies, and frameworks for learning can deliver much more value to an organization than just cost savings. As blended learning initiatives mature, the focus will be on increasing workforce effectiveness by integrating learning with performance support. These innovations will enable organizations to be more responsive to changing business demands, develop deeper relationships within and across the extended enterprise, and deliver financial results. Learning will become a competitive differentiator separating those organizations that are merely surviving from those that are leaders in the knowledge economy.

Looking Ahead

As with most people, much of what I know was learned on the job. "Learning while doing" will only intensify in the next decade. So could "learning while doing" be made easier in the future, given the technologies and tools that are now available or those that will be in the future? Absolutely! It is interesting to think about the fact that, while 80 percent of what we learn occurs ad hoc while we are doing it, training budgets in most organizations are still largely spent on the other 20 percent . . . formal training. This needs to be rethought. On-demand organizations will need to shift their focus from "bringing the worker to the learning" to "bringing the learning to the work."

So where do we go from here? Three powerful forces are converging to transform not only how we learn but also to heighten the importance of learning's role in the organization: rapid changes in the marketplace, advances in technologies, and changing lifestyles and workforce demographics. In response to these multiple interacting forces, I believe that learning will change dramatically in the following ways:

- Learners will be empowered to shape their learning experience, rather than passively receiving it.
- Learning will become embedded in process workflows, enabling learning while doing.
- The focus will expand beyond individual learners to enabling teams with collaborative learning environments.
- Learning will become a key vehicle to enhance relationships across the enterprise and its entire value chain.

These are very different ways of thinking about learning for most organizations. Let's explore these facets of learning in an on-demand environment in a little more detail.

Empowered Learners

Today, most learning is designed to deliver a consistent, uniform experience. The curriculum is typically structured and prescribed by the institution. The role of the instructor is to convey information. The role of the student is to receive and apply this information. We've all had experiences like this where we've attended a class to learn something new.

In the future, I anticipate that learners will be increasingly empowered to shape when, where, and how they learn. Leveraging today's technology, power is shifting to the consumer. For example, a user today is able to independently address his or her specific learning needs with search engines versus referring to a course catalog. With this in mind, I feel that instructional professionals will need to rethink the notion of a course as the primary deliverable for their craft. Nevertheless, organizations will continue to define learning paths, assess value, and reward outcomes in support of overall organizational objectives, but learners will have greater flexibility as to how they achieve those objectives and consequently impact business results. Even in the future, classrooms will not go away. However, the classroom experience will focus on applying or practicing the concepts being taught, rather than being just a means to transfer information.

Technology and new delivery options will enable just-in-time access to information within the context of the individual's role or task being performed and the amount of time available. This type of learning delivery will profoundly impact productivity. Learners will become both consumers of learning and producers of content in their areas of expertise. They will be expected to update organizational data sources with the latest insights from real-world market experiences so that others within the enterprise can benefit and leverage that understanding, enabling breakthrough thinking and innovation.

Embedded Learning

In most organizations today, learning typically is focused on providing information before an action or event—"learn, then do." As technology evolves to transparently weave learning into our work, learning opportunities will be triggered automatically at the time of an action or event—"learn while doing." Content will be delivered within the context of a person's role and interests, seamlessly embedded into workflow. Dynamic, personalized, role-based "workplaces" will include access to both formal and ad hoc learning, such as performance support, collaboration, and expertise location. Thus, learning will be available when you need it most.

We are already beginning to see movement toward embedded learning through enterprise-wide portals. These access points are designed to give users a single, consistent interface, tailored by job role, to access content, applications, business processes, and people. Advances in technologies will further embed learning into our lives. Smart devices, contextual search capabilities (for example, context recognition, personalization filters), and multi-sensory input and output options (for example, virtual reality, voice recognition, and language translation) will allow individuals to access learning around the world and around the clock. For example, personal digital assistants (PDAs), laptops, and mobile phones have become a requirement to keep up with the growing demands of today's fast-paced business environment. Advancements in these mobile devices are making them even more practical, not only for on-the-go communication, but also for just-in-time information sharing and learning.

Collaborative/Group Learning

In the future business environment, only those organizations that are able to innovate "on demand" will excel. For this to happen, however, organizations need to discover how to tap people's commitment and capacity to learn at all levels—individual, team, organization. Peter Senge, chairperson of the Society for Organizational Learning, stated this most eloquently when he said, "Organizations learn only through individuals who learn. Individual learning does not guarantee organizational learning. But without it, no organizational learning occurs."[1]

As I mentioned earlier, individual professional development is essential. However, management best practices today involve the use of cross-functional teams, dynamically formed around specific projects and customer requirements. Technology, such as expertise locators, instant messaging, and community tools, can be applied to support teaming across boundaries of time, space, and geography. If an organization creates a safe environment where people can share what they've learned, learning will also facilitate feedback into the organization, enabling a culture where the learner contributes to institutional knowledge. The ability to do this well will be a key differentiator in the future market environment.

Extended Enterprise Learning

In the future, organizations will need to integrate horizontally across functional organizations and processes not only inside the enterprise but outside as well. Learning will serve as a key enabler of this integration process—it will become the glue that binds the extended enterprise community.

As all senior leaders know, the linkage between strategy and execution won't occur without everyone understanding the strategy. Access to learning opportunities is critical for employees. Equally important is the education and collaboration with the extended enterprise, including customers, partners, and suppliers. Accelerating learning opportunities will help suppliers better understand your organization and how they can help address your requirements. Similarly, business partnerships are built on trust, awareness, and appreciation of each other's unique capabilities. Learning methods can also be applied to marketing and customer support programs to deepen client relationships by increasing their understanding of your products and services.

Summary

I see a future where a learner's experience will be profoundly different. Learning will be relevant, delivered just in time and in context to the role or task being performed. Learning will be much more compelling and interesting, engaging multiple senses. Learning will be adaptive to learning styles and more accessible to those with disabilities. Learning will become increasingly more collaborative, enabling real-time access to subject-matter experts and communities of interest. Finally, learning will be continuous, with learning moments embedded in work and life.

People's desire to contribute and be productive at work, to continue to grow and thrive professionally while balancing the demands of family life and other interests will not change. The winners will be those organizations that create the most effective environments where work, life, and learning are all integrated and where learners are empowered. This has profound implications for how organizations should define, manage, and deliver learning. Are we thinking about learning this way? Will we be ready?

Note

1. Senge, Peter. (1990). *The Fifth Discipline: The Art and Practice of the Learning Organization*. New York: Currency, p. 139.

A JOURNEY OF E-LEARNING EFFORTS

David Barton

When I look back on our e-learning initiative at Michelin, how I got involved, and the direction that it is beginning to take, I am truly amazed. The rate at which technology is changing and the number of vendors offering variations of these technologies is astounding.

Our venture into e-learning started like many companies', with growing competition, fewer people, large application implementations, and users scattered in multiple locations. I have been interested in computers since my company first began using them in the early 1980s. I am by no means a computer expert, but instead someone who realizes the possibilities that they offer to many aspects of the business, including training.

A First Foray into CBT

I was first approached one day in 1997 by the head of our new document management initiative. He came into my office and started drawing boxes and arrows on a whiteboard, described the new system, and told me that we would have to train everyone in North America. I knew this would be an enormous task, especially when he said that it would have to be completed in the next few months. As with other projects, I started looking at how we might accomplish this task via instructor-led training. It became apparent to me right away that, given the time limit, the number of users, and the lack of available human and physical resources, we would have to consider another alternative. At the time, computer-based training (CBT) was available from vendors, but most of it was pretty basic and not very interesting. Another problem was that there was no off-the-shelf content available for the manner that our system had been modified. I decided that we should find some available internal resources not currently being fully utilized to apply toward learning an authoring tool and create some simple CBTs. To add to the initial complexity, the CBTs would be delivered on our new intranet. We found an employee who was between assignments and was willing to give it a shot. She learned the authoring tool pretty well and created some decent training modules based on the current instructor-led materials. I took the finished product to our information technology group and asked them to put it on the intranet. They laughed at me. They told me that we were pushing it already with the creation of our intranet and that there was no way that we were going to put non-approved stuff on their production servers. I could not understand what the problem was. Why was the potential not as obvious to them as it was to me? They were intelligent people and they seemed to care about the company.

Thus began my uphill battle to create what seemed to me the only reasonable and cost-effective way to provide training to the entire North American audience in a short period of time. After a number of meetings with information technology, IT security, and the telecommunication group, we finally put the CBT online. It was cool, but there were problems. First of all, the person who created the CBT had no prior experience, no real passion for the subject or the technology, and was doing it to fill time. No buy-in! Second, our infrastructure had not been fully tested and was not ready for the technology. Third, I was trying to do all of this too quickly, without paving the way and getting the involvement of the necessary groups. We were marginally successful, but obviously we had a long way to go.

Another Attempt at CBT

When we moved to our "common desktop environment," pre-assessments were given to all users to determine their knowledge of the new products. Anyone requiring some level of knowledge was trained in classrooms and was also required to attend training for advanced requirements and applications (such as Access®). A training vendor was hired to accomplish the task. The training required that all facilities furnish a conference or training room (modified to house computers) for at least a month. Managers and users alike were irritated by the disruption and time away from work. The training was OK, but the costs were staggering. I decided at that point that if I ever had a future say in how training for a large implementation would be accomplished, I would do it better and more efficiently. I got my chance about a year after the document management implementation.

I was asked again to provide training to all computer users, this time for our new Microsoft Office® products. The year was 1998. We were upgrading from our current version of Microsoft Office to a completely new version. I was teamed up with an American colleague in France to provide the training as part of a global team. It was decided early in the project that we would use our computer hardware provider as consultants and project managers. As before, the approach was to provide instructor-led training to all global users. But this time, I was able to convince my colleague in France to explore the possibility of using CBT. Instead of using off-the-shelf content, the global team opted to create custom content that better matched our altered applications. In turn, it was also decided that delivery would be through CDs in a classroom environment. Unfortunately, this did not meet the North American office's needs, so I decided to seek out a CBT vendor who could provide off-the-shelf content to be delivered through our intranet. The global team created some good-quality CBT and offered to have it customized for online delivery. We agreed, but once again the results were not so good. We took perfectly good content and tried to force it to work in an unproven environment. When this did not work, we were left with just over a month to implement an alternative. Our computer hardware company suggested that we buy a server from them, loaded with off-the-shelf content, like the one they were successfully using internally. After several battles with the purchasing department and IT, we bought the non-standard server and installed it on the system. By this time, we had a training website on our intranet and were able to provide a link to the limited learning management system (LMS) on the server. Although it was not an overwhelming success, we were able to provide the training to our user population on time and at savings that would have been at about half the cost of doing classroom sessions were it not for the extra costs of a difficult change management process.

Getting the Right People Together

As we continued to struggle with the use of computer-based training, I found that other groups in North America were involved in similar struggles and had experienced similar results. With the support of the director of training and development, we assembled an internal group to attempt to pull these resources together. We named our group the Technology Enabled Training (TEL) group. Our mission was to get our arms around the various computer-based training activities that were taking place in the company. We were tasked with learning from each other, preventing duplication of effort, and providing guidance to others in the company interested in using computer-based applications to train their users. It took a couple of years to assemble the best mix of people to make this team effective.

We began by inviting users involved in computer-based training initiatives to join. But it was quickly discovered that we were continually running into some of the same roadblocks (such as determining who was the key IT representative needed), so we invited a couple of different IT professionals to join the team . . . but then ran into different/other IT roadblocks due to the complex internal IT structure as well as the willingness of the representatives to serve once they were identified.

After a lot of discussion and false starts, we discovered that there were several additional groups of IT professionals required to successfully implement computer-based training. Our latest group now included IT representatives from IT security, telecom, IT infrastructure, and the person responsible for the IT budget. Finally, the dream team! Well, as far as the IT members were concerned, this was true. However, we were still having a tough time getting our requests through the purchasing department. We then added representatives from various other users groups, including sales, training and development, production, and other support groups that included most of the IT and purchasing areas. With this approach and this team, our success rate increased significantly.

Project Implementation

We have since implemented a number of major projects over the past several years with varying degrees of success. These include our Financial Management System, our Document Management System, and our Human Resources Management System. A variety of approaches have been used that include custom CBT and electronic performance support systems (EPSS) blended with classroom training for key users. These approaches are beginning to be more accepted by the users and, in many cases, requested by the managers.

For example, training for our financial management implementation was accomplished with a combination of custom CBT and classroom training. The CBT was used as a prerequisite to classroom training for the end users. Again, the idea of training people only electronically on a new application was rejected and scoffed at by the management group and users. We trained key users to provide module-specific training to local end-users, thus eliminating the need to send everyone to a central location. The CBT is being used on a continuous basis to provide the initial training for new

users, as well as for recertification training for current users. One
year later, the project manager, who was also involved in the original project, asked that all product upgrade and new user training be
accomplished through custom EPSSs.

I am responsible for the training administration module of our
Human Resource Management System. When it was implemented
in 2001, I was tasked with providing training for the Training Administration Module and training consultation for all of the other
modules. I proposed a blended approach, using key users and custom EPSSs to provide the initial, as well as the ongoing, training for
all modules. But the idea of using EPSSs as the primary delivery
method was rejected by the other module leaders and by our project
manager. Regardless, I proceeded with this approach for the Training Administration Module, which was my responsibility. When
the project manager saw the product and realized the cost savings
that we would realize, he asked that I provide the same training for
all of the other modules. No problem, except that we only had
about a month and a half to make it happen! But after much hard
work, in the end we were successful with the training, and, after-
ward, we decided to offer blended training approaches specific to
each module.

One year later, I was asked to help provide a similar approach
for the upgrade, but this time globally. The result: we were able to
train users in seven languages, in the majority of our user countries
around the world, for about one fifth the cost of traditional classroom training.

Conclusion

As I look ahead, I am optimistic that we will continue to make
progress at an increasing rate. More and more of our management
is realizing the benefits and savings that blended approaches afford.
We are gaining more knowledge and insight through our membership in the MASIE Center Member CONSORTIUM and through
the hard knocks that we have experienced with our implementations and TEL efforts.

In summary, I would like to list some of the key "do's and don'ts" that we have discovered during our journey down the rocky road of technology enabled learning:

Don't

- Insist that one approach fits all situations.
- Force technology, when another approach is better.
- Work in a silo. Get ideas and other points-of-view.
- Close your eyes to new ideas.
- Rush (easier said than done).
- Think that you can work around IT and purchasing.
- Continue to separate e-learning from the "normal" learning strategy.
- Try to implement everything at one time.
- Always pick the most elaborate and expensive approaches; sometimes less expensive alternatives are adequate (or better) for your situation.
- Say never. What is not possible today may be in a few months.
- Give up. It takes persistence to make progress.

Do

- Form a team of users and support groups.
- Involve user managers early in the process.
- Try new approaches.
- Spend time helping everyone understand what you are trying to do.
- Market, Market, Market!
- Add something new as often as possible—make them want more.
- Tie the training to business needs.
- Consistently show results. Make a big deal! It may not be as obvious to others as it is to you.

- Make training easily accessible. It should be intuitive to the user.

- Listen to feedback. Even though your approach is great, it may need some tweaking!

Even as I write this reflection, the budget has been cut for two major projects and another is being threatened. This almost turned into a rant instead of a rave. My gut reaction is to throw up my hands and give up. But no, instead, it makes me more determined than ever to be more creative in helping upper management understand the benefits and cost savings possible through the use of technology.

Yes, budgets are getting tighter, profits are thinner, resources are scarcer, and there is less time available for accomplishing training and development. But on the other hand, technology is getting better, bandwidths are wider, content is more engaging, and users are more computer savvy! Sounds like a great time to make significant gains, doesn't it?

GOING GLOBAL AT MCDONALD'S WITH E-LEARNING

Mike Hendon

McDonald's is one of the most recognized brands around the world. With over 30,000 restaurants in 128 countries and 1.7 million employees speaking thirty languages, McDonald's elected to utilize e-learning as part of its blended learning solution. With a worldwide network consisting of more than 250,000 trainers, it is most important to the system to assure that consistent messages and consistent training occurs. And as one can imagine, the nature of the business and the demographics of the McDonald's employee base also require ongoing training and development.

Value Proposition for e-Learning

There are many business challenges that fit into the value proposition of why McDonald's chose to consider e-learning as a part of a blended approach to learning. The business challenges faced by McDonald's include turnover, the training required to keep a ready workforce, growth of the existing product line and new products, new processes, the impact of the use of technology in the restaurant, product integrity and safety, and career development of the staff, including promoting from within and deploying best practices. System-wide, McDonald's uses crew trainers to train new restaurant crew members (employees who work in McDonald's restaurants). McDonald's prides itself on the consistency of its brand, image, product quality, and taste around the world. To make this happen, there must be consistent training each and every time a person is trained. With over a quarter of a million crew trainers worldwide, one can determine that this is indeed a formidable task. To make this consistency happen, a blended approach of e-learning combined with the "shoulder to shoulder" training conducted by the crew trainer was determined to be the most appropriate solution.

Training has always been a part of McDonald's culture because Ray Kroc, the founding father of the brand, strongly believed in the development of employees. In fact, he created one of the first corporate universities, Hamburger University. This has now expanded into six additional Hamburger Universities that serve all areas of the world. As with other global processes, this ensures the consistency of the brand. Many a weary traveler looks forward to a recognizable and assured quality product. In addition, training this large number of people demands a cost-efficient and easily maintainable methodology. The implementation of global curricula and the ability to easily update the curricula materials efficiently at the many locations requires some form of electronic distribution. Based on the business case for each country, this is currently being implemented throughout the world with a mixed solution of stand-alone personal computer systems using CD-ROMs and hosted solutions.

With a total of 1.7 million employees and a substantial portion of these being crew members, the decision was made to focus first on the crew and the crew's training. Other options including addressing the restaurant managers, whose restaurants for the most part are connected to the Internet, and the consultants in the field, who typically have Internet connectivity both in their offices and on the road. This would have been easier to do. However, this did not align with the business initiatives of McDonald's and therefore was not considered an early option.

Global Challenges

Even with the good reasons for an integrated learning experience, including the availability of e-learning for employees globally, the challenges for making this modality available can be overwhelmingly difficult. These challenges are multi-faceted—some as simple as where to locate the computer in the restaurant, especially when there is no crew room or only minimally available space, and others as complex as what level of connectivity can be made available at the restaurant and what is the value proposition for doing this.

Fulfilling the language requirements of the major countries has historically been an issue and continues to be so today. The concerns surrounding what languages are needed and how the requirements of each country should be addressed are always on the forefront of thought. And of course, there is always the thorny issue of funding— who pays for the localization of the content? Many of these answers are being addressed today with the decision to focus on the restaurants in the "Big 13" countries of McDonald's business. This strategy encompasses almost 90 percent of the restaurants and represents twelve languages. Language was one of two major obstacles to the total implementation of e-learning. The second was the required investment in hardware (for example, personal computers for the areas that elected to go with a stand-alone system) and the technology infrastructure for those that were willing and able to invest in a hosted solution.

In making e-learning available around the globe, as McDonald's has accomplished with its traditional curricula of self-study, class attendance, and follow-up work with a coach, an organization has to make the decision for how to treat different languages. This level of treatment needed to happen with e-learning as well. Some companies have the luxury of declaring a single language as the "business" language. This tends to be possible the higher the level of position in the company for which the learning is intended. This is because many times the language is a requirement of the person in the role or of the role itself. However, not all companies are able to make this declaration or can have this decision supported globally, nor will the level or nature of their audience allow for this.

Globalization and Localization

While the areas of globalization and localization may appear to be similar, they are vastly different and must be treated accordingly. Expectations must be determined and accommodated. Much of this is geo-political and is learned along the way, sometimes with a significant learning curve, and it is almost always difficult to manage.

Globalization is defined as designing and producing products that can be adapted to local markets around the world without the need for redesign. *Localization* is defined by our organization as adapting a product to a specific local market or region with the end result being a product that is integrated into the end-user's cultural and language conventions. This requires extracting language elements, regional and cultural elements, and business and legal requirements.

Two specific examples related to developing e-learning modules and localization follow. When working with different English-speaking areas of the world, there was at first much debate about whether or not to build the e-learning modules using "Commonwealth" English or "American" English. Our partners told us that there is no such thing as "Commonwealth" English, only English, and Americans should adapt. To help avoid the different "versions," it was decided to use the term "International" English. This required its own glossary, much like what had been done previously with multiple forms of Spanish. It also required working with several areas of the world to determine what was acceptable in terminology and linguistics. Our partners from these areas of the world let us know in no uncertain terms that if the materials were not in "Commonwealth" English, then they would not be welcomed or used. Of course, this helped us in reaching our final decision. Fortunately, an acceptable decision was made with their input and also in response to the fact that, due to the specific operating system employed, these "Commonwealth" English speaking groups were to be the only groups that would use the modules. Forcing them to translate from "American" English would not have made good business sense. In this regard, the ultimate decision saved money and satisfied the affected areas of the world, and the push for disseminating e-learning around the world continued without interruption.

Another language-related example dealt with the correct interpretation of the word "straw." As you can imagine, straws are important to McDonald's products. To one country, a straw is an instrument used to assist in the drinking of a liquid. To another, it was completely different. Solving this "simple" dilemma required discussion among several people representing multiple countries and coming to an agreement for a mutually acceptable definition and spelling within the glossary. By agreeing up-front, we produced a win/win for this area of the world, and the cost of country-by-country localization was avoided.

Benefits and Measurable Results of Localization

The McDonald's strategy has been to "think global, plan international, act local." As exemplified above, one of our most important learnings is that local interest must become an integral part of the process for any globalization effort, and especially for localization, to be effective.

When handled via this strategy, the outcomes to be achieved are fourfold:

1. Alignment of local development of e-learning products with worldwide initiatives
2. Prevention of duplication of efforts
3. Using resources more effectively
4. Taking advantage of economies of scale

Experience shows that, when localizing content, measurable results of the above can be achieved, with savings in both time and budget. An important aspect is reducing or eliminating downstream costs that will need to be multiplied time and time again based on the number of countries developing similar products or developing products that have to be modified or adapted to multiple audiences who are using different operating platforms. Therefore, if e-learning products are designed for multiple country use and can be shared, the cost of localization can be kept to a minimum.

Another positive aspect is that there will be greater buy-in, acceptance, and support of the product if the country becomes actively engaged early in the process. This means they must dedicate resources to assisting in the design, review, and quality assurance testing of the product. An example of why this is important is that in our formative days of e-learning, we began a pilot that was conducted in six countries and included four languages. We followed a very regimented implementation process for the engagement of the countries. Part of this regimented process was a requirement made to our supplier that their localization/translation vendors use in-country localizers and in-county reviewers. In working with our international audience and on their review of the product, we discovered a major disconnect with the localization effort. Vendors had disregarded our requirement for in-country localizers and had instead used technically competent localizers from another country. This created a significant issue in credibility with all concerned. By the localization/translation vendor not using in-country localizers, the perception by the respective country was that McDonald's Worldwide Training, Learning, and Development had not abided by the mutual agreement and had not followed the protocol established for each party's respective participation.

Possible positive measurable results include employer image and people commitment. It is important that McDonald's be viewed as an employer of choice and an employer that looks after its people. Much work has been done internally and is now available relative to job competencies and to the related training that will allow an individual to grow to his or her aspirations. Many of the top executives of the corporation began as crew members years ago and have climbed the ranks to where they are today.

Another measurable result is greater consistency in the training delivery by being able to achieve economies of scale. McDonald's uses a network of country, division, regional, and corporate employees to deliver training to its multiple audiences. Consistency is the key to success in protecting the brand.

The Role of Governance

A governance body is an essential element in making any global implementation successful. This, along with a top-down "push" for implementation, a plan of action, and an implementation toolkit, tend to be the keys to moving this process forward. The implementation toolkit must contain a detailed and systematic plan, the required support needs, a timeline, and the estimated investment in time and resources for the success of the implementation.

The governance body must also be of sufficient stature, strength, and force to carry decisions throughout its organization, country, and area of the world. It has been determined that at McDonald's, the highest-ranking training leaders were to participate. This group, charged with delivering feedback and input and for the direction of learning, was first called the Curricula Collaboration Team. Since then, it has expanded into a decision-making body and is now known as the Global Training Board. The members of this board are global heads of training and/or heads of human resources and training and have defined roles and responsibilities in making decisions regarding all curricula, diagnostic tools, and modalities for delivery of training.

A Hamburger Is a Hamburger Is a Hamburger

One of the more noticeable characteristics of McDonald's is that every customer, at every location, no matter where in the world, can be assured of a consistent experience and a quality product. To be able to support this, there is considerable work behind the scenes within the delivery network of the seven Hamburger Universities globally, professors, instructors, managers, and trainers to ensure that this occurs on an ongoing basis. Training a workforce of over 1.7 million employees is a formidable task and one that must assure accuracy in content and delivery of the training product. e-Learning affords McDonald's this opportunity.

SIMULATION AT THE SECRET SERVICE

As Real As It Gets

Paul L. Nenninger

Prologue

September 11, 2001. I arrived at Secret Service Headquarters in downtown Washington, D.C., around 7:45 a.m. EDT. I joined several other agents in a conference room for a board meeting. One of the last to arrive announced that a plane had just crashed into the World Trade Center. Across from me sat a lady who was formerly the special agent in charge of the White House. She pointed at me and said, "You know all about that." As we gathered up our personal effects, I explained that the training center had been crashing planes into the White House since 1998 on a simulation program provided by the military. It was done to test the security responses of the various agencies that interact to provide security and support to the White House.

Training Via Simulation

I get energized about simulations. They represent one of the very best ways to train when the actual training ground is not available for a variety of reasons. A simulation gives you the chance to train multiple times with minimal set-up time. Trainees have said that the ability to conduct back-to-back exercises is a great luxury. The lessons learned are not lost by hours of delay as the next live scenario is put in place. You can train with one or many and have the simulation play the additional roles. The training is never canceled because of bad weather or because the training ground is under repair or is being used by someone else. As long as there are workstations available, simulations are available on demand. The flexibility available to training with a simulation allows for quick changes. If trainees fail early in an exercise, the simulation can be quickly reset, remediation offered, and the same simulation generated immediately.

Variety is another advantage of simulation. Any training facility for live exercises is limited by what exists there. Even the most inventive people are limited by the space and terrain available in the real world. In a simulation, you can expand those possibilities; you can add or remove buildings, roads, people, vehicles, trees, bushes, and other obstacles.

I had the pleasure of working with a really great group of people at the Secret Service James J. Rowley Training Center's Security Incident Modeling Lab (SIMLAB). I was also in charge of the program in its early stages. The Service had a very good piece of analytical software for simulation called the Joint Conflict and Tactical Simulation (JCATS) built by the Lawrence Livermore Lab. The Joint Chiefs of Staff Joint War Fighting Center at Fort Monroe, Virginia, distributed the software to the Secret Service. This is an outstanding example of cooperation between civilian and military sides of government. The program was dynamite at analysis. One of the only drawbacks was the screen image. The simple line drawing representations of people, vehicles, buildings, vegetation, and so forth did not provide an appealing image to the participants and was also not very intuitive for workstation operators.

However, this simulation provided that all-important commodity: a place to practice our security plan when the actual facility was not available. As you can imagine, the White House is a high-use facility. When not available for official functions, it is usually scheduled for major repairs, renovations, or sometimes just routine maintenance. It is hard to squeeze in a live security simulation with all that goes on at the White House. Also, live simulations are very manpower intensive. Can you imagine getting all of the following scheduled to pull this off: the White House Usher's Office, White House Staff, Military Aids Office, U.S. Marine Corps, U.S. Air Force, Metropolitan Fire Department and Police Department, Federal Aviation Administration, Old Executive Office Building Staff, Treasury Department, National Park Service, Secret Service's Washington Field Office, Presidential Protection Division, Vice-Presidential Protection Division, Assistant Director for the White House, White House Uniformed Division, Technical Security Division, Intelligence Division, and the training coordinators and instructors who deal with all of the above! This would require days of scheduling the special equipment, the manpower, the site, and notices to the facility that an exercise was being conducted. Unlike simulations, with live training held at the training facility, you have to be careful not to break anything and you must avoid certain areas entirely, all of which detract from the training scenario. The idea of having a place to run a simulation, observe the action on the screen, and implement what actions you would perform as you act out your assigned role is a great asset to providing protection to the president. The actions can then be programmed into the simulation to see how the resulting reactions to the provided stimulus conclude.

Can you imagine the reaction, in today's media-frenzied climate, if in downtown D.C. a live exercise was conducted on the White House grounds? Even if it was announced ahead of time, switchboards would be overwhelmed, a small panic would ensue, and, worst of all, elements of the security plan would be displayed for the public and the press to observe. Showing your security plan and reactions to certain scenarios trains not only those participating, but also those observing. Like all knowledge, it can be used for good or evil purposes. The risk of teaching a potential terrorist anything about presidential security is not one that anyone is willing to take.

Can you imagine really crashing planes into buildings? The other very important thing that simulations allow you to do is practice something that you will never be able to do live in the real world (at least not without tremendous expense and, even then, only once) and (and this is a very important and) also allow you to practice scenarios that can be attempted by a terrorist or other deranged individual.

Just consider the logistics of obtaining a plane and then getting equipment to launch it into a particular building you want to "practice" on. It is extremely hard to disguise a catapult capable of launching a plane into a building. The element of surprise is lost. With a simulation, the trainee approaches the scenario with a mind that is stimulated by the reality of the simulation and not the massive preparation that was observed on the way to training that day. And who gets to clean up all this mess? I don't think it has taken more than five minutes to clean up the classroom after running multiple simulations over three or four hours.

The Power of Practice

"Because knowledge deteriorates rapidly unless it is used constantly, maintaining within an organization an activity that is used only intermittently guarantees incompetence."[1]

During any catastrophic event, a fair amount of time is spent getting organized, directing resources, and solving problems on the fly. But many parts of any response are similar for a catastrophe. The basics of responding to a fire, a building collapse, or a plane crash are the same; the on-scene assessment by first responders is essential to determining how much and what kind of help is needed. The lesson most often learned in the simulations is that communication is the weakest point. Resolution of any crisis rests with the timely communication of what is going on, where it is happening, and who or what is needed to help resolve the problem. This vital information must be communicated to the command structure, who can best use the information to subsequently obtain the assets essential for addressing the immediate crisis needs. The issues "why and how" are to be addressed only after lives are saved. Practice of these responses is valuable because all responses to a crisis have multiple actions. Organization, the accurate relay of information, training in the particular applicable skill, and mental preparation save time and provide confidence for all the participants to deliver their best efforts. Yes, there will be a lot of adapting and overcoming of challenges during the crisis but, as Louis Pasteur commented while looking for various answers, "Chance favors the prepared mind."[2]

I think simulation training creates a kind of situational awareness so that when something resembling the simulation actually happens, your brain recognizes the issue and allows you to perform more efficiently because you have practiced. It also allows you to focus on a particular part of a plan that you have experienced. The situation may not flow exactly as formulated, but the familiar is always easier to accept than that which is completely strange to you. How does simulation create familiarity? Practice, practice, practice!

The Value of Analysis

"Nothing is less productive than to make more efficient what should not be done at all."[3]

One of the other great things about a good simulation is that it runs in real time. The role players sometimes find that their responses are strategically correct, but that their timing and distance create a chance for failure. For example, if the role players issued orders or said that a given task could be performed in a certain amount of time, the computer analyzes the data and measures the tasks in real time—sometimes showing that accomplishing a given task takes longer than foreseen. The sooner you know this, of course, the better.

An analogy that comes to mind is Superman leaping tall buildings in a single bound. In effect, the computer shows that a considerable run must precede the leap so that enough momentum is provided to bound over the building. The time required for the run turns out to be the crucial part of the analysis. Time and distance are things that are sometimes missed in the "I can do this" thought process. When faced with a task, a hard-charging and well-motivated Secret Service employee will tell you that he or she can/will accomplish it. The Secret Service is replete with physically fit, type A personalities who will get the job done no matter what. But they are not supermen and superwomen, and the constraints of earthbound human beings are made evident in an accurate simulation.

The after-action analysis of the training by the SIMLAB personnel yields helpful discoveries. For example, while reviewing a day's training on the captured statistics, it revealed that some units in the exercise had a higher failure rate than others. Through logical perusal of the variables, it appears the sole difference was weapon and ammunition choice. In this case, it was poorly suited for the express mission. This feedback was provided at the next day's training. It was determined that changing ammunition was not a real consideration due to a superceding policy regarding that weapon and ammo choice. Changing to another type of weapon was the only remaining possibility. In fact, changing the weapon type did result in the improved performance of this unit. As a result of this analysis and running back-to-back training operation simulations with the changed type of weapon, a change in policy was recommended.

Gaming

> "I see you stand like greyhounds in the slips,
> Straining upon the start. The game's afoot!
> Follow your spirit! And upon this charge . . ."[4]

The Secret Service applied software intended for command-and-control exercises that encompassed the world and adapted it to the individual agent, civilian, fireman, staff member, and assassin. However, as good as the simulation was, the participants cried out for more sophisticated on-screen images similar to the various games they played or observed their kids playing.

One way to upgrade the sophistication level is to adapt common off-the-shelf (COTS) software to a training need. At first, SIMLAB used the game DOOM® as a stress relief tool. DOOM allowed the SIMLAB employees to have a virtual and sometimes literal "scream" to release stress produced from the tedium of programming and testing on the Joint Conflict and Tactical Simulation. The Marine Corps at Quantico once considered using DOOM as a training aid for a rifle squad. After a few games, it became apparent that teamwork produced more success than did individual effort.

We introduced DOOM to some of the special tactics units so that they could improve their teamwork. The students liked the idea of training on the game; it allowed all-weather training opportunities and compressed training time. They also liked the better on-screen image displayed by the COTS game that allowed them to feel more involved in the action.

Common off-the-shelf software also has a marked price advantage. For $20 to $40 per workstation, you have a game that can be run as a simulation. I have heard many in the training field say that they do not really want custom-built training, but instead want the ability to customize the training. Using a game for a simulation allows you to make it your own.

Progressively, other games such as Rainbow Six® and Flashpoint® were adapted to training for different reasons. Initially Rainbow Six was effective because it closely resembled the special operations units and their equipment. Two such units are the Counter Assault Team (CAT) and the Emergency Response Team (ERT). The software allowed for tactical training and highly disciplined tactics, so highly disciplined that team members must have full faith and confidence in the execution of a tactic even though they begin the exercise unseen by each other and progress through the simulation by only verbally confirming their progress. At a common point, they will emerge to reunite the team for the successful completion of their mission.

Rainbow Six

The Secret Service's experience with Rainbow Six is probably one common to gamers everywhere. In searching for the newest and latest modifications to play this PC-based game, we discovered these wonderful entities called communities. Groups of fellow gamers, whose hobby it is to produce enhancements to the game, post their results to the Internet for the community of people playing Rainbow Six to use. For the most part, these modifications or modules (mods in the gamer vernacular) are free to anyone who wishes to use them. The Training Center obtained several mods this way. Of course, we used a clandestine gamer tag (pseudonym) email address without the usual easily identified government address for contact with the community. I was somewhat shocked when a pretty accurate depiction of Air Force One came from a member of the community for Rainbow Six. Shortly after this came a Presidential limousine. The image was sufficient for use in the training scenario, even though not accurate to every detail. Therefore, it appeared as if other modifications needed for future games could be had for the asking.

Training by the special operations teams takes place in a specially constructed classroom. Workstations are isolated by partitions. Participants are required to communicate by radio just as in the real world. If phone calls have to be relayed by command personnel, phones are available and role players answer and respond. The opposing force is in another classroom nearby. The two cannot communicate. The only thing the participants know about each other is what they see on the PC screen as the scenario plays out. The training group then debriefs the exercise. For the most part, the self-critique by the special operations covers any training points that develop from the exercise. Occasionally the observing special ops instructors offer additional information.

On the first exercises performed with Rainbow Six, the trainees complained that the opposing forces were playing the game too well and felt that their advanced knowledge of Secret Service special unit procedures and training had affected the outcome of the game. But SIMLAB had planned ahead. The new opposing force was soon introduced—four clerical staff on the training center campus.

Flashpoint

Flashpoint is another COTS game that has a larger play box (the area in which the game takes place) than Rainbow Six. The play box affects what can be modified. For instance, Rainbow Six was pretty well limited to a few buildings and little or no space to drive cars. It was impossible to fly a plane due to these limitations. Typically, the Secret Service scenario includes planes, helicopters, cars, and people distributed over several miles of distance. Flashpoint allowed for the use of these larger scale operations and did so with a good mix of civilians and civilian vehicles. Limitations are the result of programming the scenery, action, and detail and need to be traded off with the needs of more space in which to run the simulation.

One of the things I observed during these training simulations was that the same multi-tasking that goes on in real life occurs in the simulation. There may be a different tactile feel at the fingertips (no weapon in hand), but the same stressors resulting from visual, auditory (both from the PC and walkie talkie), and physical coordination stimulus occurs at the PC. Voices tense up as they pass information to a team member over the radio. Radio traffic is garbled and has to be repeated. Descriptions are mangled. Directions are confused. All of this because the simulation proceeds in real time toward its programmed outcome and can be interrupted only by those who came to practice that day. In other words, the solution provided by the trainees working in concert brings the problem scenario programmed into the PC to a successful conclusion. Of course, an improperly applied strategy would have the opposite effect. The other thing that I observed is the value of the self-critique.

It is unusual if the special operations teams do not know the cause of problems that come up during the exercise.

The Value of Simulations

Like all good training, an evaluation of the process and exercise is mandatory. This has been overwhelmingly positive. Trainees like the chance to train multiple times on the same exercise, the chance to freelance from established plans to see whether a "new idea" will work. Most consider the simulation to be training with a very high value for job performance. Last, the trainees are required to give a brief description of a scenario that they would like to see portrayed in a future simulation. This comes from the knowledge that employees talk about plans, policies, and possibilities with co-workers as they socialize at work and converts that critical thinking to something more tangible. The trainee suggestions are then scanned for similarities. Sometimes the suggestions are entered as scenarios just as provided, while other suggestions are combined to make a scenario. Trainees like it when they recognize a simulation as something they suggested. It reinforces the idea that their thoughts are valuable.

Everyone dealing with training and new technology has experienced the need to sell a program. To find that instrument of change that can lead the rest of the agency or company to use and eventually embrace the new technology to better train for their jobs is important. In retrospect, SIMLAB found a leader at the grassroots level. The special operations units are admired and respected as a group because they are fitter, train more often, and have the latest in gear for performing their jobs. They are an elite group. As the special operations groups found that their military counterparts used similar software, and when possible did not launch an operation without a chance to have it simulated, they requested more and more time in SIMLAB. The experience of the special operations units with Joint Conflict and Tactical Simulation had produced pent-up energy for a "3-D" simulation and the COTS games took advantage of that desire to allow participation via a more visually appealing simulation. The special ops teams requested training time split between the analytical simulation provided by JCATS and the tactical simulation provided in a COTS game. They determined there was value in testing a plan in a very accurate simulation and practicing a successful plan in a reasonably accurate game. As they practiced more and more, the word began to spread. More calls came in.

Now there are exercises being conducted that include multiple units of the Secret Service, various command centers, and individuals. Some of the exercise is displayed on the Joint Conflict and Tactical Simulation, while other parts are distributed on Flashpoint for direct action by individual team members. The Joint Conflict and Tactical Simulation handles things like alarms, FAA radar, and threats that are considered at too great a distance to work in Flashpoint. Flashpoint handles the people on the ground taking action on observed threats or reacting to information communicated through the command centers. The respective programs make up for the inefficiency of the other. New employees practice their security planning skills on a simulation. After all have completed their work, the group critiques one another and votes on which plan appears best for running as a simulation in JCATS. Not only do you write the recipe but you bake the cake.

Conclusion

"Imagination is more important than knowledge. Knowledge is limited. Imagination encircles the world."[5]

One of the most exciting things to come out of simulation labs is the environment that it creates where you have permission to fail and to bring forth your ideas for consideration. The lab provides an environment that allows for discovery. Some parts of the simulation training have negative feedback portions—you do get killed. The more I watch the training taking place during the simulations, the more I realize that the trainee is having what educators desire students to have—that "aha!" moment of discovery. Only instead of "aha!" it may be "oops!" or some reasonable facsimile of that expression. I believe that "aha!" and "oops!" are really the opposite sides of the same coin and that this chance of discovery is so important for the critical thinking that is required for the protection of the President. If technology is adapted to the terrorist cause, then critical thinking plays an important part in countering that threat.

One of the things emphasized in these training exercises is critical thinking. The world is constantly changing. Unfortunately, the ways to wreak havoc, maim, and destroy march in unison with other change. For instance, the advent of the digital clock allowed for time bombs with a twenty-four-hour timer rather than a twelve-hour timer; the micro chip allowed for clocks with programmable settings that made possible time bombs that can be activated weeks, months, or years later. It makes you shudder to think what technology will be maligned to add to the terrorist toolbox.

I recently read a book by Bill Bryson titled, *A Short History of Nearly Everything*, where the author gives a short (thankfully) explanation of who discovered what in our world. He answers questions such as how far away is the sun; how much does the earth weigh; where did earth come from . . . you get the picture. I observed that very often the answer to those questions was found by accident as the scientist (often just a hobbyist) was looking for the solution to some other mind-boggling problem. As Secret Service personnel consider the intelligence from sources around the world and sometimes prophetic works of fiction for what the future may hold, the lab provides that experimental place where knowledge is discovered among the everyday tasks performed on the stage called simulation. The simulations allow them to let their respective fertile minds collectively and independently pursue such things as crashing planes into the White House. Simulations are where ideas come to life.

Notes

1. Rosenstein, B. (2002, July 5). Scandals nothing new to business guru: An interview by Bruce Rosenstein. *USA Today*. Available: www.usatoday.com/money/general/2002/07/05/2002–07–05-drucker.htm
2. Schrage, Michael. (1999). *Serious Play*. Boston, MA: Harvard Business School Press, p. 117.
3. Rosenstein, B. (2002, July 5). Scandals nothing new to business guru: An interview by Bruce Rosenstein. *USA Today*. Available: www.usatoday.com/money/general/2002/07/05/2002–07–05-drucker.htm
4. Shakespeare, W. (1994). *Complete Works of William Shakespeare*. Glasgow, UK: HarperCollins. p. 602.
5. Viereck, G.S. (1929, October 26). What life means to Einstein: An interview by George Sylvester Viereck. *The Saturday Evening Post*.

IT'S IN THE AIR

The Move to m-Learning

Judy Brown

When I started work in the learning and technology arena over twenty years ago, I programmed "drill and kill" (a common term for the boring, early computer-mediated learning designed to practice a specific skill) materials on a mainframe computer. There was a green screen and a limit of eighty characters per line and twenty-four lines per screen. Somehow it did work for what we wanted to do, but we often dreamt of what could be. What if everyone had access to computers? What if we had color and even graphics? In the early days I don't even recall us talking about moving graphics or sounds. That would have been too much of a stretch.

My first "mobile" computer in 1979 was the Texas Instruments Silent 700 (actually it was a portable thermal printing terminal). It did not have a screen, but rather thermal paper for the display. It did have an acoustic coupler into which the telephone handset rested to make a connection to another computer via the built-in 300 baud modem. It came in a luggage-type carrying case and required an electrical outlet and telephone connection. But it could connect to other computers.

Then in 1984 I received one of the new IBM 5155 Portable PCs with two floppy drives, a small amber display, and a weight of over thirty pounds. Was this really what portability meant?

It was another twelve years before I received my first Palm Pilot™ in 1996. This new device was indeed portable, connected to my contacts and calendar, and provided immediate access to saved information, no matter where I was. The battery lasted over a month, and most importantly it provided the contents instantly—without the need to wait for a computer to start up. Finally, everywhere I had immediate access to contacts, notes, and calendar entries. This, indeed, was portability.

Fast forward to today, where I now have a combination telephone and organizer in one device. Tasks, contacts, calendar, and notes are all readily available, plus access to browse the Internet, to communicate using instant messaging, to access tutorials, forms, or databases, to play music or listen to audio books or lectures, or to capture audio, photos, or videos.

It is time to start dreaming again about how these devices can—and will—change our lives, including both formal and informal learning. You'd better open your eyes, as mobile learning is already happening.

In this chapter, we will take a look at the mobile industry today and some examples, but more importantly, we will examine the opportunities today and tomorrow for truly any time, anywhere learning.

Today

Boundaries between work, education, and home continue to blur. We are a mobile society with employees away from a physical office much of their time. Many are already carrying mobile devices for organization and communication. Why not then for learning?

At the same time, we are well aware that only a small portion of learning takes place in the classroom. The evidence is overwhelming that mobile learning is already beginning to take hold and is no longer confined to a specific time or place. But we have only begun to tap the possibilities.

Professor Christopher Dede, Harvard Graduate School of Education, notes that "part of what makes handhelds so exciting is that they have, perhaps, 60 percent of the capability for learning at about 10 percent of the price. This next generation of handheld devices, in particular those that are Pocket PC-based, has the kind of raw computing power that laptops may have had two or three years ago, even though screen sizes are much smaller and full-sized keyboards are a peripheral add-on. This array of features means that they will be used a little differently than a laptop is used."[1]

Once these devices are a part of our daily life, it isn't a stretch to see how they can enable new access to learning and performance support.

Industry Predictions

Personal digital assistants (PDAs) are now more powerful than desktops, and even mainframe computers, were only a few years ago. Analysts predict that multipurpose handheld devices (PDA and telephone) will outsell laptop/desktop computers combined by 2005. Analysts estimate that more than 500 million mobile devices will be in use in 2004.[2]

The Gartner Group predicts that wireless "hot-spots" for mobile users worldwide will total thirty million in 2004, up from 9.3 million in 2003.[3] At the same time, enterprises are reducing wired networks and increasing wireless networks.

Nearly nine out of ten companies believe mobile computing improves workforce productivity, according to a survey published by The Economist Intelligence Unit report, sponsored by Nortel Networks. Interviews were conducted with 309 executives across seventeen industries and found that "more than 58 percent of senior executives use mobile computing at least twice a day." The report did note, however, that security and wireless integration difficulties were still barriers.[4]

Additional studies have identified productivity gains averaging as much as a half-hour per day with the adoption of connected mobile appliances.

Devices

These devices can take the form of handheld computers or personal digital assistants, mobile phones including the new Smartphones, audio players (such as the Apple iPod), video players, Tablet PCs, and even wearable devices. They can be connected through a desktop, a laptop, or a network, either wired or wireless. They can be stand-alone and possibly synchronized periodically, intermittently connected to a network, or always connected.

Most handheld devices currently use the Palm or the Windows Pocket PC operating systems. Palm devices are available from Palm-One and Pocket PC devices are available from vendors such as Hewlett-Packard, Dell, or Toshiba. Additionally, Sharp offers handheld devices using Linux, and Psion offers their own Psion EPOC operating system. Note that not all applications or development tools are available for all systems.

Other than the operating systems, the differences between devices include cost, battery life, memory, storage capacity and external media supported, weight, and displays (size and color). Many are truly multimedia communications devices and often include phone, camera, and/or audio capabilities. Many handheld devices combine phone capabilities, while at the same time many mobile phone vendors include PDA productivity application capabilities.

These portable devices can be either instantly on, or always on, and can be used anywhere—standing in line or sitting in a waiting room, in a plane or taxi, lying in bed, or any place when even short periods of time are available.

Peripherals add more capabilities to these devices to scan barcodes or radio frequency identification (RFID) tags, probes for scientific experiments, biometric input for security, and infrared beaming or Bluetooth capabilities to transfer information. Keyboard replacements, including infrared laser keyboards, are here today.

Studies have identified productivity gains averaging a half-hour per day with the adoption of connected mobile appliances.[5]

Learning

Mobile learning (or m-learning) has been simply defined as the intersection of mobile computing and e-learning. Today much of the m-learning content that is available has been ported from the desktop. Natural applications are those for which flash cards may have been used in the past, procedures and step-by-step directions, certification tests or practice drills such as for the SAT (Scholastic Aptitude Test), reinforcement, knowledge checks, content review, rote memory work, or job performance tools.

However, we are beginning to see usage that better fits the capabilities of these readily available devices. Learning management systems (LMSs) are beginning to provide support for disconnected users and download modules to the portable device, transferring results when next connected. These can either be full modules or practice modules from a "course" to be used for practice or reinforcement.

With the recent concentration in e-learning on learning objects (or bite-sized learning) and performance outcomes, these smaller learning "chunks" are relatively easily ported to mobile devices. Additional drivers include the availability of wireless connections, convenience, instant on capabilities, and automated "push" delivery. Real learning any time and anywhere is now finally possible.

Clark N. Quinn noted that "as we recognize the transition from formal courses to informal learning, from learning Just In Case to Just In Time, we are similarly recognizing the potential to move to granular learning experiences—a blend between e-learning, knowledge management, and performance support."[6]

Handheld computers have several unique form factors that suggest further intriguing educational opportunities. Klopfer, Squire, Holland, and Jenkins describe five properties of handheld computers that produce unique educational opportunities:

1. *Portability*—can take the computer to different sites and move around within a location

2. *Social Interactivity*—can exchange data and collaborate with other people face-to-face

3. *Context Sensitivity*—can gather data unique to the current location, environment, and time, including both real and simulated data

4. *Connectivity*—can connect handhelds to data-collection devices, other handhelds, and to a common network that creates a true shared environment

5. *Individuality*—can provide unique scaffolding that is customized to the individual's path of investigation[7]

There are limitations to providing learning through these devices; however, the benefits usually outweigh the challenges. Most often cited as limitations are the size of the screen and security. There are solutions coming for screen size and battery life, and the use of a personal firewall and a secure virtual private network (VPN) log-in help to address today's security issues. Note that security concerns should also include the training of users on the use of passwords and/or encryption for sensitive content.

Examples

m-Learning examples are readily available in markets in which mobile workers are a substantial percentage of the workforce, although we are beginning to see innovative examples in areas such as retail sales, which does not have a large mobile component. Medical, law, sales, banking, government, and academic examples are readily available. In fact, according to iGillottResearch Inc. (www.igillottresearch.com), the medical industry has adopted mobile devices for the largest number of employees. Universities are starting to enable enrollment, course scheduling, and e-books on PDAs.

Across all industries, content from both vendors and internal developers is readily available as well as learning materials in areas such as IT training, safety training, product and sales training, briefings, presentations or lectures, and publications.

Following are several interesting applications and examples of m-learning.

3Com University

The business of 3Com University depends on reaching internal and external sales consultants, technicians, and customers with timely information about the features, benefits, and technical specifications of its products. As an innovator in the field of PDAs, 3Com undertook a pilot project to demonstrate the usefulness of offering instant information about 3Com products to customers, consultants, and technicians who were working in the field using a Palm hand-held device.

Latitude360™, a division of RWD Technologies®, worked with 3Com to identify a strategy that would enable the Palm to deliver just-in-time information to a mobile and geographically diverse target population. Latitude360™ then developed and built two modules that contain product features, benefits, technical specifications, as well as a self-assessment where users can check their HomeConnect and OfficeConnect product knowledge. Now anyone can download data modules from the 3Com University website to the Palm and get the latest product information instantly in the palm of his or her hand. The modules can be used with any Palm. The inclusion of performance-oriented solutions like the Palm-based m-learning, combined with access to a knowledge management system, enterprise tools, a learning management system, and online testing, allows for a blended m-learning solution for 3Com University.

General Motors

Physicians in the GM health plan use Palm handhelds to quickly access reference information for thousands of drugs, improving the quality of care and patient safety and reducing healthcare costs.

The healthcare field has been one of the most aggressive in adopting mobile computing, and publishers have responded by making available reference and training materials for both the Palm and Pocket PC platforms.

IBM

IBM is prototyping mobile e-learning solutions for customers in industries such as retail and fast-food restaurants that can provide on-the-fly, on-the-go training with bite-sized content for employees. Even though IBM officials couldn't disclose the customers' identities, they are providing generic demonstrations of this retail environment solution. By making use of a barcode reader in the device to reduce input, users log in by scanning their store badges. They can then access updates and training materials on specific products. The training content might help the store employee explain to a customer the differences between two similar products or learn about a new sales procedure in a few minutes while the employee isn't busy helping a customer.

OmniLearn

The OmniLearn Learner Support System combines both desktop and mobile options to deliver and track learning and performance initiatives automatically via the Internet at a pace that is controlled by participants. Utilizing a unique workflow "push" process, OmniLearn drives all of its performance improvement and learning initiatives by delivering mini-lessons, guided practice, and assessments without taking employees away from their jobs.

Once a learner enrolls in a course, it is delivered in small pieces on a daily basis with reinforcement messages sent via email, a phone, pager, or the desktop as requested. At any time the learner can change the desired method of communication to accommodate his or her personal schedule.

OmniLearn's "push" process addresses the traditional challenge of gaining learner participation and offering continual practice. All guided practice activities provide reinforcement as part of a learner's daily work routine. The system also provides for additional learner support through tracking, two-way communication, and a learner resource page tailored to each organization's needs.

MOBIlearn Project

The MOBIlearn Project (www.mobilearn.org) is supported by the European Commission. The MOBIlearn consortium explores new ways to use mobile environments to meet the needs of learners working by themselves and with others. The MOBIlearn project consortium involves twenty-four partners from Europe, Israel, Switzerland, the United States, and Australia. Their competencies are integrated and extended by a Special Interest Group, which includes 250 of the world's leading organizations active in information technology. The consortium is targeting:

1. Workers who want to update their knowledge continually to satisfy the demands of their jobs;

2. Citizens who want to improve the cultural experience when visiting a city and its museums; and

3. Citizens who want to have simple medical information for everyday needs.

A new m-learning architecture will support creation, brokerage, delivery, and tracking of learning and information contents, using ambient intelligence, location-dependence, personalization, multimedia, instant messaging (text, video), and distributed databases. Field trials encompass "blended learning" (as part of formal courses); "adventitious, location-dependent learning" (during visits to museums); and "learning to interpret information sources and advice" (acquiring medical information for everyday needs).

m-Learning Project

m-Learning (www.m-learning.org) is a pan-European research and development program. It is aimed at young adults, aged sixteen to twenty-four, who are most at risk of social exclusion in Europe. They have either not succeeded in the education system, cannot read and write adequately, or have problems with simple calculations except in familiar contexts. They are not currently involved in any education or training and may be unemployed, underemployed, or even homeless.

m-Learning is drawing on the experience of participants in designing modular multimedia learning materials and games, informed by m-Learning's underpinning research, to develop very small prototype learning modules for delivery via a variety of handheld devices. An intelligent tutor system is also being developed that includes an assessment agent to help identify needs and learning preferences, plus a tutor agent to help personal learning planning. An example of a mobile portal addressing such topics as health and fitness, lifestyle, number skills, and word skills is available on their website.

Duke University

In the fall of 2004, Duke University provided over 1,600 first-year students with 20GB Apple® iPods to help stimulate creative uses of digital technology in various aspects of their academic life and while on campus. The goal of the program is "to facilitate the use of information technology in innovative ways within the classroom and across campus." See www.duke.edu/ipod/ or cit.duke.edu/about/ipod_faculty_projects.do for examples of how faculty are using audio-based resources in their classes and the beginnings of "podcasting" initiatives.

Wake Forest University

Mobile medical students at the Wake Forest School of Medicine use Palm handhelds during clinical rotations to easily access critical patient and reference data—patient lists, demographics, diagnoses, procedures, and reference databases from the Internet—thereby improving the quality of patient care.

Wake Forest University has been a leader in the experimentation with, and adoption of, handheld devices in the classroom. They have developed ClassInHand (classinhand.wfu.edu/) and DataInHand (datainhand.wfu.edu/), applications that provide for remote quizzing and feedback and for remote data collection. Both are available as free downloads for the Pocket PC platform.

Harvard Medical School

Harvard's mobile medical students stay informed with Palm or Pocket PC handhelds. Access to personalized data—course calendars, announcements and communication, class notes and syllabi—improves Harvard's program quality, student productivity, and student-faculty communication.

University of California, San Diego

UCSD faculty and students are testing how wireless handheld devices can better connect students to faculty and to each other. They have developed and are testing two applications: ActiveCampus Explorer and ActiveClass. ActiveCampus Explorer displays a map with a list of nearby sites, the location of their nearby colleagues and their availability, and a means to record information about physical spaces. To better engage learners, ActiveClass enhances classroom interaction through the anonymous posting of questions, polling, and other information. As expected, they are finding improved performance with better engaged learners.

Boston Museum of Science/MIT

"Hi-Tech Who Done It?" was an experiment conducted in January 2004 at the Museum of Science by MIT's Teacher Education Lab (education.mit.edu), led by Eric Klopfer, who developed this mystery at the museum. Players physically move throughout the museum's exhibit halls using their location-aware handheld computers to collect virtual clues, interview virtual characters, and collaboratively investigate a simulated mystery. The game uses location-aware handheld technologies to embed players in lifelike situations and provide opportunities to engage in critical thinking about scientific situations. The device identifies the specific locations of the players and provides information relative to role and their location at the time.

Teams were comprised of parents and students. Some of the comments from this experience included:

- Mother of middle-school-aged daughter: "This has been the best experience—having in-depth conversations with my daughter about logic and science."

- A woman suggested that this kind of thing should be offered to corporate groups because it would make a good team-building vehicle because in the game you form investigative teams and only certain roles can access certain information, so you learn the importance of working as a team.

Academic ADL Co-Lab

So far, most handheld learning applications have been applications ported from the desktop. The Academic Co-Lab believes that a powerful handheld learning environment might capitalize on the *portability, social interactivity, context sensitivity, connectivity,* and *individuality* of ubiquitous devices to bridge real and virtual worlds. Working with Professor Kurt Squire, the research examines a handheld computer simulation platform designed to exploit the opportunities inherent in handheld technologies. With GPS and wireless capability, the platforms enable the development of "augmented reality" simulations, that is, simulations that provide a virtual context layered on top of a real-world context. The handheld computer provides a window into the virtual context that is sensitive to information being supplied to it by the real world. Over the past two years, this platform has been used with nearly five hundred high school and college students, as well as with students in informal learning programs through the MIT/Education Arcade's augmented reality gaming platform.

The three applications currently being deployed in Madison, Wisconsin, are

1. *Environmental Detectives*, an environmental disaster simulation game where players participate in a real-time simulation-game based around a toxic contamination in a local watershed. Students must combine real-world (characteristics of the landscape) and virtual-world data (virtual readings, interviews with virtual characters) to identify the cause of the contaminant and design a solution to deal with its effects.

2. *Taken Off Campus*, a virtual tour mystery game where players try to uncover the mystery of a rash of burglaries around the UW-Madison campus. Players literally run around the UW campus interviewing characters and investigating landmarks to piece together the puzzle of the stolen valuables. While presented as an entertainment application, this game is designed to explain the history of UW-Madison, share common history and folklore, and enculturate new students into campus life.

3. A *history time travel game* where players virtually travel into the past and into the future to try to reverse the flow of history after a wormhole has appeared and altered Madison history. Players learn about the architecture and history of Madison, including its days as a frontier town, controversies surrounding the late great architect Frank Lloyd Wright, and the controversial riots in Madison in the 1970s.

Although these three applications have differing objectives and different use scenarios, they carry common elements that can be used in any general distance learning application. Specifically, they use *engaging backstory*, *differentiated character roles*, *reactive third parties*, *guided debriefing*, *synthetic activities*, and *embedded recall/replay* to promote both engagement and learning.

Opportunities

Now that these mobile devices are part of many of our lives and growing at a fast pace, how can they be further utilized for learning and performance support? Penetration of mobile workers is growing in most sectors. Add to that the frequent travelers, telecommuters, multi-site workers, and non-office workers. Figure 1 shows the number of mobile workers as a percentage of total workers across a number of industries.

Figure 1. Mobile Workers Per Industry Sector

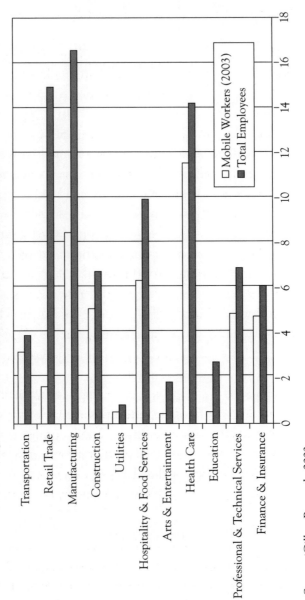

Source: iGillott Research, 2003.

Additionally, the average worker in the United States spends only two days per year in formal training programs. Imagine how you can reach your workers with learning opportunities when and where needed.

In traditional learning, examples such as the classroom support application at Wake Forest or at UCSD are beginning to appear. Personalized reinforcement and performance support such at that offered by OmniLearn are available today. This supports the "IV drip" of learning that Elliott Masie of The MASIE Center has been talking about for some time. (Elliott Masie refers to the IV drip of constant information. The "drip" can be increased or decreased depending on need, but is always there and available.)

Based on the information in Figure 1, one would assume that healthcare, manufacturing, and hospitality and food service would be the areas to target. However, some of the most innovative examples cited above are coming from retail trade, arts and entertainment, and education. These are the new arenas with new opportunities. I would have initially thought of the mobile worker or the executive to target with m-learning, but am closely following the m-Learning Project in Europe that is targeting the unemployed, under-employed, or even homeless.

New employee orientation is a good example of an opportunity for all industries to make learning opportunities available as needed. On completion of specific tasks or meetings, certain contact information or data can be transferred, and based on that information, additional tasks can automatically be scheduled. Or by using location-based information, mentors or coaches nearby can quickly be identified.

Tomorrow

We are just at the infancy of the possibilities of true any time, anywhere learning—m-learning. Professor Chris Dede refers to this as "ubiquitous computing, where the virtual world travels through the real world with you" (www.gse.harvard.edu/news/features/dede02012004.html).

The line is also beginning to blur between handhelds and wearables. New devices the size of handhelds, but as powerful as laptops, are also being introduced. We are moving from the Pocket PC to the "PC in our pocket." These devices will definitely continue to change and even become incorporated into our clothing, but the fact that we can have constant access to the world of knowledge opens doors about which we have never even dreamed.

In September 1991 in *Scientific American*, Mark Weiser declared that "the most profound technologies are those that disappear. They weave themselves into the fabric of everyday life until they are indistinguishable from it."[8]

With global positioning and wireless location capabilities, we can access just the information we need based on our location in a museum, gallery, city, or even sports location. Purdue University's e-stadium initiative now provides access to up-to-the-minute statistics, player and coach biographies, and other pertinent information. Just think of what we will be able to access for learning with location-aware devices.

Instant communication will be readily available, which should be a boon to coaches and mentors. Speech will become more popular with hands-free access, and enhanced eye-wear will provide improved visibility.

Expect to see mobile devices serve as tour guides for museums, travel, and historic sites. Useful language translators are also on the horizon.

Input capabilities will continue to improve with voice and better handwriting recognition. Expect the biggest improvements to be in the screen displays, with roll-up screens currently being built in test labs.

The World Wide Web Consortium (W3C) is working on a basis for adapting to device presentation capabilities so that content only needs to be created once for multiple-sized screens. Groups are also working on specifications for input and output choices anywhere on any device, any time.

Additional work needs to be done on the pedagogical implications of mobile computing for learning and performance support, and we also must better understand the needs and behaviors of mobile users. But I am very excited about the future of lifelong m-learning. Perhaps we will even see the convergence of e-learning and m-learning into "me-learning." Isn't that where we really want to go?

Notes

1. Dede, C. (2004, February 1). *Handheld Devices for Ubiquitous Learning.* Harvard Graduate School of Education News [Online]. Available: www.gse.harvard.edu/news/features/ dede02012004.html

2. Keenan, R. (2003, September 4). *IDC predicts strong mobile phone growth in 2004.* CMP Media LLC. [Online]. Available: www.embedded.com/showArticle.jhtml?articleID=14400016 &_loopback=1

3. Gartner Press Release. (2004, February 18). *Gartner Says the Number of Hot Spot Users Worldwide to Triple in 2004; Enterprises Must Implement a Wireless Strategy.* [Online]. Available: http://www4.gartner.com/5_about/press_releases/pr17feb2004a.jsp

4. Thomas, D. (2004, January 15). Mobile computing improves productivity. *VNU IT Week* [Online]. Available: www.itweek .co.uk/news/1152053

5. Hollis, E. (2004, March 17). m-Learning: The next wave for training and development. *CLO Executive Briefings* [Online]. Available: www.clomedia.com/content/templates/clo_nl_ execbriefs_content.asp?articleid=429&zoneid=101

6. Quinn, C. (2003, March). Flexible learning objects. *Workplace-Xpert* [Online]. Available: www.n-email.com/trimax/flexible_ learning_objects.htm

7. Klopfer, Squire, Holland, and Jenkins. (2002). Environmental detective. Games2Teach. [Online]. Available: http://cms.mit .edu/games/education/Handheld/Idea.htm

8. Weiser, M. (1991, September). The computer for the 21st century. *Scientific American.*

Part Three

Preparing Ourselves, Our People, and Our Organizations for the Future

The two articles in Part Three encompass the vision of two of the most recognized visionaries in the learning field, Sam S. Adkins and Wayne Hodgins.

Learning in the Bright Air: The Learning Technology Trends of 2015 by Sam S. Adkins

Sam's specialty is learning technology research and thus his "tech watch" is a detailed sneak peak into eight emerging technologies, how they are being employed in the learning industry, and what their impact is on our profession. Note that all of these technologies are interrelated, are converging in hybrid products, are getting "smarter" every day, and are available in the marketplace today. You probably have heard about how knowledge being generated by the human race is growing at exponential rates and doubling every two years . . . and how the complexity and volume of data is also growing. In our world, this means that learning will be pervasive. Begin exploring and experimenting with these technologies now— they are the foundation and key to our future platforms, careers, and profession.

Into the Future of meLearning: Every One Learning . . .
   Imagine If the Impossible Isn't! by Wayne Hodgins

Wayne's exciting, powerful, and compelling vision for the future, the state where every person experiences personalized learning every day, is ripe and ready to happen—but it will take *each* of us to imagine, design, and build this future. But first, three grand challenges need to be addressed: scaling up from "any" to EVERY; scaling down from every to just right for ONE; and the readiness to respond to every LEARNING moment. He describes how we already have the enablers, the strategies, the technology, the know-how, and the working models—no magic is needed—to move from theory to practice, from probability to possibility. Why else should we heed his call? Aside from the opportunities it presents to all of us in the learning profession, it is also the ethical and right thing to pursue, perhaps even our responsibility. This is Wayne's energetic and passionate "call to action" and his accompanying work plan to allow "every one learning" to become a reality. If not now, when?

LEARNING IN THE BRIGHT AIR

The Learning Technology Trends of 2015

Sam S. Adkins

The future of learning technology is bright in more ways than one. By the year 2015, information will be pervasive and, literally, in the air all around us. The inexorable drive to wireless broadband technologies will bathe the atmosphere in every part of the globe with pulsing bits of data. Smart chips loaded with vital information will be embedded in the everyday objects that surround us. The air will be teeming with ambient information. Raw data will be available virtually everywhere waiting for a human mind to transform it into knowledge during the act of learning. Learning will be pervasive.

Predicting Advances in Technology

Based on learning technology trends today, it is possible to predict the state of learning technology in 2015. General technology prediction models such as Moore's Law[1] and Kurzweil's Law[2] can be brought to bear on predicting the future of learning technology over the next ten years.

Moore's Law, named after Gordon Moore, founder of Intel, states that every eighteen months, processing power doubles while costs remain constant. Moore's Law was originally conceived as a predictor for computer chip technology, but it seems to be a good predictor of most technology advances. It is now often applied with relative success to technology in general. In practice, this usually translates to falling prices for increasingly more powerful computing machines.

Kurzweil's Law, also known as "The Law of Accelerating Returns," is named after Ray Kurzweil, scientist and prolific inventor. Kurzweil's Law states that the rate of change is actually accelerating instead of doubling at a constant rate. In a May 2003 article on *kurzweilAI.net*, Ray Kurzweil stated, "Because of the explosive power of exponential growth, the 21st century will be equivalent to 20,000 years of progress at today's rate of progress, which is a thousand times greater than the 20th century, which was no slouch to change."[3]

It is not just the technology visionaries who are predicting a brisk pace of innovation in the next ten years. Pragmatic economists are also predicting a similar pattern. For example, the well-known economist Carlota Perez, author of *Technology Revolutions and Financial Capital: The Dynamics of Bubbles and Golden Ages*, has mapped out the patterns of what she calls "Techno-Economic Paradigms" over the last two hundred years. Based on her analysis of innovation cycles, the next twenty years will be the flowering of the Information Age that started in the 1970s. She has dubbed it another Golden Age.

During this Golden Age, enormous advances will be made in all types of software and hardware technology, including learning technology. These new learning technologies will assimilate not only technology advances but also knowledge harvested from the explosion of data coming from cognitive research, developmental psychology, and the neurosciences.

All scientific disciplines are now enjoying a brisk rate of expansion. For example, there is a tenet known as Monsanto's Law in the biosciences. Monsanto's Law states that the ability to discover and apply genetic information in practical ways doubles on average every eighteen months. This explosive growth in the biosciences is transforming biology, agriculture, medicine, and the health sciences. Similar rates of discovery are occurring in cognitive science, neuroscience, and developmental psychology.

Plotting the Progression of Innovation

Innovation in software and hardware is progressing at a blinding speed. The primary innovation trend in software is toward "autonomic," self-aware, and pervasive computing. This software is referred to as self-healing because it can adapt to changing conditions automatically without human intervention. It is smart enough to detect security breaches and usage anomalies and take the appropriate action. It behaves autonomously without the intervention of a human, hence the term autonomic. Autonomic software can reconfigure entire networks to compensate for modulations in traffic. IBM is already selling autonomic computing products.

Hardware is evolving rapidly as well. The major trend in hardware innovation is the same as it has been for many years. This is the evolution toward smaller, faster, and more intuitive devices. Toshiba's 0.85-inch 4GB "hard-drive-on-a-chip," no larger than the U.S. dime, is already on the market. Phillips has begun full-scale manufacturing of a flexible display technology that can be rolled into the size of a ballpoint pen. It could hold the entire Library of Congress collection. Virtual holographic keyboards from Canesta allow users to "type" in thin air on a keyboard made of light.

There is a rapid evolution of PC technology away from desktop systems and into "computing anywhere" devices. The Tablet PC was only launched in 2003 and is already being enthusiastically adopted by workers who do not sit at desks all day. Blue-collar workers monitoring the assembly line, miners drilling for ore, and healthcare workers making the rounds have all enthusiastically embraced Tablet PCs. The tablets are converging with notebooks, PDAs, smart phones, digital video cameras, global positioning satellite (GPS) technology, and so-called affective computing devices that adapt to human interaction.

It is likely that a convergent form of the Tablet PC will be the dominant learning technology device in the academic sector by 2015. Variations of the tablet will be used by the majority of knowledge workers in the corporate and government sectors as well.

Tablets already allow natural language input and are much more efficient for character-based languages like Chinese and Japanese. Voice recognition technology will complement traditional cursive writing interfaces on the devices. Voice will allow workers and students to interact hands-free with the devices while they perform manual tasks. Elementary school children will learn to read and write on Tablet PCs running intelligent tutoring software.

Wireless-enabled tablets will allow developing countries to leapfrog twenty years of information technology progress made by the developed countries. It is no longer necessary for emerging nations to recapitulate the long process that was necessary in the past. In particular, expensive landlines and fiber optics will no longer be the requirement to achieve modern telecommunications capability.

At the current rate of accelerating change and innovation, a Tablet PC will be cheaper than buying textbooks by 2015. Not only that, but the device will carry thousands of books and simulations. It will be connected to the global network twenty-four hours a day and have native contextual collaboration technologies that link students with peers, teachers, experts, and parents. It will be "loaded" with adaptive and intelligent learning technologies that will personalize learning to that particular student's cognitive makeup.

Applying tenets of both Moore's Law and Kurzweil's Law, and even adjusting for inflation, it is plausible that such a device would cost less than $20.00. In contrast, paper-based textbooks are rising in price by 8 to 10 percent a year. This is due to the rising costs of raw materials, physical printing, inventory storage, and distribution costs such as transportation and shipping. It is entirely possible that a Tablet PC will cost less than a typical textbook if such a thing as a "textbook" survives obsolescence by 2015.

It is reasonable to expect that the world's educational and philanthropic institutions will be willing to spend $20.00 to buy powerful learning machines for every man, woman, and child on the planet. That includes what we now consider economically, cognitively, or physically challenged students. The software and hardware will adapt to a wide range of individual differences along the human learning spectrum. UNESCO's goal is to achieve universal primary education (UPE) in all countries by 2015. Universal design applied in new learning technologies will ensure that universal education also means universal access.

Barring global political upheavals and repressive government obstruction, every man, woman, and child on the planet should have access to the entire collected knowledge repository of the world by 2015.

Pinpointing the Patterns of New Learning Technologies

While there is a wide range of new learning technologies in development, it is possible to isolate the major technology patterns that will dominate learning in 2015. There are now eight primary learning technologies emerging, as shown in Figure 1.

Figure 1. Primary Learning Technologies

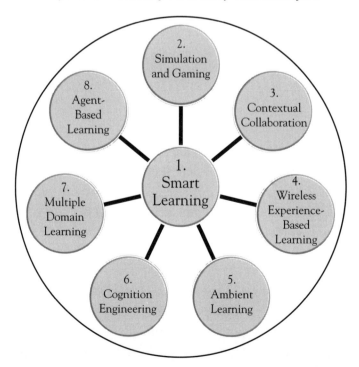

All of the technologies shown in the figure are on the market today. These technologies are highly interrelated and are increasingly used in hybrid products. For example, simulation and gaming are now often combined with smart learning technology, cognition engineering, and rudimentary agent-based technology. The content embedded in ambient learning is often simulation and collaboration. Mobile learning-ware is often indistinguishable from ambient learning in the context of field-force automation or business activity monitoring technology.

In 2004 it is still possible to differentiate learning products that are predominantly categorized as one or the other of these categories. The current state of these emerging learning technologies will be described in greater detail in the following sections. By 2015 it will become increasingly difficult to differentiate these technology trends because they will be assimilated into convergent learning products.

The central "convergence vector," or final destination where all innovative emerging learning technology is heading, is *smart* or *intelligent* learning. This is a type of technology that fuses personalized instruction with cognitive science and computer technology. The goal of intelligent learning technology is to achieve the results that were once possible only with one-to-one mentoring.

1. Smart Learning Technology: Making a Difference, One Person at a Time

In the commercial and academic sectors, there has been a long-running debate about whether one form of instructional media is more effective than others. The debate has never been resolved. Some studies show "significant differences" (statistical term for verifiable data) and other studies show "no significant difference." Yet a great deal of significant difference has been achieved with new intelligent learning technologies such as cognitive tutors.

Perhaps the best-known commercial products that use methods culled from the latest cognitive research are the "smart toys" sold by

LeapFrog. The company uses a variety of multi-sensory, multiple learning domain techniques in its early childhood learning technologies. In a study conducted by LeapFrog in three Los Angeles Unified School District (LAUSD) schools,[4] students who participated in the LeapFrog SchoolHouse Literacy Center Program outperformed students in the control group by 37 percent in key reading predictor tests. Pre-kindergarten students using the LeapFrog School-House Literacy Center made a 74 percent gain in early reading skills over children who received the standard district literacy program materials. The LeapFrog products are enjoying brisk sales, proving that there is a ready market for smart learning technologies.

Since these smart learning technologies target instruction to individuals based on their specific cognitive characteristics, they have also been successful at treating and mitigating learning disabilities. A good example of this in the early childhood market is the Fast ForWord products developed by Scientific Learning. These products are designed to help all children learn to read and use language more effectively. They have also proven to mitigate the learning disabilities of dyslexic children.

An example of smart learning technology in the later grades is the Quantum Intelligent Tutors marketed by Quantum Simulations. The Quantum Intelligent Tutors are embedded in the electronic textbooks sold by Holt, Rinehart and Winston (HRW). HRW offers Quantum Intelligent Tutors for a range of sciences taught in high schools and middle schools.

Benjamin Bloom[5] identified one-to-one mentoring as the most effective teaching method. He found that the average tutored student's achievement is better than 98 percent of classroom students. Bloom quantified this achievement by what's known as the Two Sigma variation. A sigma variation is a metric used to quantify the improvement in performance over the baseline performance, in this case the top 2 percent of classroom students.

Traditional educational systems are not designed to deliver one-to-one mentoring, and the cost of such a practice is out of reach for even the richest countries. Smart learning technology promises to achieve this level of performance. Impressive "significant difference" has already been achieved with Intelligent Tutoring Systems (ITS). In over three hundred studies conducted primarily by government agencies, the positive sigma variations achieved with intelligent learning technologies have clearly been identified.

Intelligent Tutoring Systems were once found only in government or research environments. Smart tools, smart toys, and intelligent learning platforms are now available in the consumer, corporate, and academic sectors.

One company bringing very sophisticated and cost-effective smart learning products into the commercial sector is Stottler Henke Associates, known as SHAI. They are a pioneer in early military Intelligent Tutoring Systems and are now selling these products in the broader market.

SHAI sells packaged ITS products and cognitive tutor authoring tools used to create ITS products. For example, their SimBionic tool is a visual authoring tool designed for "creating sophisticated situation assessment and decision-making logic that uses artificial intelligence (AI) reasoning techniques." One of SHAI's packaged intelligent products is called Read-On! The product is designed to improve literacy skills and has achieved extraordinary results. People can increase their reading skills by several academic grades in a matter of months.

Another ITS vendor is Sonalysts. One of their products is marketed as ExpertTrain, a learning technology that uses artificial intelligence techniques to create adaptive learning environments and context-sensitive coaching. The product uses what the company calls "expert tutors" and "synthetic coaches" to provide individualized instruction to students in highly contextual learning scenarios.

ITS experts at the Institute for Defense Analysis maintain that at the current rate of progress in ITS technology, new ITS products will achieve full Two Sigma status sometime in the next two to three years. Some researchers, such as Albert Corbett at Carnegie Mellon, claim that cognitive tutors have already surpassed the Two Sigma threshold. In other words, they generate results better than those produced by human-to-human tutoring. Corbett commented in his 2001 paper, entitled "Cognitive Computer Tutors: Solving the Two-Sigma Problem," that "Results suggest that cognitive tutors have closed the gap with and arguably surpass human tutors."[6]

These smart learning technologies do not have lessons or tests. Assessment is deeply fused with the learning experience. There is no predetermined sequencing, and interactions are generated in real time during the run time. This is an example of what is known as agent-based learning technology, also known as smart learning technology. The interactions between an agent-based learning technology and the student are conducted with natural language. These products are already in commercial use. Smart learning technologies will reach their pinnacle in fully developed intelligent learning agents.

One factor that will accelerate the demand for intelligent tutors is the No Child Left Behind Act passed in the United States in January 2002. Vendors who sell cognitive tutors for very young children contend that the use of these tutors at a very young age lays the foundation for effective lifelong learning.

For example, there are now many intelligent learning products that diminish the challenges faced by children with learning disabilities. These products intervene at an early age. They help level the playing field for children who would otherwise fall further and further behind in school. Many learning disabilities and cognitive disorders extend into adulthood. Children who overcome barriers early in life stand a good chance of being successful learners throughout their lives.

The No Child Left Behind Act has a very direct correlation with the use of effective learning. By law, schools must pay for private tutors for students who are unable to achieve performance standards in the traditional classroom. Schools will find that it will be much cheaper to deploy ITS technology during the initial instruction than to pay for human tutors later.

Of course, it is equally plausible that the tutoring companies will be able to use ITS technology to meet the performance improvement requirements of the law. Another possibility is that next-generation intelligent tutors will achieve results that are better than human tutoring.

According to Carnegie Learning, students using their Cognitive Tutor products often outperform other students on real-world problem-solving skills. This cognitive tutor technology is growing in popularity and is already being used with over 300,000 students in over one thousand schools throughout the world.

New generations of smart learning technologies are assimilating the explosion of data available from recent cognitive research and integrating a wide range of emerging technologies such as the multi-user gaming, embedded ambient learning, collaboration, and simulation. Simulation and gaming are increasingly used as the "carrier wave" of smart learning technology.

2. High Fidelity Learning: Simulation and Gaming

Simulation and gaming are not necessarily synonymous. Educational simulations, particularly in the corporate sector, tend to focus on fidelity rather than gaming as the primary experience. Yet most modern computer games use a high degree of simulation. The word "game" is rarely used to describe corporate learning simulations (gloss terms such as "business simulations" are preferred), but the two concepts are increasingly conflated.

A range of simulation methods and technologies is being adopted in the commercial sector. Business process simulation is the foundation of the booming Business Process Management industry. Training simulators that immerse users in the operation of complex machines are now common in the industrial sector.

Until now, flight simulators and the technology to make the simulators were out of reach for all but the military and aviation industries. The same kind of technology, only delivered on PC-based systems, is now being used wherever large, expensive, and dangerous machines are operated.

GE Capital I-Sim, a division of GE, now sells a range of simulators and services that are used by trucking companies, fire departments, heavy machinery firms, mass transportation companies, emergency vehicle operators, and public safety organizations. The technology that was once used to save lives in the military is now doing the same in the commercial sector.

Highway accidents involving trucks are one of the leading causes of occupational fatalities in the United States. It is only in the last two or three years that technology has been available for trucking firms to mitigate that statistic. Now trucking firms routinely send both new and experienced drivers to the simulators to hone driving skills. In these simulators, truckers gain experience under a variety of hazardous conditions.

Vcom3d sells simulation products that use a graphic representation of a human mentor, known as a virtual avatar, to sign in American Sign Language (ASL). The firm sells authoring tools that generate ASL-based content to academic, corporate, and government organizations. The ASL avatars communicate a wide range of learning content to students and employees. They are now often used to fulfill the "reasonable accommodation" requirements mandated by accessibility laws. Verbal learning content delivered to hearing employees is ported to the avatars for ASL delivery to hearing-impaired workers.

Simulation in the healthcare industry is growing at a rapid rate. Patient education, medical device training, patient simulators, and surgical procedures are now more likely to include simulation than any other learning form factor.

Some of these healthcare learning products combine several sensory modalities into the learning simulation. For example, Immersion Medical has pioneered haptic, or sense-of-touch, learning products in the healthcare industry. A nursing student can actually feel the way a needle pierces skin tissue without experimenting on human subjects. The student uses an input device that functions like a hypodermic needle. Vibrations are generated in the simulated needle that mimic the way a real needle functions. Previous to these kinds of simulators, healthcare students used oranges to practice injections.

The Medical Learning Company markets a product called Syn-Patient. The synthetic patient incorporates sophisticated speech technology developed by NeoSpeech. According to the company, "SynPatient provides continuous voice interaction in a rich multimedia environment featuring images, sounds, video, and voice." These synthetic patients are becoming intelligent and can mimic an infinite number of medical conditions.

The biosciences are prolific users of immersive simulation technology. Students and researchers now can "walk through" molecular structures and study atomic and molecular phenomena from any angle. Product designers now use similar technology to collaborate on evolving industrial products in what has come to be known as "knowledge-based engineering" (KBE).

Announced in late-2003, MIT has a new simulation and gaming initiative they are calling the Education Arcade. The goal of the initiative is "to transform the way video and computer games are used in the classroom." The Education Arcade expands on the Games-to-Teach Project funded by the Microsoft iCampus initiative. Games-to-Teach developed a suite of conceptual frameworks to support learning across a wide range of subjects. The project demonstrated that simulation, gaming, and learning content could be successfully integrated into effective learning products.

Educational gaming, once commonly referred to as edutainment, now comprises a significant proportion of products sold by the educational publishing industry. According to the Entertainment Software Association (ESA), the current market for edutainment is 5 to 6 percent of the total $16-to-$18-billion global gaming market, now worth over a billion dollars worldwide.[7] Edutainment is developed by both gaming-oriented vendors and educational publishers.

The gaming industry has long been on the forefront of simulation and collaboration innovation. They have now embarked on a path toward what they call "massively distributed multi-user collaboration" in which several thousand users can play the same game over the web. There are now dozens of gaming environments that allow large numbers of users to interact with each other in a shared virtual world.

The gaming industry is also now collaborating closely with the U.S. military in the quest for "asymmetric collaboration" technology. Asymmetric collaboration is described as simulation and gaming technology that adapts to randomly unfolding developments, hence the term asymmetric. The technology learns, and to reach its full potential will require sophisticated agent technology still in prototype stages.

Probably the most sophisticated simulations that have emerged in the last few years are the products that target the affective learning domain. Innovative companies such as SimuLearn, WILL Interactive, Kaplan, and Insight Experience are bringing affective learning products to market that imbue ethical behavior via simulation.

Simulation is the current method of choice for learning products dealing with particular subjects in the affective learning domains such as ethics, teamwork, innovation, leadership, conflict management, and motivation. Simulation excels at this and generates an almost visceral learning experience. All corporate role-playing simulations tend to tap into the affective domain. The most sophisticated products do this by using agent-based learning technology.

One of the better-known simulation products that deals with the affective learning domain is SimuLearn's Virtual Leader®. Virtual Leader uses complex artificial intelligence routines to control the behavior of virtual characters. These virtual characters have a large repertoire of verbal responses. The product pulls from a library of over two hundred body gestures and facial responses designed to elicit behavior from the real participants.

WILL Interactive sells simulation products designed to teach adults and children about the consequences of their actions. WILL Interactive's patented interactive behavior-modification programs are already used in "a wide range of pressure-filled realistic decision-making situations, including lifestyle choices, crisis negotiation, antiterrorism, and now school violence."

3. Communities of Contextual Collaboration

In the technical sense, the term "contextual collaboration" refers to the seamless integration of various collaboration technologies with productivity applications and platforms. In a literal sense, the technologies are accessed in the context of a learning experience or a work task. Collaboration technologies include chat, instant messaging, virtual meeting rooms and classrooms, presence awareness, web conferencing, application sharing, and device awareness.

All the major platform vendors, including Sun, Oracle, IBM, and Microsoft, now offer native, integrated contextual collaboration technology "in the box." In other words, the technology is included with the purchase of these platforms. Cisco entered the fray in late-2003 when they purchased Latitude, a popular web conferencing and virtual classroom product.

The significance of this competition for collaboration technology is that contextual collaboration, e-learning, and learning technologies are now native to the most common platforms. Best-of-breed collaborative products from vendors such as Bantu, Centra, CollabWorx, Groove, Appian, WebEx, EMC's Documentum, and Open Text are used by a variety of academic, corporate, and government agencies.

The original idea of "communities of practice" has evolved into a conceptual location now commonly called WorkSpace. Vendors who sell products in this category tend to combine graphical user interface metaphors for space, time, and collaboration into their product interfaces. In these new interfaces, collaboration is now conducted in the WorkSpace.

One of the founding fathers of modern knowledge management, Ikujiro Nonaka, now advocates that knowledge creation takes place in an abstract (almost metaphysical) place he calls "Ba."[8] In his theory, this place can be a physical, virtual, or mental space but is usually a combination of these spatial domains. It is a nexus formed by individual and organizational learning.

The real significance of contextual collaboration is less about the technology and more about the "humanization" of the connected world. Now innovative companies like Tacit Knowledge and AskMe are merging presence awareness with expertise management. These products actively "mine" for expertise in an organizational structure using a variety of techniques such as presence awareness and expertise profiling. The real impact that this is having on learning is that human expertise is now "lighting up the switchboards" of these expertise management interfaces. The web has come alive with the presence of humans.

It is well known that up to 80 percent of the knowledge needed by a worker to complete tasks on the job comes from a co-worker. Contextual collaboration technology now traps that expertise, and in many ways captures both informal learning and organizational learning. It is very likely that these tools will supplant first-generation e-learning and knowledge management.

4. Wireless Experience-Based Learning: What Are You Doing Now?

Wireless technology is probably the fastest-growing learning technology trend. Wireless technology is being adopted across academic, corporate, and government sectors. Although it is a very mature trend in Asia and Northern Europe, other countries are catching up fast.

While the technology spreads rapidly throughout the globe, learning product vendors are pouncing on the opportunity. Vendors are innovating extraordinary new learning technologies that take advantage of the trend. Those technologies include a laundry list of new technology jargon, such as augmented reality, performance-ware, learning-ware, field-force automation, radio frequency identification (RFID), performance support, business activity monitoring, and a new product category called "tele-collaboration."

Wireless networks are spreading rapidly in higher education institutions, corporations, and government organizations. Learning products tend to follow rapidly as the networks take hold. Next-generation mobile device technology such as smart phones, wireless PDAs, wireless gaming devices, video-enabled cell phones, and

Tablet PCs are the devices that are already beginning to dominate this landscape.

Learning products that leverage these devices tend to focus on the real-time experience of the user as the focal point of learning. This is usually called experience-based learning, but a variety of terms are also used to describe this type of learning, such as active learning, engaged learning, situational learning, contextual learning, problem-based learning, and scenario-based learning. All of these stress the importance of the learner's experience within a real-world context as the primary condition required for learning. Combined with wireless connectivity to information, this type of learning is proving to be quite effective.

One of the first product areas to adopt wireless technology is language learning. Language acquisition products from companies like EnglishTown use text messaging and voice chat in their commercial learning products. Vendors sell smart phone and PDA software that can translate foreign phrases in real time. Tourists and businesspeople alike can enter a phrase in their native tongues and have the smart phone "pronounce" the correct phrase in the language of their choice.

Mobile-Mind sells a range of products for the academic sector, including American Sign Language translators and K-12 test-preparation products that are delivered on cell phones. But students don't use these devices to study per se. They use them while they perform daily activities, in school and out of school. Learning comes in "bursts" on the device. Scantron used to be known for paper-based quiz and survey scanners, but is now a strong player in the mobile learning product industry. Texas Instruments is perhaps the current leader in the global market for wireless devices in classrooms.

Teachers in classrooms can watch what students are doing with the wireless devices and selectively route information to students who require assistance. Students using cell phones equipped with instant messaging can silently send each other information during class. Teachers and professors are now quite aware of this and sometimes ban cell phones from class to prevent cheating. More progressive teachers are embracing the behavior as a collaboration opportunity and bring their own cell phones to class to participate in this new form of experience-based learning.

One of the most innovative uses of wireless technology in learning products is coming from the new industries that have emerged with these new technologies. There are now several technologies that "transmit" learning content, including cellular transmission, direct satellite feeds, and a range of radio technologies such as radio frequency identification (RFID), wireless fidelity (Wi-Fi), ZigBee, and Bluetooth. A range of devices now taps into those transmissions, including smart phones, wireless PDAs, Tablet PCs, satellite-enabled devices, and handheld RFID readers.

RFID probably holds the greatest promise for experience-based learning. There are two types of RFID technology: passive and active. Passive RFID products are usually low power chips, or smart tags, that passively wait to be scanned. Active RFID products include their own power source and seek out scanners, other smart tags, and other devices to create what is sometimes called "meshes" of information. RFID technology got a boost in 2003 when the U.S. Department of Defense mandated that all military inventory be tagged with RFID chips. Wal-Mart's decision to require the same thing from its suppliers by 2005–2006 contributed to the acceleration effect.

It is now estimated that the majority of workers in the United States will use some form of wireless productivity device by 2006. About 10 to 15 percent of so-called "office workers" in the U.S. government are already using mobile technology. The government has just embarked on a formal telework initiative that will accelerate this trend. It is likely that up to 50 to 60 percent of the government workforce, civilian and military alike, will be mobile, in the technical sense, by 2006.[9]

Over 3,800 mechanics at Honda use the Nomad Expert Technician System from Microvision. The Nomad is a wireless, wearable computer system with a head-mounted display device that beams an image directly on the retinas of technicians. The system provides mechanics with access to manuals, procedures, mentors, and repair information *while they work on cars*. According to Microvision, learning embedded in a mechanic's work experience not only mitigates the need for formal training but reduces the time it takes to do common tasks by an average of 40 to 50 percent.

Almost every large industrial vehicle now includes on-board mobile technology. The average Caterpillar tractor now has five IP addresses. Farmers use the technology combined with GPS signals to accurately plant and fertilize crops. Mine workers use the combined technology to locate ore, machines, and workers with great precision.

FieldCentrix is one of the new breed of field-force automation vendors. Their FX Mobile product is a workflow software product that uses wireless-enabled handheld computers, laptops, and PDAs to automate a wide range of field service processes. With FX Mobile, service technicians receive work orders electronically on their mobile devices. "It then guides them, screen by screen, through the job—prompting them to perform standard tasks, take notes, and even record future recommended repairs or activities."

Closely linked to wireless experience-based learning is a new type of learning technology called *ambient* learning. This technology fuses learning content directly into the physical environment of the workplace, at the exact location of a worker, and often inside the device, machine, or vehicle being used by that worker. The primary distinction between the two, at least for the time being, is that experience-based learning focuses on *what* a person is doing, while ambient learning tends to focus on *where* the person is doing it.

5. Ambient Learning: Surrounded by Smart Objects

Learning technology known as "embedded training" or as "onboard trainers" has been used by the U.S. military for several years. This is performance support and learning content that is accessed in vehicles or on machine consoles. Lockheed develops embedded training technology that automates human performance assessment using "speech recognition, keystroke analysis, and eye tracking."

They also develop technology that provides "real-time diagnosis of operator and team performance and computer-assisted coaching."

While this technology is becoming much more sophisticated and is rarely used yet outside the military, a new form of this kind of embedded learning is also taking hold in the corporate sector. The newer form, called ambient learning, has an affinity with traditional embedded training but embeds the learning into chips mounted into a range of objects, called *smart objects*, such as machines, appliances, vehicles, and sensors. The term ambient is defined as "surrounding, or existing on all sides." Hence ambient learning is a form of learning that surrounds the person working in an environment populated by these smart objects. Ambient learning is a term more common outside the United States and is a derivative of the technology known as ambient intelligence, now widespread in Europe and Asia. Ambient intelligence is defined by the Advisory Group to the European Community's Information Society Technology Program (ISTAG) as "the convergence of ubiquitous computing, ubiquitous communication, and interfaces adapting to the user."[10]

Ambient intelligence and ambient learning were able to take root in these regions due to the wide availability of advanced short-range and long-range wireless technologies. As wireless broadband technology becomes widely available in the United States throughout 2005, ambient intelligence and ambient learning will migrate to the American shores. Ambient learning can be experienced anywhere a student or worker is in the presence of a smart object or device that has been outfitted with wireless network connectivity and computer technology.

Since these smart objects are increasingly being used in industrial environments, jobs that were once considered blue collar are now becoming information-centric jobs. Manufacturing, mining, construction, mechanical maintenance, and field-based jobs are now becoming "connected" through mobile technology. This kind of technology is now spreading far beyond the stereotypical user, defined as a white-collar worker sitting at a desk. Voice technology, for example, has extended software to warehouse personnel.

The VoiceLogistics products sold by Voxware are now used by inventory management personnel at companies like Haggar Clothing, 7-Eleven, and PETCO. Workers literally talk to the software as they operate warehouse machinery. In turn, the software interacts with the workers in real time on such tasks as determining the optimal route to inventory and advising workers on inventory supply.

Vocollect's Talkman product is used by companies like Dreyer's Ice Cream, Giant Eagle, and Food City. The product has been able to increase productivity by 10 to 18 percent in these deployments. The productivity rates shot up 50 to 60 percent when combined with handheld RFID scanning technology.

Tablet PCs are now being used in the daily workflow of many professionals who traditionally were not computer users. The devices are now popular in the healthcare industry and allow nurses and doctors to access interactive performance support while they interact with patients. One task that has been automated is the determination of risks involved with drug interactions. This can be a complex task, and medical errors are common in this area of healthcare. These errors can be virtually eliminated using the Tablet PC.

Ambient learning can also be embedded in software and software-based work processes. Knowledge Products sells a product called OnDemand that allows customers to literally fuse learning content and simulation directly into a real-time work experience of an individual worker. The product is embedded in any 32-bit application such as SAP, Siebel, or PeopleSoft. In late 2003, PeopleSoft chose Knowledge Products as the core learning technology for their products. This gives PeopleSoft's eleven thousand global customers access to this kind of ambient learning.

Another product that automatically generates software-based embedded ambient learning is RWD's Info Pak. The Info Pak technology automatically generates procedural work processes, including embedded Visio diagrams of the procedures, as an expert uses the application. It then tracks the most common tasks that users have trouble performing once the ambient learning is in use. It is an iterative process that virtually eliminates the need for formal training.

One of the more sophisticated ambient learning products is Epiplex, sold by Epiance. According to the company, "It auto-generates business documentation, animation, e-learning content in any language or style or format desired, eliminating over 80 to 99 percent of human effort required in creating or maintaining content." It accomplishes this by automatically capturing the computer tasks performed by a user. The product is able to reduce operating and process deployment costs associated with software applications by up to 50 percent. Data collected by the company shows that Epiplex can increase productivity by up to 80 percent.

Ultimus sells a workflow management product that includes a technology called a FloBot. The FloBot is an agent-based software technology and comes to the assistance of a worker in the context of a particular task. The FloBot "knows" where the worker is and what task the worker is attempting to complete.

According to Ambient Insight, a learning technology research firm, these new ambient learning products are in very high demand now due to the cost savings they generate for customers. Customers are able to dramatically reduce formal training, cut the development time of learning content by 40 to 50 percent, and reduce the time a worker needs to look for information by up to 80 percent. Productivity gains range from 50 to 80 percent, depending on the targeted process.[11]

Going forward, ambient learning will be embedded everywhere in the work environment, including machines, equipment, vehicles, and inventory. Similar learning content is already being embedded in smart appliances for consumers. Consumers can already buy refrigerators that provide nutritional mentoring and tips on cooking skills.

6. Cognition Engineering: Mapping the Mountains of Metadata to the Internal Terrains

In many ways, information integration, data storage, content management, and knowledge management technologies have "opened the flood gates" and now information is being aggregated at staggering rates. According to results from a 2003 UC Berkeley study, information is now doubling every two years.[12] As information aggregates into mountains of raw data, new methods must be found to utilize that information in ways that are semantically meaningful to humans.

In order to map to the semantic content of human cognition, this growing mountain of information must integrate with the internal information processing capabilities of the human mind. Extraordinary progress is now being made in sophisticated data visualization and human cognition research. This cognitive engineering technology could also be called *human comprehension technology.*

Cognition engineering is the next step after knowledge engineering. It is technology designed to determine meaning for humans and make that meaning accessible to human minds. It is a learning technology designed to translate large amounts of raw data into meaningful metaphors and analogies. Those metaphors are then mapped onto computer images and diagrams that humans can comprehend.

Cognition engineering is thus a technology that combines advanced data visualization and modern cognitive science. Both disciplines are now producing very clear-cut knowledge about how the mind processes information in general and how the mind can process aggregations of massive amounts of data.

The information emerging from cognitive science is now growing at exponential rates. Almost all of this information will have a direct impact on learning technology. Child development researchers now know that babies only a few minutes old can mimic facial expressions of caregivers. Developmental psychologists have discovered that adults can actually rewire their neural structures late in life if they learn new skills. Both of these facts contradict previous research that described babies as swimming in "blooming, buzzing confusion"[13] and adults with brains that lacked plasticity. The consensus among modern developmental psychologists is that humans learn all the time, from birth to death.

Extraordinary findings are now being assimilated from new research fields such as change blindness, false memory, mirror neurons, and personality assessment. Change blindness studies show that a great deal of information can be missed when a person is distracted or focused on specific objects. False memory has proven to be quite resilient and has shown that people can hold very strong beliefs about experiences that never happened. Mirror neurons may explain why simulation is such an effective learning method. The brain of a person just observing another person perform an action, such as a procedural skill, will fire neurons in exactly the same pattern as that fired if the person performed the action directly. Personality assessments and emotional quotients have now begun to spread rapidly through the corporate and government sectors. These are essentially affective cognitive state assessment instruments that provide an enormous amount of data about a person's emotional state of mind. A worker's emotional quotient has a direct correlation to productivity.

These kinds of "pure" cognitive assessments are being merged with sophisticated data comprehension technology. The most advanced technology in this area is simply called *visualization*. However, the other sensory modalities (touch, smell, sound, and taste) are also being integrated into these technologies.

The Mitre organization is working with international military researchers on a wide range of technologies that are designed to transform massive amounts of data into comprehensible images that can be digested by human minds quickly and efficiently without losing saliency. This is a tall order, but it is now essential as data repositories grow more quickly than humans can develop ways of understanding the data. The research done at Mitre is applied in a variety of real-world technologies, such as flight simulators, conventional task analysis, knowledge management, and data visualization.

There is a new type of technology known as *expertise mining*. It is closely linked with automatic content categorization technology. These technologies automatically identify expertise (human or otherwise) and discern "meaning" from large amounts of structured and unstructured data. Companies like AskMe and Tacit Knowledge specialize in expertise mining, and their products are used by customers to map human expertise on expertise nodes, otherwise known as expertise maps. Expertise maps are usually depicted as network diagrams showing the presence of people with specific knowledge sets and their connections with other experts and co-workers.

Companies like Autonomy, Appian, and Entopia provide products that can sift through massive data stores and automatically generate taxonomies and meaningful content repositories. Innovations include the ability to sift through all types of data, including voice and video.

Geospatial data now available from GPS and space-based imaging technology has resulted in a huge amount of highly detailed data about geographical features of the planet. This data is "crunched" in a number of ways, but it is also reproduced with a great deal of fidelity.

Insight's VizServer incorporates a unique visualization paradigm they call Star Trees. According to the company, the product is "a scalable enterprise solution that offers users the most effective method for visualizing and exploring large information collections." The USDA uses Star Trees to display census data for about two million farms across all fifty states and contains data on more than three thousand counties.

The Semantic Web is perhaps the most promising technology relative to processing massive amounts of data into meaningful information. The Semantic Web is an infrastructure that allows software and machines to "reason" about information on the web. It is an extension of the current web and not meant to replace it. The U.S. government is one of the early adopters of the Semantic Web. New companies such as Semaview, Intellidimension, and McDonald Bradley are already developing products for the new XML standard.

The Semantic Web was originally conceived by Tim Berners-Lee, the leading innovator of the World Wide Web. Berners-Lee envisions the Semantic Web as an extension of the current web that is enhanced or expanded to include more contextual information about the meaning of content. Berners-Lee has stated, "The Semantic Web is an extension of the current web in which information is given well-defined meaning, better enabling computers and people to work in cooperation."[14]

Semaview is developing "personalized information management" products and services using the Semantic Web. They are "focused on creating the next generation of knowledge management tools using the latest technologies such as agent-based computing, machine learning, and the Intelligent Internet."

Social Networking Analysis (SNA) software is a new type of technology that is gaining ground in corporate and government sectors. SNA is essentially an automated "community of practice" mapping technology that maps the complex relationships of people, roles, and organizations. It can quickly identify how organizations really work and which people play the most vital roles in an organization.

One implication of this new type of comprehension technology is that it appears that a new form of notation is emerging in the culture. Like musical notation and mathematical notation, it is an abstraction of a type of conceptual reality. It is well known that mathematics is notoriously difficult for children to learn. Evolutionary psychologists have suggested that it is because it is a relatively new form of notation in human culture.

Social Networking Analysis experts warn that new notation skills are required to make sense of the social and expertise maps generated by these technologies. They are concerned that managers could come to the wrong conclusions about work activity in an organization if they misinterpret the maps. It may take some time for humans to master this new form of notation.

7. Multiple Domain Learning: Multi-Dimensional Learning Domains and Multi-Sensory Technologies

In 1956, a group of educators led by Benjamin Bloom identified three overlapping human learning domains: *cognitive* learning, *psychomotor* learning, and *affective* learning. They represent the knowledge, skills, and beliefs, respectively, of a human performer. The integrated framework of these three domains has since become known as Bloom's Taxonomy.[15]

Even though these three domains are tightly integrated aspects of human learning, traditionally only the skills and knowledge domains have been part of the corporate training focus. Training professionals have shied away from the affective domain because of its complexity. Until very recently, it has been prohibitively expensive and impractical to develop learning technologies that mapped to the affective domain.

Now new learning technologies have emerged that are automating learning designed for the affective domain. Aero Innovation sells a battery of assessment instruments that can measure the combined skills, knowledge, and affective states of a human. The use of their products clearly illustrates that more than just skill and knowledge are required to do complex tasks. Aero says, "As so often happens with ATC (air traffic control) trainees, the individual may have all of the skills and knowledge normally required but be unable to put them together in the confusion of a complex incident." In essence, their affective skills, or emotional abilities, may be inadequate to deal with complex situations, regardless of their physical and intellectual abilities. Learning technologies and training methods designed to enhance affective skills can now overcome these shortcomings.

Situational awareness (SA) is a term coined in the mid-1980s to describe the human experience of performing psychomotor tasks in real time in the context of complex operational information that includes both facts and beliefs about a situation. It is interesting that Aero Innovation, after decades of research and product development, has come to the conclusion that assessing and training a worker in complex operations requires that generic, non-specific simulated experiences must be used.

They claim that training and assessing a worker in the actual operational environment will not accurately assess or prepare a worker for that job. "To avoid confounding basic aptitude with the effect of prior training in specific tasks, the elements that comprise the test must be unlike any real-world activities such as operating computers or controlling specific vehicles." Instead they use a generic set of hand-eye coordination tasks that they claim are better suited to measure aptitude.

The company, ERGO/GERO, has created a measurement tool it calls the Ideal Observer to measure performance relative to situational awareness. The Ideal Observer is a simulated worker that is used to model optimal skills, knowledge, and affective performance. It is then used as a baseline to compare real human performance.

VirTra Systems is a company that originally developed solutions for the U.S. government and is now taking its products into the commercial sector. The products could be viewed as mere virtual reality generators if it weren't for the fact that they also generate real stimuli for users, such as smell and touch. According to the company, "The system provides not only quality video and digital audio, but also astonishes people with the sense of smell! Guests smell evergreen trees while passing through a forest, or the aroma of coffee in a virtual vacation, or even smell candy or chocolate." The system provides a variety of chemical scents to heighten the experience.

8. Agent-Based Learning: Virtual Co-Workers, Advisors, and Learning Assistants

Intelligent Automation is also a pioneer in agent-based learning technologies. Agent-based learning technologies function as virtual co-workers and allow complex information to be offloaded to an intelligent software program that then assists humans in very complex tasks such as flight control, traffic management, and asymmetric security threats. There is a tendency to associate these programs with human behavior, and thus they are often given names usually given to people, such as Cybele or Diva.

According to Professor James Hendler, former chief scientist of the Information Systems Office at the U.S. Defense Advanced Research Projects Agency (DARPA), "Agent-based computing focuses on the development of distributed computational entities (software agents), which can act on behalf of, mediate, or support the actions of human users and autonomously carry out tasks to achieve goals or assist the activities of the users in achieving those goals."[16]

Agent-based learning technologies are often described as intelligent, adaptive, and even perceptive. Essentially, they are designed to learn. Once they are sufficiently intelligent, they are used by humans as learning technologies. They are now being used in a variety of learning products such as Intelligent Tutoring Systems, embedded trainers, automated helpdesk personnel, and virtual mentors.

Zoesis builds animated cartoon characters that "are expressive and appear to be intelligent and understanding of the human viewer/user." The company uses artificial intelligence technology developed at Carnegie Mellon University "to enrich characters' simulated minds, bodies, and speech."

In July 2003, DARPA funded a "cognitive computing" project called Perceptive Assistant that Learns (PAL). The technology is being developed by over twenty companies. The goal is to "spawn AIs that attempt to encapsulate the knowledge that an administrative assistant might amass while helping an executive. Knowledge would be gathered by learning rather than using a historically brittle knowledge base." By "learning to help around the office by observing and interacting with office workers, PAL aims to automatically configure itself to the user." DARPA hopes that PAL will increase the productivity of workers by automating knowledge acquisition.[17]

Lockheed Martin's Advanced Technology Laboratories is developing a range of agent-based technologies. One of their products is called Dismounted Guardian and is designed to protect individual ground troops in the field. According to Lockheed, the Dismounted Guardian is "a mobile, agent-based, situational-awareness system capable of executing on wearable or handheld computers. The system will autonomously alert users of enemy unit threats; nuclear, biological, chemical events; minefield locations; and degraded/inoperable equipment, as well as mission-performance contingencies."

Agent-based simulation is the foundation of many innovations in the gaming sector, such as the popular Sims®games from Maxis.

In February 2003, Douglas Lowenstein of the Entertainment Software Association (ESA) commented that "Artificial intelligence—a central part of advanced game design—is now so advanced that characters in the games have their own independent, autonomous personalities that players interact with. It may not sound like much, but when you see it and engage with it, these games provide an astonishing level of interactivity that no other form of entertainment can ever achieve."[18]

Verity is a company that sells virtual human experts to both corporate and government clients. The U.S. Defense Logistics agency uses this technology to mentor users and employees. Even civilians can "talk" to a Verity NativeMinds avatar called Phyllis at the Defense Logistics Information Service website. Phyllis greets all visitors with a friendly verbal welcome, and she will gladly answer questions.

Now a wide range of technologies are being developed that encode behavioral aspects into virtual humans. There is a broad category of products known as *affective computing*. There is a specific product category of affective computing called *affective learning technology*. It is used to target the affective learning domain.

MIT's Media Lab is developing a learning companion that is designed to mitigate belief systems that undermine learning accomplishments in children. The project is funded by the National Science Foundation. This is not a tutor per se, but an affective companion that tries to alleviate frustration and self-doubt in young learners. It does this by first establishing a relationship with the child. It then attempts to ascertain the cognitive state of the child and then interacts with the child, depending on that cognitive state.

It is usually second nature for any person to be able to determine the emotional status of another person, providing there is access to a wide set of visual, verbal, and environmental cues. It is seldom possible to see the body language of another person in online situations. New agent-based technology, currently on the market, can gauge a person's emotional status by analyzing his or her voice or text-based conversations.

Utopy sells "emotion detection software" called SpeechMiner, designed primarily for call centers. The technology can provide "global emotional analysis of employees and customers or micro-analysis of specific agents and customers." The SpeechMiner software also tracks a human worker's vocal performance for compliance. "You can leverage SpeechMiner to ensure that agents are properly reading all disclosures, that no misrepresentations are made, and that customers respond in the proper fashion. You need to sustain your organization's reputation as well as prevent customer lawsuits."

Mindfabric also integrates emotional analysis into its automated customer support products. "User emotion analysis deciphers user emotions from their interactions with self-service systems or contact center agents." The technology is able to recognize a variety of emotional cues by deciphering voice inflection, tone, and cadence.

AnthroTronix uses agent-based technologies to help children overcome physical and cognitive challenges. AnthroTronix, funded originally as a start-up by the government, developed a product called "CosmoBot" that is "designed for clinical rehabilitation and special education." This technology is being used to help children with special needs; one use of their robots is early intervention with autistic children. The robots are infinitely patient, considerate, responsive, and consistent.

The significance of these new technologies is that they are now being used to provide adaptive counseling, rehabilitation, mentoring, and tutoring to individuals based on their particular needs. The technology "senses" the human's skills, knowledge, and cognitive emotional state. The agent-based intelligence then responds with appropriate behavior designed to enhance learning.

Fast Forward to 2015: Learning in the Bright Air with the Help of Our Personal Learning Assistant

Peter sits on a hill in Tanzania overlooking the Serengeti. He is a first-year medical student and he is doing his homework. Today, one of his professors wants him to practice making intravenous injections into a patient's arm. On his Honda Tablet Mainframe he is running a simulation of a patient who has come to his simulated doctor's office to get a Tetanus shot. He is wearing a tiny head-mounted display device that projects 3D images directly on his retina. Peter welcomes Mrs. Tumpe and asks her to sit on the stool. She chides him for being so formal and asks him to call her "Akili."

Peter wears thin, transparent, "smart" gloves with sense-of-touch haptic sensors. He can literally feel the objects in the simulation, including the texture of Akili's skin. He picks up the alcohol bottle in one hand and the cotton swab in the other. The haptic technology allows him to feel the weight of the bottle and the liquid shifting as he turns it over on the swab. He now smells alcohol. His Honda computer is equipped with olfactory software, mandatory now in all medical learning technology. He dabs Akili's arm, picks up the syringe, and moves it toward her arm.

At this point, Badru, his personal learning assistant, "freezes" the simulation. In crisp Maasai dialect, Badru tells Peter that his bedside manner is in need of improvement. Peter now notices the look of concern on the patient's face and recalls that the patient did move away from him when he lifted the syringe. The PLA reminds Peter that most people are anxious about injections, even with today's relatively painless syringe technology. Badru tells Peter he will have to improvise this human interaction when the simulation begins again.

The simulation resumes and Peter softly tells Akili "this won't hurt a bit" and jokes that, "then again, that is easy for me to say" while smiling and holding eye contact with her. Her body language relaxes and she smiles at Peter. As he penetrates the skin with the needle, he can feel the tip puncture the outer layer and Badru tells him to "ease up to avoid going any deeper." Peter injects the medicine and withdraws the needle. Badru tells them both that in the old days medical students had to practice with oranges to learn this skill. Mrs. Tumpe's eyes go wide when she hears this, and they all laugh.

All of the technology that is described in this 2015 scenario is available now in 2004 in some form or another. The least-developed technology in 2004 is the personal learning assistant and perhaps, to some, the least believable aspect of this scenario. Current agent technology has just begun to produce truly intelligent affective agents. Will agent technology be ready by 2015 to make this scenario a reality? It has to be.

There are compelling reasons that make the development of very smart personal learning agents not only inevitable but also crucial. Time is running out. The knowledge being generated by the human race is now growing at exponential rates and doubling every two years. The human mind will not scale to comprehend the volume of data that will exist within two to four more years.

The complexity of that data is also growing. Layers of technology-based agents are now absolutely necessary to navigate, understand, and communicate the massive amounts of complex data being aggregated. This layer insulates the human mind from the increasingly familiar condition now known as "cognitive overload."

These layers are already in use today and getting smarter every day. One example is IBM's WebFountain technology. According to IBM, WebFountain "collects, stores and analyzes massive amounts of unstructured and semi-structured text." That is somewhat of an understatement; it is capable of analyzing twenty million web pages in any of twenty-one languages per day. IBM indicated that WebFountain would have the entire World Wide Web "mined" by the end of 2004.

A software-based interpreter of complex healthcare data is a product called Iridescent. Iridescent was developed at the University of Oklahoma. It not only analyzes data, but it also generates hypotheses about that data. Iridescent can already analyze and hypothesize about the information in the 4,600 journals and 12.7 million records in the Medline database. Due to the recent explosion in medical knowledge, Medline is now growing at over five thousand abstracts a year. Human researchers can no longer assimilate this data. Iridescent was invented to insulate the human mind from this complexity. There is now no turning back, nor should we want to. We need these agents.

These software agents are learning, fast. They sift through massive amounts of complex data and mull over near-infinite numbers of variables and patterns in the data. They communicate those patterns in a natural language and a human-like manner geared to specific human beings. They are assimilating smart learning technology that adapts to a single human individual and provides highly targeted personalized interaction. They are evolving into personal learning assistants.

By most estimates, there will be over seven billion people on the planet by 2015. Each one will have a personal learning assistant of some kind. They will learn and laugh together in the bright air.

Notes

1. Moore, G. (1965). Cramming more components onto integrated circuits. *Electronics, 38*(8), 114–117.
2. Kurzweil, R. (1999). *The age of spiritual machines: When computers exceed human intelligence*. New York: Viking.
3. Kurzweil, R. (2003). *Understanding the accelerating rate of change* [Online]. Available: www.kurzweilai.net/meme/frame.html?main=/articles/art0563.html
4. LeapFrog (2003). *Effectiveness study*. Los Angeles Unified School District. [Online]. Available: www.leapfrogschoolhouse.com/content/ research/ER_TheLiteracyCenter_LAUSD.pdf
5. Bloom, B.S. (1984). The 2 Sigma problem: The search for methods of group instruction as effective as one-on-one tutoring. *Educational Researcher,13*(6), 4–16.
6. Corbett, A.T. (2001). Cognitive computer tutors: Solving the two-sigma problem. *Proceedings of the 8th International Conference on User Modeling 2001*, 137–147. London: Springer-Verlag.
7. Entertainment Software Association. (2001). *State of the industry*. [Online]. Available: www.theesa.com/releases/SOTI2001.pdf
8. Nonaka, I., & Konno, N. (1998). The concept of "Ba": Building a foundation for knowledge creation. *California Management Review, 40*(3), 40–54.

9. United States Office of Personnel Management. (2003). *The status of telework in the federal government*. [Online]. Available: www.telework.gov/documents/tw_rpt03/status-toc.asp

10. Gupta, M. (2003). *Ambient intelligence—Unobtrusive technology for the information society*. [Online]. Available: www.pressbox.co.uk/Detailed/7625.html.

11. Adkins, S. (2004). *Ambient learning reaches the states*. [Online]. Available: www.ambientinsight.com/whitepapers

12. Lyman, P. (2003). How much information. [Online]. Available: www.sims.berkeley.edu/how-much-info-2003

13. James, W. (1890). *The principles of psychology* (2 vols.). New York: Henry Holt (Reprinted Bristol: Thoemmes Press, 1999).

14. Berners-Lee, T., Hendler, J., & Lassila, O. (2001). The semantic web. *Scientific American, 279*(5), 35–43.

15. Bloom, B.S. (Ed.). (1956). *Taxonomy of educational objectives: The classification of educational goals: Handbook I, cognitive domain*. New York: Longmans.

16. Hendler, J. (2002). Agent based computing for autonomous intelligent software. *Software Tech News, 4*(4). [Online]. Available: www.softwaretechnews.com/stn4-4/agentbased.html

17. Johnson, C.R. (2003). Darpa AI research focuses on "cognitive computers." *EEtimes*. [Online]. Available: www.eet.com/at/im/news/showArticle.jhtml?articleId=18308837&kc=6383

18. Lowenstein, D. (2002). *Remarks of Douglas Lowenstein at the Electronic Entertainment Expo*. [Online]. Available: www.theesa.com/DLE3SPEECH.html

INTO THE FUTURE OF meLEARNING*

EVERY * ONE * LEARNING . . .
Imagine If the Impossible Isn't!

Wayne Hodgins

While the numbers are staggering, the dream of adaptive personalized learning for every person every day and thus the brightest future ever imagined lies immediately in front of us and within our grasp. As will be outlined in this article, the vision for a future world state where every person experiences personalized learning every day is clear, but has arrived prematurely, is inequitably distributed, and remains unseen by most. This is no longer just a dream, but a probability. The daunting part comes when you do some simple math:

> 6.3 billion individuals × 500+ languages × the # of tasks performed × 24 hours × 7 days a week = a REALLY big number!

The exciting part comes when you start to imagine what our world would be like if we increased the effectiveness of learning for everyone all the time by customizing the learning to fit each person and each situation. This future is ours for the choosing if we can muster the courage to ignite the transformation from vision to reality

---

*This work published by permission of Wayne Hodgins.

by simply imagining that this bright future is now possible and begin shaping its design and implementation. The trick is that it will take all of us to imagine, design, and build. If you can imagine this previously impossible dream now, you are already part of the solution. Read on to find out more on how to join and aid in this quest.

What If the Impossible Isn't?

A rhetorical question is defined as "one asked solely to produce an effect (especially to make an assertion) rather than to elicit a reply," and I am definitely out to produce an effect! The effect I expect to produce is twofold: first to convince you that this grand vision *is* possible and within our grasp. Then, once you believe, my intent is to show the three "grand challenges" or obstacles on this path to personalization and suggest some strategies for successfully confronting these challenges. By the very act of imagining this to be possible, we begin the journey to transform this vision into reality. By working now to resolve the grand challenges, we will all live to see the grand vision materialize in amazing improvements and be rewarded with the knowledge that we made a difference and made our world a better place through better learning. If you are already a believer and share both the belief in the impossible and the vision for a planetary state of personalized learning experiences for every person every day, you may want to skip right to the Grand Challenges sections to learn more about these and to get started at resolving one or more of them.

Introduction

meLearning: Changing the World with Personalized Learning for the Planet

Let's start with the end state we want to reach: personalized learning experiences for every person on the planet every day. While I'd be the first to note that learning does not have nor need any prefix, let's use the term "meLearning" to note this state of personalized learning experiences.

The title of this article is the same statement I'm going to end with—"*Imagine if the impossible isn't?*"—and that is precisely what I'd like you to do while you are reading this. Imagine if meLearning experiences really *are* possible at the planetary scale. Imagine the reality of seeing a day, not that far from today and definitely in *our* working lifetime, when every person on the planet can experience personalized learning multiple times every day.

> Shut your eyes, take a deep breath and hit the "SUSPEND DISBELIEF" button for a moment before continuing.

It won't be easy to accept that the impossible isn't and you may need to suspend disbelief for the remainder of the time you are reading. But just *allow* for the possibility of meLearning at this scale. If you insist, you can go back to disbelief again at the end of the article. However, I'm betting that by the time you have finished reading and reflecting on the points raised here, you too will be a believer, and furthermore you will want to join in the meLearning crusade!

Surely you must be joking, Mr. Hodgins?! (with apologies to Richard Feynman). I could not be more serious. It is not lost on me that these are most critical and sensitive of subjects, and let me assure you that I appreciate most deeply just how serious these goals and issues are. I treat them with the utmost respect and sense of humbleness. I do not take them lightly, nor distance myself from them, and have decided to devote myself to helping with this transformation from impossible dream to practical reality for the remainder of my time on this planet. I'm hoping you too will be compelled to join in this transformation; it will surely take all of us to do so.

The Vision: What, Why

Why Believe? Why Now?

In my reflections of the past few years, I've not only imagined that this vision for meLearning at the planetary scale could be possible, I've come to believe that it is *inevitable*. But for those who are not there yet, why should you believe? Well, consider that much (most?) of what we previously thought could never happen has happened within just our lifetime:

- We've put people on the moon, and now we're headed for Mars and beyond.
- We've mapped the human genome, and not only done so but in an order of magnitude of less time than predicted.
- Using Malcolm Gladwell's "tipping point" observations, New York City was able to go from having the worst crime rate of any city to having one of the lowest.
- The Berlin wall and the Soviet Union both came crashing down.
- The "net effect" or "Law of Plentitude" as described by Kevin Kelly in "12 Rules for the New Economy"[1] has been causing unprecedented adoption and growth of new economies.
- Moore's Law[2] continues with apparently no end in sight (in spite of numerous predictions of its imminent end several times).
- Ray Kurzweil's "Law of Accelerating Returns" wherein it appears that almost all evolutionary trends from technology to human development are all accelerating *exponentially*.
- The Human Cognome project, which is the "mapping" of the human cognitive process and capability. This is being worked on by Dr. Robert Horn,[3] who is developing work parallel to what led to the human genome advancement and which is connected with what is often referred to as NBIC or nanotechnology, biotechnology, information technology and cognitive science,[4] or NIBC.[5]
- Heck, we may even have solved the vexing problem of the blinking 12:00 o'clock on most VCRs and other consumer electronic devices!

If you are reading this, you would most likely find several of the reports listed above to be fascinating reading. For example, Ray Kurzweil's paper on "The Law of Accelerating Returns" provides some very compelling evidence that should make us believe the "impossible" is not. In short, this law has shown how the evolution of almost everything is happening at an exponential pace. Even exponential growth is increasing exponentially! Exponential growth is not something we are typically familiar with, but Ray puts it all into very practical and profound focus in this excerpt at the beginning of his paper:

> "The future will be far more surprising than most observers realize; few have truly internalized the implications of the fact that the rate of change itself is accelerating. Because we are doubling the rate of progress every decade . . . it is not the case that we will experience a hundred years of progress in the twenty-first century; rather we will witness on the order of twenty thousand years of progress (at today's rate of progress, that is)."[6]

This is *not* to suggest that there is nothing left on the "mission impossible" list, including some that have been there for a very long time, such as world hunger, world peace, and world health. But consider that while meLearning at this scale has also been on this list of impossibilities for a long time, removing it from this list would also remove most of the others on the list! Over time, meLearning would provide much of the cure for the root cause of these other world problems. That is why learning is so important and an imperative that we really have no choice but to take on.

And just why is believing and imagining so important and relevant? Because we do not typically put much effort or work into something we don't believe in or that we think is impossible. Yet by imagining and believing in our dreams, we begin and accelerate their transformation to reality. Let's start believing!

Embarrassing Richness of Enablers

Another change that convinces me that meLearning is now within our grasp is that we have reached a point in human history where we are drowning in an embarrassing richness of *enablers*. In this context, enablers are simply defined as anything that converts something from impossible to possible. And not just "technically possible," such as in the lab or for the chosen few or for the privileged or the highly skilled. Rather, anything that enables anyone who so wishes to be able to do something that he or she otherwise could not. Enablers would include such things as:

- *Affordability*: when something that was previously too costly becomes affordable at the scale and by those who would most benefit from use. For example, the application of Moore's Law to almost any computer technology we use today.

- *Knowledge*: when we "discover" something we didn't know previously that enables us to do something we could not or did not know prior to this discovery.

- *Skills and Abilities*: when we are capable of doing something we could not do before.

- *Tools and Technology*: tools, equipment, software, and devices that enable us to do something we could not do before.

- *Standards*, which enable such changes as:
  - Interchangeable parts
  - The Industrial Revolution in manufacturing
  - HTTP, HTML, XML, and TCP/IP, which enabled the Internet and the web
  - Standard paper size enabled copiers, printers, fax machines
  - Phone telephony networks
  - Common rail gauge enabled transportation of goods to extend anywhere
  - VHS standard, which sparked the tipping point of VCRs, video rentals, entire video industry

- *User Interfaces*: the point of interaction between ourselves and the tools and technology we use that makes it possible for almost anyone who wants to be able to use it, for example, graphical user interfaces on computers and modern automobiles.

And we *should* be embarrassed! We have apparently failed to notice that most of what we assume to be impossible has become possible. Compounding the problem, these out-of-date assumptions, combined with our lack of imagination and creativity in adopting, adapting, and applying these enablers, have resulted in our complete squandering of opportunities to creatively apply and benefit from these enablers. In particular, there is almost a complete lack of impact on learning and performance improvement. We've had almost *no* appreciable change or improvement in learning for *hundreds of years*!! Learning has somehow emerged through the past revolutions including the "electricity revolution" (more than one hundred years ago), the "semiconductor revolution" (only about forty-five years old), and appears to be weathering the current Information Revolution with no discernable effect! We cannot, we must not, let this continue any longer.

However, this is also a time of a major change for which our focus needs to migrate from those who have been creating the enablers to those who are implementing them. It now befalls those who implement the enablers, which by definition is all of us, to determine what problems these enablers will be applied to and how. The inventiveness, the creativity, and the innovation must now come from the masses, all of us, as we seek to solve problems through our creative application of this rich supply of enablers. Innovation and large-scale change occur with the creative application of the enablers and often from the "lay person" or the average person and the consumer community.

Why Has Learning Been Immune to This Bounty of Enablers?

In light of the diverse and rich volume of enablers we now have and the exponential rate at which new enablers are arriving daily, why hasn't learning, education, or training improved significantly in the last hundred years? Try what I'd call the "great-grandparent test." Imagine taking your great-grandparents to most any institution, industry, or practice such as your workplace, your car, your house. They would typically be amazed and puzzled by much of what they saw. Yet, take them to most classrooms, even show them "e-learning," and they would tend to feel very comfortable and right at home!

Where is the innovation and change in learning? Whiteboards versus blackboards? Books read on the screen instead of on paper? Slides projected from a computer instead of a slide projector? What effect have any of these had on the effectiveness of learning? The relevance of learning? Are we getting any better at facilitating the learning process and increasing the resultant skills, knowledge, and abilities of the learner? I don't see any evidence pointing to almost any improvement in the past century at least. Why? I believe that this is primarily because we feel that we have been everything that is "possible" and we have been consumed by trying to incrementally improve the tried-and-true models we know. Could it be that we are so busy "perfecting the irrelevant" based on what was previously possible that we have not reconsidered what IS now possible?

However, rather than dwell on the past, let's look forward now to the future.

Imagine Where We Will Be in 2050??!!

Of course, imagining the future is not easy. To some degree we probably can't imagine where we will be in 2050. Consider for example that it took only forty-four years to go from the Wright Brothers' first flight to Chuck Yeager breaking the sound barrier. In 1900 it was impossible for most to even imagine such a thing as human flight. Or was it? But it happened! Although it is probably difficult or impossible to imagine the *specifics* of the future, I am neither advocating nor suggesting that we have improved our ability to literally *predict* the future. Instead, our learning from the past, such as with the previous example of man's ability to fly, can teach us that the impossible is only a momentary condition. Most things *can* and do happen, although often in ways that we do not anticipate. So the lesson is to imagine a future that we believe is best and do a lot of "imagine if" speculation—and not let the fact that many of these seem impossible at the time be a necessary deterrent.

Just as it was impossible in 1900 for anyone to imagine people flying at supersonic speeds, it is impossible in 2004 to imagine that planetary meLearning is possible. Yet my argument is that, right up until the time of its breakthrough, a revolutionary change is deemed to be impossible and comes as an unexpected surprise. Any truly new innovation is initially distinguishable from magic. The lesson learned should be that we need to dream bigger, not smaller, and prepare for a premature arrival, sooner than expected.

Future Success Comes from Innovative Approaches, *Not* from Copying Prior Success

It is also very revealing and beneficial to study how human flight came about and where the breakthrough came from after thousands of years of trying to "flap harder." We did not learn how to fly by mimicking other examples of "experts" or success such as birds or animals that can fly. Success came from understanding what enables things to fly, such as air flow and lift and wing design, and then we developed innovative ways of achieving flight such as with fixed wing design, propellers, jet engines, new lightweight materials, and other creative ways to match our unique conditions. In the end, success came after we stopped trying to flap at all. Our innovation and creativity were *not* in "flapping" but in flying. Our breakthroughs in being able to achieve planetary meLearning will come through similar innovation and creativity, *not* from copying how learning has been successful previously.

What's the Point? Why Bother?

Why do we need meLearning? To solve problems. Big, small, and every size in between. Yours, mine, and *every* one else's. To match supply with demand. We are already experiencing exponential grown in the demand for learning. Let's also take another full step back and ask, "So what?!" What effect would this have? Why would this matter? What would this change? In a word, and one I don't use lightly, *everything*! Why? Because, when you "peel the onion" by removing all the layers of symptoms and get down to the root causes of most problems, big or small, the long-term solution is inevitably . . . LEARNING!

This isn't a new observation of course. For example, taking the case of world hunger, most have heard the ancient Chinese observation that if you feed a starving person a fish and a loaf of bread, you've fed him for a day. If you teach him how to fish, grow wheat, and cook, you've fed him for a lifetime. Learning is equivalent to the latter; it addresses the long-term solution. As with most profound change, it really *is* that simple.

A Critical Caution: Don't Confuse Symptoms with Causes!

While the remainder of this chapter is going to focus on addressing the underlying causes and cures, we must *not* ignore the treatment of equally real and immediate needs and symptoms. *Please*, let's be sure that we continue to support and augment the great people and organizations who work tirelessly and often thanklessly on these "symptoms." For example, let's be sure that when someone is starving, or dying of disease, or being beaten, that we provide every possible and immediate intervention to resolve the problem.

Let's make sure we address both short-term and long-term needs and problems concurrently. Similarly, let's not make this more complicated nor drawn out than needed. Let's make sure that, when people need quick answers to solve their immediate problems, they get them in a timely and highly relevant fashion. However, it is equally imperative that we also have some of us working on the root causes and developing the longer-term solutions to these problems. If not, we are destined to be treating symptoms forever and fighting a losing battle over time. The world's problems are gaining ground on us and getting worse with the rapidly growing population numbers, expansion of diseases, reduced food sources, declining environments, and so on.

As critical and necessary as it is to be addressing these world problems, let us also recognize that success in increasing the effectiveness of learning also addresses the most positive of opportunities: overall quality of life for all of us. Whether this is through increased productivity, increased sense of self-worth, greater progress and accomplishments, improvements to culture, fine arts, improved creativity and innovation . . . the foundation is continuous LEARNING. The adage about a rising tide raising all boats applies to the overarching and spiraling positive benefits from improving our own capability and the effectiveness of learning.

But Really, WHY?

One of the compelling reasons why we must transform this vision into reality and take on these grand challenges is simply that it is the morally and the ethically right thing, perhaps even the responsibility for those of us who are the privileged few on the planet to be able to extend this same access to everyone. Getting "any" to "every" one. Yet equally important and compelling is the fact that personalized or meLearning is also the right thing to do for very "enlightened self-interest" reasons of business, governments, and academia. Having meLearning operating at a ubiquitous level globally will create enormous new markets, extend virtually all existing markets to reach anyone and everyone who wants or needs them, and therefore benefit not only learners, but all those in the "supply chain."

Analogies for Understanding

When trying to imagine a future that does not currently exist or one that is significantly different than currently in practice, the use of analogy is extremely helpful and almost required to make the transition from old models to new ones. Therefore, before we move on to looking at strategies to successfully realize this grand vision of meLearning, let's look at two analogies, one simple and one more complex, which many people I've worked with have found insightful and valuable as they developed their working understanding of meLearning.

Serious Play

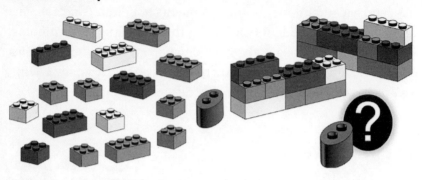

The analogy of LEGO™ blocks is often used when first introducing new paradigms such as modular content, learning objects, and mass customization. I'll use content for the example in this analogy, and therefore the individual LEGO™ pieces represent the smallest piece of raw content (for example, text, graphics, audio, and video).

Raw objects can be used for different types of assets. For example, a photo could be used on a presentation screen, but it could also be used in a multiple-choice question. These assets can be snapped together and pulled apart as needed, enabling almost infinite flexibility to create logical assemblies of individual content objects to meet the learning needs of individuals. The assets begin to take on properties and functionality and are then ready to be assembled into learning objects.

The whole content object model is a relatively simple taxonomy and can best be explained graphically, so I have been using the diagram in Figure 1 for many years. To gain a basic understanding of this model and its powerful ability to be a meta model, here is a very brief explanation. Starting on the far-left side, the content in these first two levels has very little context and therefore this content also has the maximum reusability. These are perhaps the two most important values of this model because it means that we can have *both* reusability *and* context, and so the content can be used in almost any context and for almost any purpose. However, the content pieces are so small and have so little context that they are relatively "useless" by themselves. Moving to the right in this diagram,

Figure 1. Content Object Taxonomy

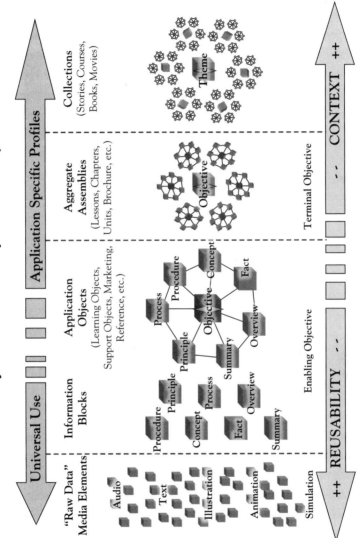

context is added not so much within the content itself, but rather through the design of the solution to a given problem and the process of carefully selecting and assembling each of these smaller components into subassemblies and more complete solutions. These designs and assemblies, which are created in response to a given problem or need, are sometimes referred to as "application profiles" and would now become content that is more specific to such purposes as training, marketing, engineering, and so forth.

It is most important to note that this taxonomy is very generic in that it applies to content overall and not just that used for learning purposes. For a more complete explanation of this model and other details of learning objects, please refer to the paper "The Future of Learning Objects," located at www.learnativity.org.

From LEGO™ to Buildings: In Search of a More Powerful Analogy

While the Lego™ example is useful in its simplicity, the construction industry may provide a much more robust analogy. On average, 85 to 95 percent of all materials in every building built in the past ten years, commercial and residential, are pre-built components. Things like doors, windows, cupboards, sinks, ceiling tiles, and light fixtures are all manufactured to meet specific standard dimensions and attributes. This means that almost all of the material in any building is pre-manufactured and sitting in a warehouse awaiting delivery *before* the building is conceptualized, designed, or built. In many respects, creating a new building is really a complex assembly project. The more one considers the comparison between the building industry and the emerging content object economy, the parallels become more apparent. These same component "building objects" can also create dull, uninspired, "cookie-cutter" housing or office buildings. This underscores the importance of architects, designers, engineers, plumbers, electricians, artists, craftspeople, and customers. Objects, like building components, enable enormous creativity. However, their effective use demands careful conceptualization, specification, selection, and assembly.

Transforming Vision into Reality

Grand visions have grand challenges. Experience has taught me that the best start to a solution is a clear articulation of the problem. Hopefully, the prior sections have given you a clear vision of a future of me-Learning and you are willing to allow for the possibility this can be achieved at the planetary level. While a clear view of the future is necessary, it is insufficient by itself and won't give us the future we seek. Therefore, the rest of this article will be devoted to clearly articulating the problems or challenges standing between today's world and that which we can now imagine possible in the near future. I ask you to take these challenges as a "call to action," and to assist with this I will also suggest some strategies for successfully resolving them. My hope and wish are that you will be able to not only remember these three challenges, but also share them with others as you encourage them to share this vision and work with us to make it come true. To help with that, EVERY * ONE * LEARNING is used to represent each of the challenges and create a phrase to capture our collective call to action.

Three GRAND CHALLENGES: A Call to Action and a Work Plan

1. EVERY: Scaling Up from "Any" to EVERY

- Bringing the capability of any time, anywhere, anyone to EVERYone, EVERYwhere, EVERY time.
- Equalizing the "distribution of the future" by ensuring and enabling access for all.
- Connecting every person, place, and thing.

2. ONE: Scaling Down from "Every" to "Just Right" for ONE

- Transforming the state of "any" (see number 1 above) to a state of "just right" for every unique learning moment.
- Just the right people, just the right information, just the right way, just the right time, via just the right medium, just the right location, and so on.
- This is about good enough and just enough.

3. LEARNING: *Readiness to Respond to Every* "LEARNING *Moment": Faster, Better, Cheaper*

- When the learner is ready, the learning resources will be too.
- Join forces with others who have come to similar conclusions, such as the Computer Research Association, which recently (2002) concluded at its "Grand Research Challenges" in computer science and engineering that the grand challenge was to have "A teacher for every learner."[7]

Strategies for Future Success: How to Get There from Here?

OK, if the first step to solving a problem is to define its attributes, then the second step would be to lay out some strategies for resolving them. There is not sufficient space within this article to provide much detail, but I intend, especially with your requests, to develop many of these strategies as articles in their own right in subsequent print, websites, web logs or blogs (a personal website typically updated daily using software that allows people with little or no technical background to update and maintain the blog), and wikis (mass contribution web pages that allow users to freely create and edit webpage content using any web browser). In the interim, and to help you formulate actionable plans and solutions of your own, here are some suggested strategies for tackling each of the grand challenges.

1. Standardize Standards. To make this vision of meLearning and sustained human performance improvement a reality, standards are essential enablers that provide for basic abilities such as interoperability, reusability, manageability, accessibility, durability, and affordability.

History has shown rather conclusively that the takeoff point for any new era or innovation includes the adoption of common standards. Examples would include railway track gauge, telephone dial tones, videotape formats, email protocols, and the Internet and World Wide Web. Similarly, we can see that without such common adoption of standards, the market stalls. Consider the historic battle between VHS and Beta that delayed the explosion of the video industry. Or look to current examples such as the lack of common standards for DVD recorders or instant messaging. These stories often start out with proprietary specifications from an individual company or source. Unfortunately, this often means that emerging technologies are built using proprietary specifications and will not work well with other similar or competing products. Since these technologies often do not meet the needs of end-users, the market typically drives the various leaders from business, academia, and government to work together to develop common "standards." This allows a variety of products to co-exist. This convergence of technologies is very important for the consumers of these technologies. Products that adhere to standards will provide consumers with wider product choices and a better chance that the products in which they invest will avoid quick obsolescence.

In the world of learning, common standards for things such as content metadata, content packaging, content sequencing, discovery, learner profiles, and run-time interaction are requisite for the success of the knowledge economy and the future of learning. Breaking from the tradition of conflict, in the case of learning technology standards, there has been a wonderful lack of competing standards. Even with this significant advantage, it has taken many years of extremely hard and thankless voluntary work by many individuals and groups from the world learning community such as AICC (Aviation Industry CBT Committee), ARIADNE (French acronym for a large European consortium for the sharing and reuse of content in repositories), Dublin Core (a large metadata specification), IMS (Instructional Management Systems), and countless other acronyms. They have designed and developed these specifications and are now being ratified, generalized, and globalized through standards bodies such as IEEE (Institute for Electrical and Electronic Engineers) and ISO (International Standards Organization) to create fully accredited standards.

As a result, and with a nod of thanks and appreciation to these efforts, robust accredited standards and working reference models such as the Advanced Distributed Learning (ADL) Shareable Content

Object Reference Model (SCORM) are now available and are being implemented every day around the globe in real-world situations with scalability. The attention therefore now shifts to the many issues and questions of how we will integrate these standards into our current projects and plans for the future.[8]

2. Start with Simple Rules. It is worth further noting that the success of the web and Internet came from *not* having a carefully laid out and predesigned master plan! Rather success has "emerged" from having some fundamental principles, some simple rules, and some common standards (HTTP, TCP/IP, HTML, and others). This was much more organic in nature, and we now understand this to be an example of "emergent behavior." The lesson for us to take away from this is to be most careful not to try to over-plan or over-manage, but rather to have some simple rules and some basic principles and then to expect the unexpected in the form of "behaviors" that will emerge. From these emergent behaviors, we can "breed success" of a continued and sustainable variety by providing the feedback loops to help select those that work and we like and to reject those that do not. Note too that this makes it critically important to know what success looks like! Hence the importance of establishing an overarching "vision" and providing just enough details to clarify the primary purpose or value proposition, while avoiding being too detailed in the specifics, which would constrain our ability to imagine the future.

Leonardo da Vinci's drawings and descriptions of "flying machines" far preceded the invention of the airplane and the infamous Wright Brothers' first flight. We don't regard da Vinci as the inventor of the airplane but we certainly can see the role he played in creating the vision.

This is a good example of the difference between imagining the future and predicting the specifics of what it will look like and how it will happen.

This was my rationale for providing the prior details on the grand vision and grand challenges facing meLearning. In this way we have a model of constant "course correction" and adaptiveness. Although we may most often be "off course" in terms of some predetermined ideal, we will—much more importantly—be able to stay "on target."

3. *Adopt Creative and Constructive Destruction.* Change of the magnitude required to successfully achieve meLearning will require that we have the courage to adopt a "creative destruction" approach. As per a book by this name a few years ago, we will need to put most of our sacred cows on the barbeque! Many of the constraints that are preventing us from making more forward progress with learning are those imposed by our ingrained models, concepts, and assumptions. Many of these have been practiced for so long we are not even aware of how deeply and thoroughly they have penetrated our thinking, our ways of doing things, and our solutions. For example, we will need to tear down such longstanding pillars of the past as the traditional document model; our models for storing, filing, and retrieving; software applications; the course model of instruction; instructional design; and the notion of pre-manufactured, mass-produced products. To many observing, this will be seen as simply destructive and will be met with fierce opposition. However, this is neither without purpose nor simply to be destructive. This is to meet a most creative and necessary need to rethink, redesign, and reimagine many of our models. To paraphrase Einstein, you can't solve problems with the same things used to create them!

Let's look at one example in more detail. Our habits and methods for storing digital data files are based on our historic solutions for storing physical objects such as books, documents, wine, and building supplies. Most computer filing systems mimic the file, folder, filing cabinet model, often (as in most operating systems such as Apple Mac and Microsoft Windows) right down to having physical depictions of these artifacts (file folders, for example) as graphic representations on the screen. Most of us are very familiar with this model, and it certainly helped make filing things on a computer for the first time more intuitive. However, this asset is now increasingly a liability when it comes to filing, and especially when retrieving the information you want from even your own computer. Haven't we all had the experience of not remembering in which file folder we might have put the data we want? Was it in "docs 2004" or "project 34–256" or "files from work"? Furthermore, what happens when you want, as is often the case, to be able to put the same file in different folders? As David Gelernter[9], one of my favorite thinkers, said recently: "Storage space and computing power are dirt cheap; our task isn't to use them efficiently, it's to squander them creatively. The important challenge in computing today is to spend computing power, not horde it." This is very good context for this discussion on changing our desktop metaphor away from the "1940s Steelcase file cabinets" toward a "narrative information stream," as Gelernter puts it.

This example demonstrates the basic premise of how we can create new solutions by creatively "destroying" our former models. The best file folder system? None at all. The best file naming convention? Each file "tagged" with what is formally known as metadata. This is simply the information that would describe the attributes or characteristics of every file—things like name of the author(s), date last worked on, revision number, file name, and so on. With this metadata available, you can simply ask for the files that match a certain set of criteria and not even know (or care) exactly where they are stored. What I Need—When I Need it—Where I Need—Who I need. WIN—WIN—WIN—WIN. Creating the new through the constructive destruction of the old! Keep this in mind as you read on. Warning! Creative Destruction Ahead!

Strategies for Grand Challenge Number 1 (EVERY): Scaling Up from "Any" to EVERY

> "The future is here. It's just not evenly distributed yet."
> *William Gibson*

Over the past century or more, we have a preponderance of evidence to show that we have successfully completed the "proof of concept phase" when it comes to reaching what could be described as "the state of any." We have the transportation systems to move physical goods and people; the telecommunication system, Internet, and web to move text, pictures, voice, and data; and the power grid and batteries to power most of this. Advances in such areas as ease of use, improved interfaces between people, systems, and machines, and supporting standards for interoperability have made all this relevant and accessible to the lay person and not the unique domain of technicians or especially skilled individuals. Putting this all together, we have proven that it is possible to get anything and anyone, anywhere at any time, and to connect just about any two or more places, people, or things. However, while true conceptually, and practiced pragmatically by a minority of the world's population, we now face the truly grand challenge of bringing this state of "any" to *every* person, place, and thing.

The fact that this state of any is even possible is worth celebrating! Let's be sure to acknowledge and marvel at this accomplishment. Let's acknowledge those who have helped to make these prior dreams a reality and encourage them to continue to work at improving and extending these capabilities. However, let's *also* remind ourselves that if you are reading this, then you (we) are likely among the privileged *few* who have this capacity of "any."

And therein lies grand challenge number 1: Getting the state of any to every one, every place, every time. Equalizing the distribution of access to technology, information, other people, knowledge, and expertise. Based on the low rate of success or "unequal distribution of the future" to date, *much* more needs to be done. In my opinion this is not only a grand challenge, but it is a grand imperative for us all—an imperative that we can all contribute to and one that we will all benefit from resolving.

Sometimes Good Enough Is (Good Enough); Sometimes It Isn't Even Close!

A friend and colleague, Gunnar Brückner, former CLO of the United Nations Development Programs and now CEO of Coaching

Platform Inc., recently reminded me of the great phrase he says he hears a lot in Latin America: "Lo perfecto es el enemigo de lo bueno," which means "The perfect is the enemy of the good."[10] These are words to live and learn by, as it is all too easy to constrain the scale and reach of our work and success by holding it back until it is perfect. This is not to suggest that quality does not matter or is not important, but rather to suggest that, when solving problems, having something to use that is in less than ideal form is almost always going to be more valuable than not having it at all or having to wait for it. It will be important to keep this in mind during our quest toward EVERY * ONE * LEARNING. We will realize this vision much faster and more completely if we choose to use a strategy of "good enough" to continuously create and deliver the best learning solution possible at the time and then work to continuously improve on this with each successive solution.

However, let's also be clear that, when it comes to information and learning, getting to most of the people, most of the time is *not* good enough! In the Information Age and in any free and self-determining society, access to information needs to be an inalienable right of every person and the responsibility of us all to ensure for our fellow citizens of the world. In the case of learning, this includes the need to consider *every* one of us as "special" and with unique needs, not just a small percentage of the population. It's not enough that we are getting the available enablers to some of the people some of the time, or even most of the people most of the time. The only acceptable goal is *every* one, *every* where, *every* time!

This is also an imperative because without such a state of universal, ubiquitous "any," then we are *all* constrained in terms of the success and benefits and value we can gain from such a state. This is in part related to the often observed "net effect" or the "Law of Plentitude," which is based on the observation that *adding* greater numbers of members *multiplies* the value to each member. Kevin Kelly provided an excellent example of this in "12 Rules for the New Economy" from *Wired* magazine[11]:

"Consider the first modern fax machine that rolled off the conveyor belt around 1965. Despite millions of dollars spent on its R&D, it was worth nothing. Zero. The second fax machine to roll off immediately made the first one worth something. There was someone to fax to. Because fax machines are linked into a network, each additional fax machine sliding down the chute increases the value of all the fax machines operating before it. So . . . each additional account you can persuade onto the network substantially increases the value of your account. When you go to Office Depot to buy a fax machine, you are not just buying a US$200 box. You are purchasing for $200 the entire network of all other fax machines. The fax effect suggests that the more plentiful things become the more valuable they become."

Combine this with the previous discussion of Kurzweil's Law of Accelerating Returns and you begin to get a sense of just how powerful these trends are. In the case of learning, we can envision similar exponential returns when we start to assume that we are all learners and all teachers all the time. When this is enabled to improve with every use, when every time we have a learning need it is met, and when we aren't learning we are helping others to learn directly and indirectly, then we get what Doug Engelbart so cleverly called "getting better at getting better" in his talk on "the unfinished revolution" at Stanford (see www.bootstrap.org/colloquium/archives/transcripts-original/col_transcript_s02a.htm). Better yet, we are getting better at an exponential rate! So our end-state goal is clear and attainable: *every* person, *every* thing, and *every* place. And the reasons to do so include the "enlightened self-interest" of every one of us as well.

Connecting Everything to Every One; Everything Is "Just" a Node

One of the fundamental characteristics of innovations that have truly changed the world is that of connecting things, especially data and people. Trains, planes, and automobiles, television, telecommunications, the Internet, and the World Wide Web have fundamentally altered our transaction space as well as the nature and diversity of our interactions. Metadata (the attributes describing every person, place, and thing) and the taxonomies and ontologies that follow will be the key to enabling this connectivity. On the technical and system architecture side, it will likely be new paradigms of what is being referred to as the "Semantic Web," the adding of meaning and relevance to what we know today. As my colleague Dr. Dan Rehak from Carnegie Mellon likes to remind me: "Everything is 'just' a node!" and I've come to believe that we need to take this to a literal level of creating ubiquitous connections between every person, place, and thing. Perhaps one of the most recent and compelling examples or arguments for doing this is the success of the World Wide Web and Internet. A world where every person and every file can be connected directly, one to one; indirectly through webs of such connections; and one to many.

Think of the impact on learning, learners, and learning content. Think about every learning object connected to every other learning object, able to communicate, pass data, and manipulate the other. Think about a world where control of content is truly put into the hands of every individual or his or her designated assistants, where everyone in need of a given skill or knowledge can be connected directly with those who have it. What will it mean to have potentially billions of authors and publishers? It would mean that we would have much more conversion of the tacit knowledge that each of us is generating continuously into much more accessible, shareable, and useable explicit knowledge. It would mean that we could start to do some serious personalized data mining and pattern recognition to discover how we do things best, how we learn, what predictably determines success, and many more such examples of continuous improvement of learning, finding, and performance.

Mass Contribution from "The Rest of Us"

So where is the supply of "everything" going to come from? In order to achieve the immense scale that meLearning demands, and to sustain this indefinitely, a model that could be characterized as "mass contribution" will be required. A state wherein we all play a role in both the creation of, and the consumption of, everything. Imagine that we are *all* authors, all programmers, all inventors, all contributors to the world knowledge pool. This is *not* to infer that we will all have the talent to be professionals at these tasks, nor that we need to make this a significant and formal part of our jobs. Instead, this means that as it becomes easier, more intuitive, more automatic, and more transparent (all requirements for this to all work) for anyone to be such a contributor, we all become creators and contributors and gain an "unconscious competence" in these roles as we just go on with our regular lives.

Early forms of this (although likely crude by future standards) can be observed in the volume of content more and more of us are creating daily with such things as email, spread sheets, databases, word processing, slides, photographs, phone conversations, digital cameras, web cams, and cell phone cameras. These are increasingly activities of the masses, you and me, and not the strict domain of professionals and experts in these fields. It is a great example of the "good enough" strategy. Is it more important that we have great grammar in our emails and impressive graphics in our slides or that we capture, share, and reuse our ideas, opinions, and innovations? While I would hope that we all strive to improve such things as grammar and slides, it is far more important that we are capturing our knowledge in a way that can be stored, shared, discovered, and improved by others. The goal isn't to replace programmers or authors or illustrators. The goal is mass contribution of our ideas and knowledge. What's more, this scales infinitely.

Mass Contribution of Metadata

There is no question that metadata is a critical foundation and essential enabler for this transformation and the solution of these grand challenges. Massive amounts of metadata will be required to make this all possible and to have the ability to discover the "right stuff." Many question whether it is even possible to gather anywhere close to the volume of metadata required. Much of this is based on the misunderstanding that most metadata has to be manually created, and thus part of the answer lies in increasing the amount of the automation for the metadata generation and processing. However, another intriguing part of solving the metadata supply problem is mass contribution. In particular, we have a current example of mass contribution of metadata that provides us with a compelling and currently working model: music CD metadata.

When you insert a music CD into your computer, you may have noticed that your music player either tells you or asks you to connect to something called "CDDB," which stands for CD Data Base, and, if you do, then you see all the metadata for the music on that CD—the names of the songs, their length, artist name, and so forth. You may have assumed, as most do, that all this metadata is on the CD itself, but it is not—and instead comes to your machine via the Internet from this CDDB. But have you ever wondered where all this music metadata comes from? Most have also assumed it is provided by the music publishers; wrong again. In fact neither the publishers nor the music companies provide *any* of this. It all comes from people like you and me. It is managed by the Gracenote company, which is an organization that runs a business model based on selling the software to the music player software companies and online services. Built into their software (what shows up inside the music players and online music sites) is a "submit" button that taps into Gracenote's database, which contains detailed information about every track on essentially every CD produced just about anywhere in the world. About a million users per day (often several times a day) use it to find out about their tracks. They also contribute about seven thousand submissions per day to the database by clicking on the "submit" button that references the CDDB. Of those seven thousand submissions, about 1,500 make it into the database each day. Those 1,500, a mix of new CDs and updates to already-cataloged CDs, have survived several thousand filters that weed out spurious submissions, automated voting logic to select the most likely accurate version from among near duplicates, plus human screening when needed. Within hours of a popular new

CD's release, Gracenote receives between ten and one hundred submissions of information about it. Now how is *that* for mass contribution?! Faster + Better + Cheaper!! In addition to a great example of mass contribution of metadata, Gracenote is also an excellent example of the kind of business models we will see much more of in the future—those that combine the seeming impossibility of an "open source" type of approach in the form of CDDB with a very profitable business in licensing the technology to use this metadata.

Mass Contribution from the Professionals

Mass contribution also includes the experts and more traditional sources of creating content, code, and so on. Perhaps the most compelling example is the explosion in the volume and accessibility of software code brought on by the so-called "open source" approach just mentioned. While too often over-hyped and misunderstood, in its simple form open source is about mass contribution by enabling anyone to contribute software code to a repository or license work using something like Creative Commons[12] in such a way that it is available to anyone else who wants it. This is causing more and more people to start a project by doing a good search for any existing code or content and then using this as the starting point for their work, rather than starting from nothing. They might simply assemble a new solution from nothing but pre-existing materials, or they might use some as is while modifying others or create brand new code or content. This is not merely the sharing of code, nor even just contribution. This is a spiraling of continuous improvement as others take what you have produced and improve or extend on it.

Nor is this restricted to software code. It is being applied to the mass contribution of content as well. Recent examples include:

- The decision by the British Broadcasting Company (BBC) to make its entire archive of all video images (one of the largest collections in the world) available for free to the public. Does *that* qualify for mass contribution?!

- In April 2001, MIT announced that it would be posting the content of some two thousand classes on the web and dubbed the program Open Courseware. The MIT OCW project would make everything, from video lectures and class notes to tests and course outlines, available to anyone with a browser. Does *that* qualify for mass contribution?!

- Since 1996 in Europe, the ARIADNE consortium (www .ariande-eu.org) has had thousands of member teachers and professors contributing learning resources into a repository for sharing and reusing learning objects. As of last year, they had over five thousand specific and well-developed learning objects, in more than ten languages, from more than twenty countries, and in more than fifteen local installations. Does *that* qualify for mass contribution and distribution??

If you think this only applies to "digital stuff" such as content and code, think again. Have you considered how Amazon and eBay represent the mass contribution of physical goods? Has so much ever been so easily available from so many to so many?

Spiraling Improvement

What does this all have to do with learning? Everything! Just start to imagine if you, or a person or agent helping you, could pick and choose "just the right" bits of content from these sources, combined with some of your own, and assemble this all into a usable package designed and built on-demand for a specific purpose or problem. Imagine such things as personalized books, websites, lessons, charts, graphs, slide shows, software applications, and on and on, and you start to see that what we formerly thought of as content and a fixed product really becomes a dynamic service that is *extremely* valuable. This is the realization of the part of the vision about having just the right learning resources available for each learning moment. Even more powerfully, this is all sustainable, scaleable, and transferable— with no end in sight! By enabling everyone to contribute, we make serious advances toward resolving the grand challenge of *every*. The explosion of the volume of information, code, tools, and photos is another one of those things that is literally increasing exponentially every day. So this future has already arrived, and we just need to work at distributing this capability to *every* one on the planet.

Strategies for Grand Challenge Number 2 (ONE): Scaling DOWN from "EVERY" to "Just Right" for ONE

While reaching the state of "any" is a great and incredible accomplishment in itself, it is but the first important step toward reaching the end state of planetary personalized learning. Even once we have accomplished the previous grand challenge, number 1, and we have *every*, the next challenge is to scale down the focus from *every* to just the right *one*.

Think about it this way: Do you want to talk with anyone or everyone? Do you value any or every piece of content? Do you need any or every bit of software code? Do you benefit from any or every piece of equipment or technology? Do you want it at "any" time? No! You, like all of us, want it *just right*, just for *you*: just the right person, just the right information, just the right place, just the right technology, just the right medium, just the right code, and all at just the right time! This is when learning occurs—at the level of *one*.

> Your parents were right by the way. You ARE a snowflake. You're completely unique.
> Just like every other snowflake![13]

Getting to this state of "just right" for *one* has a fundamental requirement that is still very scarce: the ability to predict what is needed, by whom, and where, when, and how to deliver it. This requires a way to capture, share, protect, and recognize the patterns of our individual preferences, that we have good optimization and adaptive capabilities, and that we have an effective feedback loop that enables constant "course correction" of both people and machines by knowing what is working and what is not.

The state of "any," on the other hand, is a state of plentitude, and the problem becomes that of overwhelming choice. There is a primary need for what could be called "decision support." Let's appreciate how fortunate most of us are to have such a "problem" and let's work on the previous challenge to ensure everyone has this problem and how to solve it. Please note that the emphasis here is on both decision (one needs to be made) and *support*! Successful solutions will augment our ability to make smart and good decisions and *not* have them made for us or without our permission!

Once again, this is not a new idea. Most have probably heard of the notion of "just-in-time" learning, and we can certainly relate personally to how wonderful having everything "just right" would be for ourselves and those around us. What *is* new and what I'm suggesting has changed is the possibility that this is now an achievable goal. Surely this is worth pursuing?! Can we possibly continue to choose otherwise?

There is a risk that this grand challenge could be perceived as being "greedy" or wanting it all or looking to achieve perfection. But this is about good enough and just enough—reaching the state of "just right." Successfully attaining this state requires an inversion of focus from searching to finding and developing a capacity that some have described as "on demand" or WIN-WIN: What I Need—When I Need It.

From Mass Production to Mass Customization

When it comes to learning (and most other things), it is increasingly critical to acknowledge the need for not just diversity, but also uniqueness. The needs of every person are different every day as each faces new and unexpected situations. Not just in rooms with desks and computers, but on the train, in the field, on the job site, in the car (under the car!), or any other place where problem solving, working, and learning occur. And not just for managers, not just students, not just a privileged few, but everyone, everywhere, every day.

In spite of statements to the contrary, for the past hundred-plus years, education and training have been in denial of the need to recognize that each individual is unique and different. We've evolved a model for education and training that matches the mass production model that aims to produce consistency, whereas what we really need now is the opposite in the form of mass customization and uniqueness. The past model worked very well, and we have spent over one hundred years perfecting it to a high degree. However, today as we move into the new so-called Information Age or Knowledge Economy, there is a need for a revolution in learning in a scale that will likely dwarf that of the Industrial Revolution. What has changed? What is the core cause that makes this degree of change such an imperative? The unexpected has become the norm. Mass customization is required, and not monolithic consistency of mass production. *Readiness to respond to the unexpected* is the fundamental capacity now required. Fortunately, there are now sufficient enablers in the form of innovative new technology, standards, conceptual models, and methodologies that bring this previously impossible goal into the realm of possibility.

Getting BIG by Getting *Small* and Just Right

As visions go, they don't come much bigger than this one for "me-Learning," yet surprisingly one of the fundamental strategies for success appears to be how well we can "get small" with our approach to learning and just about everything else.

Getting small is one of the largest and most pervasive meta trends I've seen, specifically the trend of breaking down all the previously monolithic models we have created for everything from content to software code to jobs into very small, standard components. After getting everything down to these small, standard components, what makes this massive scale of personalization possible is described as *mass customization: customized* because every solution is a unique assembly of "just the right" people, materials, content, technology, and so forth, and *mass* because this is for the masses, EVERY one.

In simple terms, this model of mass customization starts by taking everything from content to software code to equipment to human competencies down to the very smallest possible size (and not one bit smaller, as Einstein noted). These smallest possible objects are the "raw assets" that can then be made into more refined and functional, although still very small, standard components. These standard, reusable components can be pre-made and put "on the shelf," inventoried, ready, and able to be carefully selected and assembled into a complete custom solution of just the right solution of resources needed to match any given individual need and situation. It promises to have a *much* greater impact on our world and be much more of a revolution compared to mass production and the preceding Industrial Revolution. How can we get to mass customization? By applying some of the ideas already mentioned, namely:

- *Standardized Uniqueness:* Although it sounds like an oxymoron, standards are critical for mass-customized uniqueness. Fortunately, more and more standards for mass customization are emerging, including XML, RDF, metadata, sequencing, content packaging, competencies, and digital rights.

- *Getting It Just Right:* The dream of adaptive personalized learning will not happen just by "getting small"; the small components only become valuable when they are carefully selected and assembled into well-designed, just-right, solutions.

- *Capturing Experience:* When technology is able to capture and learn from its own experience and from its user, it gains a critical new power: accurate prediction of what will be needed next, in terms of information it can provide or suggestions it can offer. With it, learning is truly as adaptive as the technology itself.

- *Understanding Learners:* Personalization of the learning experience requires knowing something about the learner. To avoid redundancy, the system must know what the learner already knows. To assemble relevant learning experiences, it must know about the learner's past experiences, learning preferences, career goals, and more. Personal profiling enables new approaches to productivity. Thus security and trust become critical attributes of this future. It is no coincidence that the planned future of the World Wide Web, known as the "Semantic Web," has at the top of its architectural model a level known as the "Ring of Trust."

Getting Small Is a Very BIG Idea!

It is easy to conclude that it would be impossible to have true uniqueness for learning and performance an achievable goal. As noted in the introduction to this chapter, do the math—there are over six billion unique individuals on the planet, they speak hundreds of different languages, work at thousands of different jobs, live under different conditions, have different budgets. Multiply these together and you get a *very* big number, one approaching infinity in relative terms. Yet the resources available to address these billions of learners are very finite. There are only so many teachers and instructors and a finite number of resources. And of course a *very* finite budget to support all this. Impossible, right?

Matching demand with supply, the best solution would be to take a customized approach and create a truly unique solution for each learning situation. However, this is clearly impossible, as customized solutions typically require that we start fresh and develop everything as a "one off" solution and one that is not reusable. Surely it would be impossible to meet the almost infinite requirements of the learners by using the slowest and most expensive solution. Or is it?

There are in fact examples where the use of common or standardized components enables the creation of infinite and unique solutions quickly and efficiently. Simple yet powerful examples would include:

- *Language:* Unique and infinite numbers of thoughts can be expressed with written language using a very small standard set of letters in the alphabet (twenty-six in English, thirteen in Hawaiian), a finite number of words in the dictionary built by combining these standard letters, and all assembled with the rules of grammar to apply these meaningfully (hopefully!).

- *Music:* Unique and infinite songs can be written and played using a small standard set of twelve notes, which in turn can be assembled using some "rules" into collections such as chords, which are further mixed and matched with rhythms that deal with beat and time, plus melody and pitch. And this enables almost any kind or form of music from rock to jazz to classical and from Indian to Brazilian to Chinese.

- *Construction Industry:* As detailed in the "from LEGO™ to buildings" analogy we used earlier, unique and infinite numbers of buildings can be designed and built using standard modular components that are carefully selected from catalogs and warehouses.

- *Living Things:* We have recently made new discoveries about how all living organisms are created from four basic elements that are combined in unique twisted pairs of DNA. Most recently we believe we have "decoded" the combinations of these four letters that create the code for the most unique of all entities—life!

There are many lessons to be learned from these and other examples, and clearly this is an indication that the model I am proposing is scaleable, sustainable, transferable, and one that truly enables standardized uniqueness. Of course, let's keep in mind that as powerfully enabling as these models are, they in no way infer, let alone guarantee, that good quality output or creations will emerge. We all know of examples where letters, words, and grammar have all been used quite correctly, but nothing meaningful was said. Therefore, while appreciating the power of this model, let's be sure to not confuse the enablers and the model with guarantees of quality.

"Getting Small" Working Models

In addition to these profound foundational examples of *getting small* through standardized components and mass customization to assemble unique solutions, let's now turn our attention to models we can build on top of this foundation that move us much closer to the world of learning and that are working models today. Five examples of getting big by getting small include:

- *Getting small with software code:* Almost all software is already "small" in the form of object-oriented code. However, the use of newer standards and web services is enabling code to transform from our monolithic software applications to "on-demand" assemblies adapted to fit the needs of the individual at the moment of need.

- *Getting small with equipment:* Simple examples can be seen in the form of "on-demand" products such as Dell computers, which you "design" on a website by choosing "just the right" components for your needs; the resulting customized computer is assembled and shipped to you within days and at an extremely cost-effective price. Much more complex and many more exciting examples of mass customization in flexible manufacturing are emerging for such things as clothing and even molded and machined parts.

- *Getting small with competencies:* Just as the value of information is in having the right amount at the right time, so too is the value in finding the right people, at the right time, with the right skills, knowledge, and experience.

- *Getting small with standards:* As we have already discussed, standards are critical to making this all work. This is already happening within existing standards bodies such as IEEE Learning Technology Standards Committee (LTSC) and the Advanced Distributed Learning Initiative (ADL) and its SCORM or Shareable Content Object Reference Model. In all these cases, specifications, standards, and reference models have been developed, which are made up of small, interoperable modules that can be individually selected on an as-needed basis and assembled into a custom solution. I am also being made aware of this same adoption of smaller and more modular standards being applied to such diverse areas as shipbuilding and even politics!

- *Getting small with content:* Learning objects are leading the way for content as they follow precisely the same mass customization model for overall content (not just learning) as was detailed in the previous Content Object Taxonomy section.

Finding Versus Searching!

I don't know about you, but I'm really not as often interested in searching as much as I am in finding. Where's that quote I want to put in, that slide I saw at the last conference? It is truly frightening to quantify the amount of time that more and more of the workforce is spending *unsuccessfully* searching for the information, tools, and people they need to do their work. In my anecdotal research of the topic, it is estimated that for the average worker this is about 28 percent of the workday! Whatever the number, it is far too high for most of us and is directly impacting learning effectiveness and productivity. We are seeing more and more examples of new technologies that can extend our ability to find what we need, when we need it. You have probably started to see the ability to find things "like this," which is a powerful extension to our traditional searching. In the case of learning, this means that we can ensure that we are getting better and better at having the right resources at the learner's fingertips at the right time.

Personalization—Putting It All Together with the Magic of Metadata

Unlike current experiences many have had with metadata, in the future most will be derived automatically and will adequately describe every piece of data, every object, every event, and every person in the world. Objective metadata, almost all of which can be generated automatically, describes physical attributes, date, author, operational requirements, costs, identification numbers, ownership, and so on. Subjective metadata are the more varied and valuable attributes of a learning object and are determined by the person or group that creates the metadata. The label on a can of tomato sauce provides *objective* metadata; your opinion of whether that tomato sauce worked well as an ingredient in your favorite recipe is an instance of *subjective* metadata. It is especially the subjective attributes of metadata that create the ability to capture what is otherwise tacit knowledge, context, perspectives, and opinions. Leveraging and extending beyond metadata we are seeing tremendous work and advances in developing the vocabularies, taxonomies, and ontologies that bring the true power and ability to get it all "just right."

iMOTO

To explore and understand these terms, as well as to provide more pragmatic strategies on how to get started, let's look at five specific key areas that tend to form a foundation on which everything else is built. With apologies for introducing yet another acronym into our language, but to make it easier to remember, I've used the acronym "iMOTO" to represent these five categories. iMOTO stands for Identifiers, Metadata, Objects, Taxonomies, and Ontologies, and here is a brief overview of each one:

- *Identifiers:* This is comparable to having a unique part number for every item, assembly, or collection. It is critical that when implementing metadata standards, there be a process and a capability to create an ID to every asset, no matter how large or small, that will be used or referenced for learning.
- *Metadata:* This is perhaps the best understood of these five areas, and we have already addressed it. In summary, if you want to find it, refer to it, share it, or use it, metadata is needed.
- *Objects:* Refer to the previous section for more details on learning objects and the Content Object Taxonomy.
- *Taxonomies:* These are general principles of classification. While it is useful to organize content into categories, it is even more powerful to structure and organize metadata categories into ordered groups of relationships known as

taxonomies. Most of us learned about taxonomies in biology class when we studied the classification of plants and animals into a hierarchical structure of kingdom, phylum, class, order, family, genus, and species. Metadata taxonomies allow different systems and structures to be recognized, translated, compared, cross-mapped, linked, and understood.

- *Ontologies:* Ontologies are the relationships between items classified in a taxonomy. They enable us to capture a representation of knowledge and provide for significant additional meaning and value. For example, an ontology can enable a mechanism to conclude that "because the <<Product>> is of <<type>> 'Chardonnay,' then it must also be a white wine."

What is needed in each of these five iMOTO areas is for every company or organization to develop *its own* definitions, structures, and so forth for each one of these. Time spent doing so will ensure that there is a deep understanding of how this will all work and will pay big dividends as their implementations proceed and grow.

Real World Examples of Personalization: The "TiVo" Effect

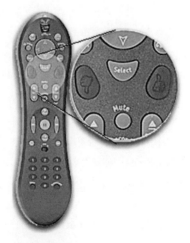

For those who are unfamiliar with TiVo™ and personal video recorder technology, it is worthy of a short explanation to show how it is already enabling an early example of personalization through pattern recognition. Simply put, TiVo and PVRs are an updated and digital version of a video cassette recorder (VCR) that replaces the videotape with a big hard drive so that instead of storing the recorded TV or video signals on tape, it puts them onto a hard drive. But the real magic and value that we would want for personalized learning comes from two "must" buttons on the remote control. As you are watching any program, recorded or live, you have the option to press either a "thumbs up" (indicating good, I like this) or "thumbs down" (meaning I don't like this). To indicate your level pleasure, you can press each button once, twice, or three times. As this information is collected into the memory of the machine, it gets better and better at knowing your individual preferences. Is it magic? Hardly. This is a simple but powerful example of pattern recognition. Finding common patterns within the attributes (metadata) of what you liked and did not like, sifting through the thousands of attributes about each show, and comparing your attributes and patterns with others with similar patterns of preferences, allows TiVo to determine with high precision just what *you* would most likely enjoy watching. This is an early but good, practical, and existing example of what "agent" technology can do and why it will become so prevalent and valuable—your own personal set of assistants, always looking to better meet your needs.

From meTV to meLearning

Now start to imagine TiVo for learning! Imagine having a learning assistant or agent always watching out for you—always scouring all available resources looking for and finding everything that matches what it has learned from your past choices, ratings, usage patterns, and so on. This is *not* key word searching. This is an example of continuous and self-improving agents (you would have many of them, each configured for specific needs or situations) that are constantly comparing your needs and situation and your preferences with what is available and providing this awareness to you for your selection and use. Also imagine that, as learners were learning, they were quickly, easily, and consistently rating their learning experiences. How well did the learning match their needs, how well did it help them solve the problem at hand, how quickly did they "get" it, how well did it adapt to their conditions, and on and on. By learners doing this analysis, patterns start to emerge and are identified, which in turn start to create a supply for that rarest of capabilities mentioned at the start of this section—the ability to accurately predicate who needs what and when. It isn't too hard to start seeing meLearning emerge here, is it? Hardly seems impossible, does it?

Strategies for Grand Challenge Number 3 (LEARNING): Readiness to Respond to Every "Learning Moment": Faster, Better, Cheaper!

> The past few thousand years have focused on inventing creative ways to augment our physical capabilities. We now begin to shift our focus to augmenting our cognitive capabilities. The results of dong so will dwarf those of the previous millennia.

Even once we address the first two grand challenges and have *every* person, place, and thing connected and enabled, even once we are able to focus *every* one down to the level of *one* unique experience, we have still to complete the journey by having learning take place effectively, efficiently, and uniquely optimized for each person and situation.

While clearly grand and important challenges, the first two are focused on access, discovery, distribution, selection, and packaging of learning resources. It is in this third grand challenge that the learning itself is addressed. The future vision here is that of "readiness for every learning moment." In a takeoff from the ancient Chinese proverb, "When the learner is ready, the teacher will appear," I am suggesting an updated and larger goal to aim for: "When the learner is ready, the learning resources will be too" so that "When the learner is ready, the learning will begin."

The phrase I used to know and love when I was a teacher was that of the "teachable moment"—that almost magical and all-too-rare experience when a student was motivated by a specific need or curiosity, when other conditions and the environment were just right, and when I was ready as the teacher to mutually experience that most special "Aha!" moment and see that spark of satisfaction in the student's eyes. LEARNING! This certainly still applies, but I want to be sure to emphasize that learning includes both the formal education and training and those situations in which learning is a very conscious act as well as the more informal and unexpected ones. Thus, the goal now becomes one of being ready to respond to every, often unexpected, learning moment.

We Are All Teachers, All Learners, All the Time

This is an enormous undertaking, and many of you will be wondering how we can realistically imagine scaling up to have a teacher for every learner. In part, the answer may lie in rethinking learning and teaching on several fronts. First, let's expand our thinking beyond the typical limitation of just education and training, classrooms and courses. Most studies that have tried to quantify what percentage of the skills, knowledge, and abilities we use to perform our jobs, live life, and generally solve problems have concluded that formal learning accounts for about 10 percent or less. And the other 90 percent of our learning? We get that from such informal sources as experience, discussions with colleagues, books, radio, TV, the web, friends, and family. Think of it as informal, continuous, and on-demand. Now start to leverage and multiply this much further by augmenting the ability for each one of us to be more useful, more of a "teacher" or a learning agent for others around us. This would not be accomplished by training everyone to be a formal or professional teacher, but rather by providing resources and enablers that would effectively connect those who have some specific skills, knowledge, and experience to those who need them—simply doing an effective job of matching supply and demand down at the very smallest of levels. It could be as simple as quickly finding the answer to a simple question on "how to" as well as dealing with more complex questions, skill development, collaboration on conceptual designs, and so forth.

To do so will require a change in our sense of and assumptions about such fundamentals as who is an expert and who is a teacher, including the virtual forms of both, such as knowledge bases, expert systems, and agents—all good examples of the need for "creative destruction," as discussed previously. Imagine if the answer and the expectation and the practice were that *every one* of us was a learner, a teacher, a learning agent, an expert all the time. Isn't this already true if you take it down to a small enough level? Isn't one definition of an expert, especially of something new and different, the person who has already tried it and done it successfully a few times more than you? Haven't you received some of your most valuable learning at the water cooler, at the kitchen table, or in the hallway?

At the risk of sounding like it would be making the challenge larger still, I think we would also want to set our expectations for the teacher-to-learner ratio to be well beyond "just" 1:1. We will want and need multiple numbers of teachers, agents, experts, and resources for every one of us, every learner, every day. Normally reserved for things such as manufacturing, business process, and consumer goods, "faster, better, cheaper" now applies to learning too!

Augmenting Our Brainpower, Not Replacing It! Thank You Very Much

I suspect that many of our experiences (as well as much research) has shown us that we are using a very small percentage of our cognitive capabilities. The future will see us put a focus on augmenting our cognitive capacities that will dwarf our past few millennia of success at augmenting our physical capabilities. This is in stark contrast to some views of virtual intelligence, which indicate that machines or robots will replace either us or our thinking, and therefore all the more reason why there is an urgent need for us to put more focus on improving our learning skills, knowledge, and abilities and a significant reason that my vision of the future is one that is extremely bright. It is not the dark, machine-controlled future that has so often been promoted in the press, in movies, and by others.

This would also appear to be a logical and predictable continuation of human evolution. In the most simple and condensed form, the initial agrarian stage of our evolution was based on pure human and animal power. The following Industrial Revolution was characterized by machine power. And the Information Age, which we are just now entering, is and will be characterized by human brain power.

We're Not Alone and We're in Good Company!

We are not the only ones who are pursuing this third grand challenge. Here are examples of others who have identified similar goals and who we should seek out and consider joining forces with or agreeing to take a "divide and conquer" approach to deal with the enormity of the workload before us in taking on these three grand challenges:

- *Computer Research Association:* In 2002, the Computer Research Association with the likes of Dr. Andy Vandam, (www.cra.org) sponsored its first "Grand Research Challenges in Computer Science and Engineering." This was the first in a series of highly non-traditional conferences where the goal was to define important questions; they identified the grand challenge to be "a teacher for every learner." You can read more of the details in the final report and associated slides and papers available at www.cra.org/Activities/grand.challenges/

- *European Commission, "ProLearn" Project:* It is noteworthy that out of all the many priorities that the European Union has to deal with, one of the largest and most common areas of focus is that of learning. In the Sixth Framework, the current five-year plan that began at the start of 2004, one of the largest projects is one called ProLearn, for which I have the privilege of being a strategic advisor. ProLearn, financed by the IST (Information Society Technology), has identified the following areas of focus:

- Interactive Media
- Learning Objects, Metadata, and Standards
- Brokerage Systems and Learning Management
- Business Models, Processes, and Markets
- Knowledge Work Management and . . .

- *Personalized Adaptive Learning:* The project description for this specific area includes the following details: "Current learning environments are typically web-based, but they usually do not take into account heterogeneous needs of users and provide the same learning material to students with different knowledge, objectives, interests, and in different contexts. Adaptive hypermedia systems build a model of goals, preferences, and knowledge of each user and use this model throughout the interaction with the user in order to personalize the structure and content of the delivered materials to the needs of that user. PROLEARN is the first initiative to integrate the variety of perspectives on personalized and adaptive learning. Currently there is no technical standard for the communication between the various personalized adaptive learning tools, as well as no metadata standard for meaningful exchange of learner model and learning content data."

Have a look at the European Commission's view on PROLEARN at: www.cordis.lu/ist/directorate_e/telearn/fp6_prolearn.htm or www.prolearn-project.org/articles/wp1/index.html.

Learning to Unlearn, Learning to Learn

At the TechLearn 2003 conference in November, Elliott Masie had one of his great interview type sessions with Dean Kamen, inventor of the insulin pump, vertical climbing wheelchair, and the Segway. I was particularly struck by one of Dean's comments when Elliott asked about how kids seem to be able to learn so quickly and well compared to some of us adults. He remarked, "Kids aren't any better at learning than we are; they just have a lot less to unlearn." Therefore, we will need to focus on developing skills for unlearning as much as for learning.

I suspect we would have a consensus that everyone is capable of learning and that human nature is a curious one, naturally inclined to learn. However, learning is also a skill and as such there are techniques, tips, and tricks to improve it. In short, we need to learn at a new and unprecedented level of speed, efficiency, and effectiveness in order to take maximum advantage of the states of *EVERY* and *ONE*.

Conclusion

The best way to predict the future is to design your own and then go build it. We (yes, that includes *you*!) are poised on the verge of transforming the dream of personalized learning for the planet into a reality. The time to *act* is *now*! Now is the time for creativity and innovative new ways. Now is the time for true transformation. Not merely tweaking the past and present models, but true systemic, holistic, and revolutionary change required to design and build nothing less than the future of learning and human performance improvement. We need more focus on innovation than invention and particularly innovative approaches to instruction and creative ways of leveraging all the enablers we have at our disposal.

Now is the time to be architects designing the future we want to see happen, developing the work plans to build it, and putting them into broad, imaginative, and unconstrained implementation. As we labor toward these goals, we will need to continuously reimagine the future. By doing so, the cycle of continuous learning and continuous improvement will accelerate the future of not just meLearning, but the world itself and all of us in it.

This fantastic transformation of meLearning at the planetary scale from a grand vision into a reality begins when we muster the courage to imagine and believe it is possible. Success will require that we commit to setting the grand challenges as achievable and necessary goals to get us there, that we summon up all creativity and innovation to design such a future, and that we start building it. For while neither is assured nor inevitable, this future *is* now possible, probable, and bright!

A future that is inclusive of literally every person, every domain, and every country. A future that spans government, academia, and business. A future that transcends and draws on the previously independent worlds of e-learning, human relations, knowledge management, and many others. A future that fuels both mass contribution from all and mass customization for all. A future where we are ready for every learning moment through the realization of the ancient promise (updated now) that when the learner is ready, the learning resources will be too.

The future is ours to choose: dark or bright? Shades of gloomy gray or a celebration of life and color? We can choose to continue on our current path of incremental improvement, treating symptoms and just surviving, or we can choose a radically better and brighter future of personalized learning experiences for every person on the planet every day knocking down those grand challenges standing in our way. Do *you* believe? Do *you* want to help build this bright future for all of us? What are *you* waiting for? Let's start believing, designing, building, and creating just such a future for us all. The rest of the world awaits our lead and that big, bright future is ours to have if we just imagine the impossible isn't.

Imagine . . . EVERY * ONE * LEARNING

Notes

1. See Wired 5.09 www.wired.com/wired/archive/5.09/newrules _pr.html
2. Moore's Law has become a common reference to the exponential nature of the world we live in. Taken in the abstract, the apparent reality is that technology doubles in speed or ca-

pability, and halves in cost about every eighteen months! See www.webopedia.com/TERM/M/Moores_Law.html

3. For a synopsis report on all this and more information on Bob's work, see www.stanford.edu/~rhorn/a/topic/cognom/tocCncptlzHumnCognome.html

4. See the full report on NIBC: "Converging Technologies for Improving Human Performance," available at http://wtec.org/ConvergingTechnologies. This is the result of a workshop from the National Science and Technology Council (NSTC), the National Science Foundation (NSF), and the Department of Commerce (DOC).

5. For a different perspective on all this, see the commentary published in *Wired* magazine at: www.wired.com/wired/archive/10.11/start.html?pg=13

6. For a fascinating and informative explanation of The Law of Accelerating Returns, see Ray Kurzweil's paper of the same name at www.kurzweilai.net/articles/art0134.html

7. See www.cra.org/Activities/grand.challenges/ for their summary report and for the slide set: www.cra.org/Activities/grand.challenges/slides/education.pdf

8. For MUCH more in-depth coverage of standards in learning, please see the recent Industry Report produced by The MASIE Center and available at www.masie.com/standards.

9. David Gelernter, professor, computer science, at Yale and chief scientist, Mirror Worlds Technologies, from his article in November 7, 2002, *New York Times*, www.nytimes.com/2002/11/07/technology/circuits/07soft.html?todaysheadlines

10. Gunnar and other equally insightful individuals have contributed such thoughts to a new (May 2004) book from Cambridge University Press edited by Marcia Conner and Jim Clawson called *Creating a Learning Culture: Strategy, Practice, and Technology* at http://amazon.com/o/asin/0521537177/thelearnativico/ ISBN= 0521537177

11. Kevin Kelly excerpt from *Wired* 5.09 www.wired.com/wired/archive/5.09/newrules_pr.html

12. Creative Commons is a relatively new way of licensing such things as content and code that enables the creator to specify how the source material can be used, reused, modified, and distributed by others. See www.creativecommons.org for more details or try it out for yourself.

13. With thanks to Professor David Wiley. During one of our typically wonderful and wide-ranging conversations, he recalled how his mother often told him that he was special, just like every other person on the planet!

About the Editor

Elliott Masie is an internationally recognized futurist, analyst, researcher, and humorist on the critical topics of technology, business, learning, and workplace productivity. He is the editor of *Learning TRENDS* by Elliott Masie, an Internet newsletter read by over 50,000 business executives worldwide, and a regular columnist in numerous professional publications.

He heads The MASIE Center, a Saratoga Springs, New York, think tank focused on how organizations can absorb technology and create continuous learning and knowledge within the workforce. He leads the Learning CONSORTIUM, a coalition of 200 Fortune 500 companies exploring the future of technology in the workplace, including JP Morgan Chase, Goldman Sachs, American Express, UPS, Home Depot, National Security Agency, McDonald's, Sears, Bank of America, and the U.S. Departments of Defense and Labor.

Elliott's professional focus has been to demystify the world of technology in order to allow organizations to use their wisdom and resources to make key choices. He has developed models for accelerating the spread of knowledge, learning, and collaboration throughout organizations. Elliott is acknowledged as the first analyst to use the term e-learning and has advocated for a sane deployment of learning and collaboration technology as a means of supporting the effectiveness and profitability of enterprises.

Elliott serves as an advisor to a wide range of government, education, and non-profit groups. He serves on the boards of trustees of several colleges, as a board member on national organizations, and as a member of the Executive Committee of Operation Respect, an anti-bullying education project. He serves as a pro-bono advisor to the Department of Defense and was appointed by the President to the White House Advisory Council on Expanding Learning Opportunities.

Elliott is known as a highly approachable speaker and trainer, blending humor, applicable stories of best practice, and high levels of audience involvement. Over the past twenty-five years, he has presented programs, courses, and speeches to over 1,600,000 professionals around the world. He lives in Saratoga Springs, owns thoroughbred horses, and travels extensively each year.

He can be contacted at emasie@masie.com.

About the Authors

Sam S. Adkins is the chief research officer at Ambient Insight, LLC, an independent learning and productivity technology research firm. He specializes in technology research that spans several converging technologies, including e-learning, simulation, ambient intelligence, advanced visualization, business process management, collaboration, wireless technology, service-oriented architecture (SOA), and web services.

Sam is a former product planner and business development manager for Microsoft's Training and Certification Group. During his eight years at Microsoft, he built the world's first commercial online learning business (The Microsoft Online Institute). More recently, he wrote the groundbreaking articles, "The Brave New World of Learning" (June 2003), "Radical Learning Technology" (November 2003), and "Beneath the Tip of the Iceberg: Technology Plumbs the Affective Learning Domain" (February 2004) in *T&D Magazine*.

Sam has specialized in electronic training for his entire professional career and prior to Microsoft worked for Authorware, United Airlines, and AT&T.

Sam can be contacted at sam@ambientinsight.com.

David Barton has a twenty-eight-year career at Michelin, North America. Most of the time (sixteen of the years) has been spent in various Quality Assurance positions within the manufacturing facility. For the last twelve years, David has served in various capacities and functional areas as a training and development manager;

he is currently responsible for planning, implementing, and managing technology enabled learning solutions.

He can be contacted at david.barton@us.michelin.com.

As an emerging technology analyst for the University of Wisconsin system, **Judy Brown** conducts research and consults on new computer directions and related technologies for all campuses in the fifteen institutions of the University of Wisconsin system. She focuses on partnerships for improving learning with corporate, government, and educational institutions and is the executive director of the Academic ADL Co-Lab (www.academiccolab.org) at the University Research Park in Madison, Wisconsin. Judy has been involved with learning technologies for over twenty years and has been involved in online learning since writing CBT applications for mainframes in 1984. She was named one of the Top 100 women in computing by McGraw-Hill's *Open Computing* magazine. For six years she wrote a technology column for the *Milwaukee Journal Sentinel* and has also written for *PC Week*, the Higher Education Cooperative Consortium, and *The College Magazine*. She helps coordinate eWEEK's Corporate Partner Program and participates in The MASIE Center's Learning CONSORTIUM.

Judy can be contacted at judy@academiccolab.org.

Vicki Cerda is a research and editorial advisor for The MASIE Center, with over twenty years of management and consulting experience as a training strategist and specialist in information technology, business, and professional curriculums. Previous to venturing out on her own, Vicki was a management specialist at Florida Power and Light. At FP&L, she was responsible for designing, delivering, and administering education programs for the more than eight hundred technical professionals in the information management business unit, along with numerous other enterprise-wide solutions that reached a workforce of over eleven thousand. In addition to her combined training, teaching, and technical experience, Vicki has a master's of science degree in management information systems as well as bachelor's degrees in both mathematics and mathematics education.

Vicki can be contacted at vicki@masie.com or vicki_cerda @hotmail.com.

After receiving his undergraduate degree in English language and literature and philosophy at the University of Michigan, **Murry Christensen** went on to a master's in creative writing and criticism, also at Michigan. Murry has worked in a wide range of media development and production environments. He has owned and managed his own interactive media companies, as well as worked in a consulting role at most of the major financial services firms in New York, and most recently managed online learning for a major global investment bank. He is a member of the Association for Computing Machinery (ACM), IEEE Computer Society, the MASIE Center Learning CONSORTIUM, and the American Society for Training and Development (ASTD). He maintains an active speaking and publishing schedule in a range of industry venues.

Murry can be contacted at mchristensen@mchristensen.com.

Nancy DeViney is general manager for IBM Learning Solutions. In this role, Nancy leads a global team responsible for advancing IBM's extensive learning portfolio and expertise, spanning consulting, integration, outsourcing, content design and development, software, hardware, research, and business partners. Previously, she was general manager of IBM Learning Services, a global business with more than three thousand employees in fifty-five countries. In this role, she was responsible for IBM's IT product training and education services businesses, serving IBM customers, business partners, and employees worldwide. She is co-chairwoman of the IBM Americas Women's Leadership Council and is a speaker at key training and customer-focused conferences.

Nancy can be contacted at deviney@us.ibm.com.

Lance Dublin is an independent management consultant, international speaker, and author based in San Francisco, California, and serving clients world-wide. He specializes in strategy development, program design, and implementation for corporate learning programs and organizational change management. He brings to his work more than thirty years' experience in adult education and training, communication and change leadership, and motivation and innovation. He is the co-author of the capstone book in ASTD's e-learning series, *Implementing e-Learning.*

Previous to his current role, Lance was founder, president, and CEO of Dublin Group from its formation in 1983 until he sold the company in 1998. Under his leadership this company became recognized for its innovative solutions to improving individual and organizational performance and effective approaches to successfully implementing large-scale change initiatives. Prior to this, Lance was the founder, Dean, and later Provost of Antioch University/West, an innovative accredited bachelor's and master's degree program serving one thousand students in the western states and Hawaii.

Lance can be contacted at ldublin@pacbell.net.

Carol J. Friday has been involved with e-learning for over seventeen years. She works for Saudi Aramco as a corporate learning consultant with the Corporate Integrated Learning Services. This new function, started in 2003, is responsible for developing and implementing corporate-wide e-learning services and coordinating e-learning across the company. Before working for Saudi Aramco, Carol worked in the Republic of Korea, Iran, and the United States as a corporate trainer, communication coach, and business advisor. She holds a master's degree and has given presentations on e-learning, communication, and ESL topics at several national and international conferences.

She can be contacted at carol.friday@aramco.com.

Mike Hendon is director of curricula and e-learning for the McDonald's Corporation. He has over twenty-five years of experience in the education and learning and development field and has held positions in academia and at all levels of corporate training and human resources. His experience and expertise range from strategy development and implementation to the latest in electronic tools and curricula development. He is responsible for the development of the worldwide curricula for the McDonald's Corporation, supporting 121 countries, thirty languages, and over thirty thousand restaurants. He is also responsible for the strategy development, leadership, and direction for the implementation of McDonald's Worldwide e-Learning Strategy, which includes multiple delivery channels, learning/content management systems, evaluation and assessment, and establishing worldwide training standards. Duties include directing the curricula and design organizations and the e-learning team; integration of training, learning, and development requirements with enterprise-wide solutions; leading research and development activities for impact to learning; and supporting worldwide business initiatives through learning and development. McDonald's Corporation recently won the e-Learning Pioneer Award from The MASIE Center for the development and implementation of its global e-learning strategy.

Mike can be contacted at mike.hendon@mcd.com.

Wayne Hodgins is recognized around the world as a strategic futurist and one of the leading experts on human performance improvement, knowledge management, learning, and training technology. With over thirty years of experience in business and education, Wayne has developed thought-provoking and visionary perspectives on how learning, technology, and standards can revolutionize workforce productivity.

As a Strategic Futurist for Autodesk, Inc., Wayne has worked with numerous Fortune 500 companies, government agencies, and high-tech companies to develop learning, training, and technology strategies. He is at the forefront of learning technology standards, serving as chair of the IEEE Learning Object Metadata working groups in the Learning Technology Standards Committee.

Wayne has delivered over 450 keynote sessions and presentations around the world for industry, government, and academia. In 2003 alone, Wayne delivered presentations on eight continents in over twenty-two countries.

Wayne can be contacted through wayne@learnativity.org or wayne.hodgins@autodesk.com.

Larry Israelite has been involved in addressing personal and business challenges through learning for over twenty-two years, working in all instructional media and in a variety of industries, including high-tech, heathcare, financial services, and business services. Currently, Larry is the director of global learning at Pitney Bowes, Inc., where he is responsible for leadership development, learning technology, and the delivery of a variety of learning-related products and services to business customers worldwide.

Prior to his current position, he was a vice president and senior consultant at the Forum Corporation. Larry also has held learning leadership positions at John Hancock Financial Services, Oxford Heath Plans, and the Digital Equipment Corporation. He holds a bachelor's degree in theatre arts from Washington College and both an M.A. in instructional media and a Ph.D. in instructional technology from the Arizona State University.

He can be contacted at larry.israelite@pb.com.

David Metcalf, Ph.D., has held a variety of positions in academic, corporate, and government organizations. He consults through DM2 Research and Design and teaches in several online university programs, including the flagship doctoral knowledge and learning management program at Walden University. As former chief learning technologist at RWD Technologies, Dr. Metcalf was responsible for the analysis, design, and strategic alignment of RWD's technology solutions for learning. Dr. Metcalf joined RWD with the acquisition of Merrimac, the 1997 spin-off from NASA's Kennedy Space Center. At KSC, Dr. Metcalf ran the Web Interactive Training (WIT) project that produced some of the earliest, award-winning, web-based training applications. He holds a B.A. in computer graphics from the University of Texas, an M.S. in computer-based learning, and a Ph.D. in information systems from Nova Southeastern University.

He can be contacted at metcalf@digital.net.

Paul Nenninger, currently a consultant in the areas of distance learning and homeland security specializing in security on the Inland Waterways, had a twenty-six-year career with the U.S. Secret Service with various permanent assignments around the country related to protection and criminal investigation. In 1997, he was assigned to the Secret Service's James J. Rowley Training Center, in Laurel, Maryland. He has served as a senior course instructor in charge of the Special Agent Introductory Training Course, the Secret Service's course on ethics, and was program manager in charge of the Security and the Incident Modeling Lab (SIMLAB). He was also the Secret Service board member for the Joint Conflict and Tactical Simulation (JCATS) Configuration Control Board, Joint Chiefs of Staff, Joint War Fighting Center, Ft. Monroe, Virginia. His last assignment was as the assistant to the special agent in charge for distance learning, delivering training content via video teleconferencing, web conferencing, and online.

Paul can be contacted at paullnenninger@aol.com.

Mark Oehlert is a perpetual student, gamer, technologist and learning enthusiast. In April of 2005 he joined The MASIE Center to work on several new projects, including the xLearn Lab and Learning 2005. Prior to coming to The MASIE Center, Mark was employed by the consulting firm of Booz Allen Hamilton as part of its Learning Team. Mark also worked for more than five years supporting the Department of Defense's Advanced Distributed Learning (ADL) initiative, serving last as the ADL Co-Lab's deputy director for communications. Mark is also the publisher of an email newsletter and a blog, both of which focus on the intersection of learning and technology. Mark's undergraduate degree (West Georgia College) is in management, his master's (Oregon State University) is in history and anthropology, and he has done doctoral work in American history at American University in Washington, D.C. He is currently pursuing a second master's degree (Boise State University) in instructional performance technology. Mark was also one of the first recipients of a research grant from The MASIE Center and is continuing that research on the future of e-learning.

Mark can be contacted at mark@masie.com.

Scott Sutker, Senior Requirements Consultant, recently joined Hewitt Associates to assist with transitioning new clients who outsource their learning and performance management systems. Before joining Hewitt, Scott worked for Wachovia and helped them build internal capacity for developing e-learning solutions and moving the corporation toward a "learner-centric" model. Projects included building new solutions with virtual classroom, learning management systems, and third-party content providers. His background includes over fifteen years of experience in training, consulting, management, and sales. Scott serves on the boards of many professional societies and the customer advisory boards of select suppliers and businesses.

He can be contacted at scott.sutker@hewitt.com.

Beth Thomas is the head of retail training for Bank One. She is responsible for all banking center training across the country and supports over 35,000 employees. Beth came from The Limited, Inc., headquarters, where for nine years she managed the Enterprise Learning Center. She supported all businesses within The Limited, including Limited Stores, Victoria's Secret, Bath and Body Works, and Express. In 2000, Beth received the TechLearn Conference Hero Award and has been written up in over a dozen magazines, including *Fast Company, Inside Technology Training,* and *Executive Technology.*

She can be contacted at bthomas6706@aol.com.

Index

The MASIE Center

The MASIE Center's Services, Events and Products as of April 2005

Learning CONSORTIUM: Don't approach Learning ALONE! Join 200 other organizations in a "conspiracy" of performance! Our CONSORTIUM provides ongoing benchmarking resources that will keep you from making poor decisions or negotiating weak contracts with suppliers. Together, we are inventing, revising, improving and evaluating the exciting field of Learning. Membership includes 365 days of benchmarking, coaching and Learning resources for your entire organization.

Annual Learning Conference: Our Fall Conference is a totally different kind of Learning event! This global conference moves beyond the training industry to explore the incredible world of Learning via provocative formats and conversations that look at how LEARNING really happens in the Digital Age and in the real lives of our employees and customers. Hosted by Elliott Masie.

MASIE Center Events: Watch our web site (www.masie.com) for upcoming events including seminars, briefings, roundtables, special interest groups, and workshops addressing the changing world of Learning, business and technology. These no-hype, vendor-neutral, intensive and highly interactive events are led by Elliott Masie. Most include a follow-up online discussion three months later. Call about having any of the offerings brought to you live or via technology. Sample programs include Gaming, Simulation and Mobile Learning, Skills for e-Trainers, e-Learning Briefing, and Rapid e-Learning Development Seminars.

xLearn Lab: A place where you can go to have an individual or a team spend HOURS "playing" and exploring the widest range of Learning technology and methodology, including gaming and simulations, digital collaboration, document and content management, rapid authoring and diverse models of Learning.

Speaking Engagements: Elliott is known as a highly approachable speaker: he blends humor, applicable stories of best practice and high levels of audience involvement. Over the past 25 years, he has presented keynotes, programs, courses and speeches to over 1,600,000 professionals around the world. Possible topics for engagements include Beyond Intranets: Knowledge Management in the Organization, The Learning Marketplace, New Models for Organizational Learning and Learning in the Digital Age.

Coaching & Consulting Services: The MASIE Center provides short-term, laser-like coaching/consulting for organizations that are either implementing new Learning solutions or companies that are developing/refining products for the Learning marketplace. Ninety-percent of our assignments involve a one-day, on-site visit and include pre and post telephone/video conferencing contact. Examples of these paid services include executive sessions with senior decision makers on strategic planning for Learning and training, third-party review of major Learning projects, and re-inventing training and Learning missions.

Learning Strategy Retreats at The MASIE Center: Each year, a half dozen companies conduct top level Learning strategy retreats at the MASIE Center using our $2,000,000 Learning technology lab, Elliott Masie's perspectives, and a very cool environment for reflection and planning in Saratoga Springs, NY. We can even blend on-site and global remote participation.

Usability Audit: The MASIE Center is uniquely qualified to analyze your Learning products for usability readiness. Our approach blends years of expertise with specialized techniques to provide an effective and unique environment for testing Learning software, content modules, Learning portals and systems. Designed specifically for Learning usability testing, our three usability labs, remote observation rooms, and video capture capabilities enable you to personally observe and track users in real-time.

LEARNING
CONSORTIUM

CONSORTIUM Member Benefits as of April 2005

Being a member of the Learning CONSORTIUM means being part of a "conspiracy" of performance. Together, we are evaluating, inventing, revising and improving the exciting field of Learning. Here is a summary of your CONSORTIUM benefits.

Event Credits: Each member organization receives two Event Credits that can be used for our annual Learning conference which is the site of the CONSORTIUM's annual meeting.

Coaching with Elliott: Each member organization receives two 30-minute virtual coaching sessions with Elliott.

Semi-Annual Meeting: This regional meeting is hosted by a member organization to discuss and collaborate on members' key Learning decisions.

Learning Retreat: Member organizations are invited to join Elliott in an in-depth Learning retreat at The MASIE Center.

Fly-Arounds: Half-day meetings are held in different cities around the globe. These meetings are hosted at member sites and Elliott "flies around" to facilitate discussions.

Monthly Calls: Each month, Elliott holds a virtual classroom or conference call to discuss key industry initiatives and concerns.

Lifelines and Collaboration: We facilitate networking and information sharing among members, including feedback on your pressing "lifeline" questions.

Research & Reports: We provide in-depth research and just-in-time reports on the Learning priorities and issues raised by the CONSORTIUM members.

Benchmarking: Our scans and surveys offer a snapshot of the Learning industry by presenting benchmarking indicators and detailed data on Learning organizations.

Reading Objects: We keep a pulse on industry issues and emerging trends with key articles of interest and other resources related to your business, technology and Learning decisions.

Ad-Hoc Research: We can help you find the information resources you need to solve your Learning challenges.

Newsletter: We keep you in the know about upcoming meetings and events, new members joining the CONSORTIUM and related news.

Member-to-Member Perspectives: We provide opportunities to work directly with your Learning industry colleagues in off-line dialogues.

LEARNING CONSORTIUM

Members as of April 2005:

3M
Accenture
ADL Co-Lab
Aetna, Inc.
Allstate Insurance Company
American Express
American Family Mutual Insurance
Armstrong World Industries
AstraZeneca Pharmaceuticals
Autodesk, Inc.
Bank of America
Bank of New York
BASF Corporation
BearingPoint
Booz Allen Hamilton
BP International Ltd.
Bristol-Myers Squibb
Canon USA
Capella University
Capital One
Cathay Pacific Airways Limited
Center for Creative Leadership
CIBC
Cincinnati Insurance Company
Cisco Systems
CNA
Colgate-Palmolive Company
Convergys
Corning, Inc.
COUNTRY Ins & Financial Services
Crowe Chizek and Company LLC
DaimlerChrysler Academy
DaimlerChrysler Services NA, LLC
Dana Corporation
David Weekley Homes
Defense Acquisition University
Defense Intelligence Agency
Dell Computer Corporation
Deloitte Consulting
Department for Education and Skills
Department of Labor
Development Dimensions International
Diebold, Inc.
Digitec Interactive
Discover Financial Services
Dow Chemical Company
Dow Corning Corporation
DuPont / Pioneer Hi-Bred
Duthie Associates, Inc.
Eli Lilly and Company
Emirates
Engenio Information Technologies
Enspire Learning
Experian
Federal Deposit Insurance Corporation
Financial Times Knowledge Dialogue
General Mills
General Motors
General Physics
Goldman Sachs & Company
Grainger
Grant Thornton LLP

Guidant Corporation
Harley-Davidson Motor Company
Harper College
HarvestRoad
HCA
Healthcare Financial Mgt. Assn.
Herman Miller, Inc.
Hershey Foods
Hewlett Packard
Home Depot
HSBC, North America
Humana, Inc.
Hurix Systems Private Limited
IBM Corporation
InCharge Institute of America, Inc.
Intel Corporation
Intellinex
Interwise
Intrepid Learning Solutions
J.D. Power and Associates
Jobs for the Future
John Hancock Financial Services
Johnson Controls
JP Morgan Chase
Kaiser Permanente
KnowledgePlanet
Kohler Company
KPMG LLP
Kraft Foods
Macromedia, Inc.
Maritz Learning
Marriott International
Marsh & McLennan
MassMutual Financial Group
MasterCard International
Maytag
McDonald's Corporation
MeadWestvaco
Meijer
Merck & Co.
MetLife
Michelin
Microsoft
Miller Brewing Company
Monitor Company Group
Morgan Stanley
Moscow State University
National Cryptologic School (NSA)
National Seminars Group
National Weather Service
Naval Personnel Dev. Command
Net Intent
New Horizons
NIIT / Cognitive Arts
Nike
Novations Group, Inc.
Office of Comptroller of the Currency
Office of the Secretary of Defense
Option One Mortgage Corporation
Oracle iLearning
Organon USA
OutStart, Inc.

Pathlore Software Corp.
Paychex
PepsiCo
Perfoption, Inc.
Pitney Bowes, Inc.
PricewaterhouseCoopers
Procter & Gamble
Progressive Insurance
protonMEDIA
Prudential Financial
Q2Learning, LLC
Questionmark Corporation
Roche Diagnostics Corporation
Root Learning, Inc.
Royal & Sun Alliance Insurance
RWD Technologies
Saba
SAP America
Sara Lee Corporation
Saudi Aramco
Save the Children
Schlumberger
Scottish Ufi Ltd.
Sears, Roebuck and Co.
Siemens Building Technologies
Siemens Logistics & Assembly Systems
Siemens Medical
SkillSoft
SSM Health Care
SumTotal Systems
Sun Life Financial
Target Corporation
Tata Interactive Systems
TD Bank Financial Group
TEDS—A Fidelity Investments Co.
Texas Instruments Incorporated
The Boeing Company
The Center for Association Leadership
The Gillette Company
The Mosaic Company
The Regence Group
THINQ Learning Solutions, Inc.
Thomson NETg
Trader Publishing Company
Transware plc
Turner Broadcasting
UBS Financial Services, Inc.
Unilever, plc
United Nations Devel. Programme
UnitedHealthcare
U. of Tx. M. D. Anderson Cancer Ctr
Universal Technical Institute
UPS
UWSA University of Wisconsin System
Wachovia Corporation
WebEx Communications, Inc.
Wegmans Food Markets
Wendy's International
Witness Systems
Xerox Corp

Pfeiffer Publications Guide

This guide is designed to familiarize you with the various types of Pfeiffer publications. The formats section describes the various types of products that we publish; the methodologies section describes the many different ways that content might be provided within a product. We also provide a list of the topic areas in which we publish.

FORMATS

In addition to its extensive book-publishing program, Pfeiffer offers content in an array of formats, from fieldbooks for the practitioner to complete, ready-to-use training packages that support group learning.

FIELDBOOK Designed to provide information and guidance to practitioners in the midst of action. Most fieldbooks are companions to another, sometimes earlier, work, from which its ideas are derived; the fieldbook makes practical what was theoretical in the original text. Fieldbooks can certainly be read from cover to cover. More likely, though, you'll find yourself bouncing around following a particular theme, or dipping in as the mood, and the situation, dictate.

HANDBOOK A contributed volume of work on a single topic, comprising an eclectic mix of ideas, case studies, and best practices sourced by practitioners and experts in the field.

An editor or team of editors usually is appointed to seek out contributors and to evaluate content for relevance to the topic. Think of a handbook not as a ready-to-eat meal, but as a cookbook of ingredients that enables you to create the most fitting experience for the occasion.

RESOURCE Materials designed to support group learning. They come in many forms: a complete, ready-to-use exercise (such as a game); a comprehensive resource on one topic (such as conflict management) containing a variety of methods and approaches; or a collection of like-minded activities (such as icebreakers) on multiple subjects and situations.

TRAINING PACKAGE An entire, ready-to-use learning program that focuses on a particular topic or skill. All packages comprise a guide for the facilitator/trainer and a workbook for the participants. Some packages are supported with additional media—such as video—or learning aids, instruments, or other devices to help participants understand concepts or practice and develop skills.

- *Facilitator/trainer's guide* Contains an introduction to the program, advice on how to organize and facilitate the learning event, and step-by-step instructor notes. The guide also contains copies of presentation materials—handouts, presentations, and overhead designs, for example—used in the program.
- *Participant's workbook* Contains exercises and reading materials that support the learning goal and serves as a valuable reference and support guide for participants in the weeks and months that follow the learning event. Typically, each participant will require his or her own workbook.

ELECTRONIC CD-ROMs and Web-based products transform static Pfeiffer content into dynamic, interactive experiences. Designed to take advantage of the searchability, automation, and ease-of-use that technology provides, our e-products bring convenience and immediate accessibility to your workspace.

METHODOLOGIES

CASE STUDY A presentation, in narrative form, of an actual event that has occurred inside an organization. Case studies are not prescriptive, nor are they used to prove a point; they are designed to develop critical analysis and decision-making skills. A case study has a specific time frame, specifies a sequence of events, is narrative in structure, and contains a plot structure—an issue (what should be/have been done?). Use case studies when the goal is to enable participants to apply previously learned theories to the circumstances in the case, decide what is pertinent, identify the real issues, decide what should have been done, and develop a plan of action.

ENERGIZER A short activity that develops readiness for the next session or learning event. Energizers are most commonly used after a break or lunch to stimulate or refocus the group. Many involve some form of physical activity, so they are a useful way to counter post-lunch lethargy. Other uses include transitioning from one topic to another, where "mental" distancing is important.

EXPERIENTIAL LEARNING ACTIVITY (ELA) A facilitator-led intervention that moves participants through the learning cycle from experience to application (also known as a Structured Experience). ELAs are carefully thought-out designs in which there is a definite learning purpose and intended outcome. Each step—everything that participants do during the activity—facilitates the accomplishment of the stated goal. Each ELA includes complete instructions for facilitating the intervention and a clear statement of goals, suggested group size and timing, materials required, an explanation of the process, and, where appropriate, possible variations to the activity. (For more detail on Experiential Learning Activities, see the Introduction to the *Reference Guide to Handbooks and Annuals*, 1999 edition, Pfeiffer, San Francisco.)

GAME A group activity that has the purpose of fostering team spirit and togetherness in addition to the achievement of a pre-stated goal. Usually contrived—undertaking a desert expedition, for example—this type of learning method offers an engaging means for participants to demonstrate and practice business and interpersonal skills. Games are effective for team building and personal development mainly because the goal is subordinate to the process—the means through which participants reach decisions, collaborate, communicate, and generate trust and understanding. Games often engage teams in "friendly" competition.

ICEBREAKER A (usually) short activity designed to help participants overcome initial anxiety in a training session and/or to acquaint the participants with one another. An icebreaker can be a fun activity or can be tied to specific topics or training goals. While a useful tool in itself, the icebreaker comes into its own in situations where tension or resistance exists within a group.

INSTRUMENT A device used to assess, appraise, evaluate, describe, classify, and summarize various aspects of human behavior. The term used to describe an instrument depends primarily on its format and purpose. These terms include survey, questionnaire, inventory, diagnostic, survey, and poll. Some uses of instruments include providing instrumental feedback to group members, studying here-and-now processes or functioning within a group, manipulating group composition, and evaluating outcomes of training and other interventions.

Instruments are popular in the training and HR field because, in general, more growth can occur if an individual is provided with a method for focusing specifically on his or her own behavior. Instruments also are used to obtain information that will serve as a basis for change and to assist in workforce planning efforts.

Paper-and-pencil tests still dominate the instrument landscape with a typical package comprising a facilitator's guide, which offers advice on administering the instrument and interpreting the collected data, and an initial set of instruments. Additional instruments are available separately. Pfeiffer, though, is investing heavily in e-instruments. Electronic instrumentation provides effortless distribution and, for larger groups particularly, offers advantages over paper-and-pencil tests in the time it takes to analyze data and provide feedback.

LECTURETTE A short talk that provides an explanation of a principle, model, or process that is pertinent to the participants' current learning needs. A lecturette is intended to establish a common language bond between the trainer and the participants by providing a mutual frame of reference. Use a lecturette as an introduction to a group activity or event, as an interjection during an event, or as a handout.

MODEL A graphic depiction of a system or process and the relationship among its elements. Models provide a frame of reference and something more tangible, and more easily remembered, than a verbal explanation. They also give participants something to "go on," enabling them to track their own progress as they experience the dynamics, processes, and relationships being depicted in the model.

ROLE PLAY A technique in which people assume a role in a situation/scenario: a customer service rep in an angry-customer exchange, for example. The way in which the role is approached is then discussed and feedback is offered. The role play is often repeated using a different approach and/or incorporating changes made based on feedback received. In other words, role playing is a spontaneous interaction involving realistic behavior under artificial (and safe) conditions.

SIMULATION A methodology for understanding the interrelationships among components of a system or process. Simulations differ from games in that they test or use a model that depicts or mirrors some aspect of reality in form, if not necessarily in content. Learning occurs by studying the effects of change on one or more factors of the model. Simulations are commonly used to test hypotheses about what happens in a system—often referred to as "what if?" analysis—or to examine best-case/worst-case scenarios.

THEORY A presentation of an idea from a conjectural perspective. Theories are useful because they encourage us to examine behavior and phenomena through a different lens.

TOPICS

The twin goals of providing effective and practical solutions for workforce training and organization development and meeting the educational needs of training and human resource professionals shape Pfeiffer's publishing program. Core topics include the following:

>Leadership & Management
>Communication & Presentation
>Coaching & Mentoring
>Training & Development
>e-Learning
>Teams & Collaboration
>OD & Strategic Planning
>Human Resources
>Consulting

What will you find on pfeiffer.com?

- The best in workplace performance solutions for training and HR professionals

- Downloadable training tools, exercises, and content

- Web-exclusive offers

- Training tips, articles, and news

- Seamless online ordering

- Author guidelines, information on becoming a Pfeiffer Affiliate, and much more

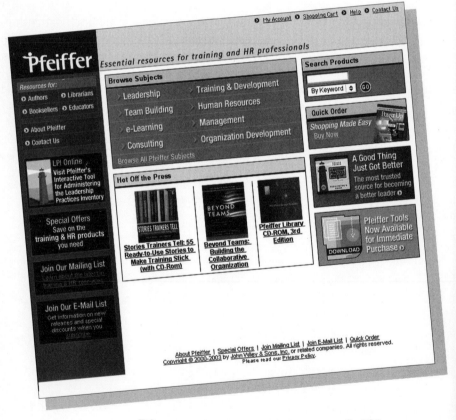

Discover more at www.pfeiffer.com